GW00599636

1

QUADRANGLES

The 17th (Northern) Division in the front line, 6 July to 11 July 1916, during the Battle of The Somme

The Division was facing Quadrangle Support Trench which lay between the fortified village of Contalmaison and Mametz Wood

Wayne Osborne

Salient Books

British Library Cataloguing In Publication Data

A Record of this Publication is available from the British Library

ISBN 978-0-9564439-2-2

Second Edition Published 2010 by

Salient Books,
21, Collington Street, Beeston, Nottingham, NG9 1FJ

info@salientbooks.co.uk

www.salientbooks.co.uk

First published 2007 by
Exposure Publishing,
an imprint of Diggory Press Ltd

Contents

Maps and Tables

Introduction

This work has come from a deep personal interest and is the culmination of many years of research. I first went out to France in April 1999 to see the Somme battlefield for myself and to find what remained of a private soldier who became a casualty on the seventh day of the Somme battle. I went looking for his inscription on Thiepval Memorial and to identify the field where he died. Though the Thiepval Memorial is massive, weighty, daunting and impressive, a name carved in stone seems to show very little for a life. So I began the search to find out what happened to Private J. Osborne 11323, 10th (Service) Battalion, Notts & Derbys Regiment.

It was initially difficult to find anything about the days after the opening of the battle. It seemed to me at the time that historians had been mesmerised by 1 July 1916 and that was all anyone was writing about. So I decided find out for myself what happened in the days 6 to 11 July 1916. The search for one man grew into a research project using war diaries from The National Archive and private papers from the Imperial War Museum. That project encompassed six days in the life of the 17th (Northern) Division and became this book.

Using the war diaries and visiting the battlefield itself, I built up a picture of what was going on in the front line between Mametz Wood and the village of Contalmaison. I have tried to make sense of events but if the story becomes confused and difficult it is simply because that was how it was. The battle was not a 'game of two halves' played out across the flat table of no man's land. The terrain was anything but flat; the weather and shelling had combined to turn the ground into a sea of mud. Communications constantly broke down and often the men at the front were out of touch with those attempting to control the battle. Despite the losses, despite the set backs and stalemates, despite events such as the suicidal attack by the 12th Manchesters, there were victories and the Division did push on and it did take its objectives.

Even today the episodes of that distant war still have the capacity to move, shake and inspire. "It looks as if it's been on the Somme" is a phrase I heard a great deal as a child and still use myself to describe an object that is battered, dented but still functioning. Northern France is so close to the UK and the cheapness of travel has brought the battlefields and the graves of our ancestors touchingly close.

I would urge anyone interested in this war to visit the Somme. The Lochnagar Crater, Thiepval Memorial, Beaumont Hamel, Delville Wood, must be seen. The peace and tranquillity of the immaculately kept British and French cemeteries should be experienced, as should the solitude of the German cemeteries. There are many places to stay in the area that offer a warm welcome. There are also some superb museums that are worth a visit. The Museum in Albert, Musée Somme 1916, and L'historial de la Grande Guerre 1914-1918 Museum in Péronne are both excellent. For those looking for something slightly different there is Le P'tit train de la Haute Somme.

Family tree research is allowing some of the ghosts to emerge from the shadows of time yet the ranks of gravestones demonstrate the sheer number of personal tales, great and small, that will never be told. Therefore, I hope that this work manages, in some small way, to give a voice to the mute headstones of the dead and to the multitude such as John R. Osborne who have no grave, no known resting place and who are reduced to an initial and surname carved in stone or who are plainly "Known unto God."

Wayne Osborne, Nottingham, 2007.

There have been some changes since this book first appeared. Thanks to this book I joined the University of Birmingham and gained my M.A. in First World War Studies. That experience brought me into contact with a number of interesting and helpful people, staff and students alike. I learned more about research and writing history, some of it too late for the first edition of *Quadrangles!* I have written other books on the Great War, including the two books about the 17th Division in the Somme Campaign that follow this one. More information has emerged, Lieutenant-Colonel Fife's diary being one gem unearthed by my friend Steve Erskine. More information will come to light no doubt and as Peter Simkins told me about writing about the Great War, "we're all working together, putting in one brick at a time."

There have been changes to the text of the first edition. Quite simply because there had to be. I had been aware of the need for the changes very early on but for one reason or another, none of which are worth writing about, the changes were not implemented in the form of revisions or as a second edition. Until now that is. This new edition of *Quadrangles* is close to what I originally intended to produce. Who knows, there may be a third...

Wayne Osborne, Nottingham, 2010.

Acknowledgements

I would like to extend my heartfelt thanks to the following people: My wife Helen, my brother Warren, Bill Williams, John Dandy, David Edwards, Emmanuel Brill, Professor Keith Case, Anne, Clare and Abigail.

Thanks to, and in memory of, my friends the late Derek Thornhill and John Brunton.

I would like to give special thanks to Dr. John Bourne, Professor Peter Simkins, the staff at the WFR Museum, Chetwynd Barracks, Chilwell, Notts, the staff at The National Archive, Kew and the staff of the Imperial War Museum. Also to Steve Erskine from the Green Howards Museum, Richmond, Yorkshire.

And last, but not least, thanks to the grand bunch of people that I have met in France during the many trips to the Somme.

Cover image: detail from a photograph in the author's collection. A group of soldiers from the Duke of Wellington's West Riding Regiment, with a young officer of the East Yorkshire Regiment.

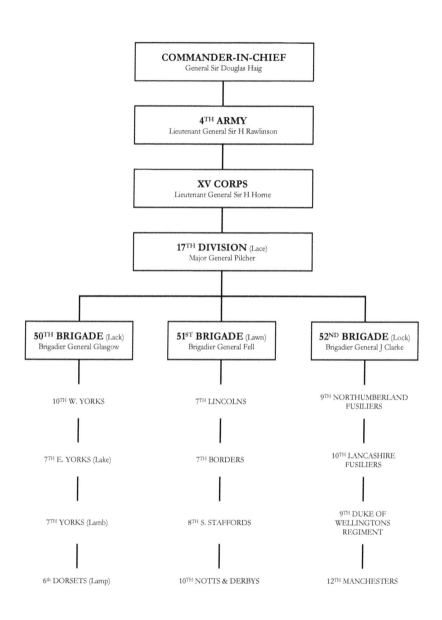

COMMANDER-IN-CHIEF
General Sir Douglas Haig

4TH **ARMY**
Lieutenant General Sir H Rawlinson

XV CORPS
Lieutenant General Sir H Horne

17TH **DIVISION** (Lace)
Major General Pilcher

50TH **BRIGADE** (Lack)
Brigadier General Glasgow

51ST **BRIGADE** (Lawn)
Brigadier General Fell

52ND **BRIGADE** (Lock)
Brigadier General J Clarke

10TH W. YORKS

7TH E. YORKS (Lake)

7TH YORKS (Lamb)

6th DORSETS (Lamp)

7TH LINCOLNS

7TH BORDERS

8TH S. STAFFORDS

10TH NOTTS & DERBYS

9TH NORTHUMBERLAND
FUSILIERS

10TH LANCASHIRE
FUSILIERS

9TH DUKE OF
WELLINGTONS
REGIMENT

12TH MANCHESTERS

1 The Chain of Command and the (simplified) make-up of the 17th (Northern) Division

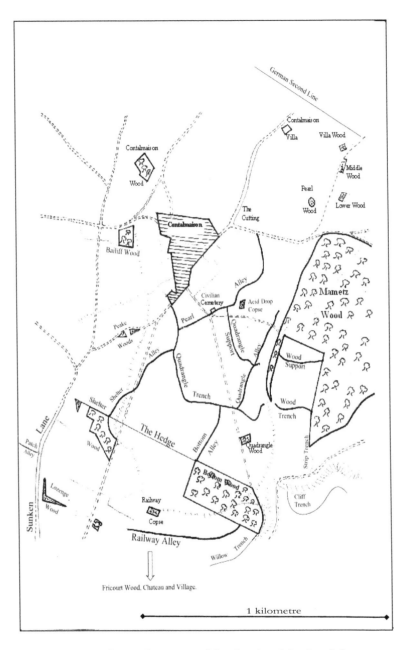

2 Main trenches and features around Quadrangle and Quadrangle Support
Map reproduced from a variety of sources
NOTE: *Contour lines and some trenches have been omitted to simplify the map. It must*
be remembered that the terrain is anything but flat.

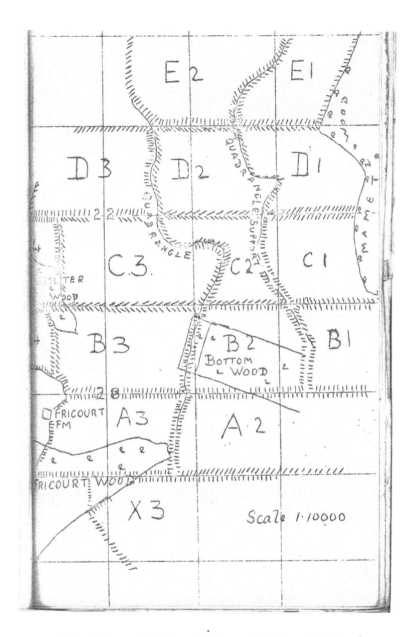

3 A contemporary, hand drawn, trench map of the Bottom Wood area.[1]
It gives a good idea of the kind of maps that were available to the front line troops.

[1] TNA: PRO. WO95/2002. 7th East Yorks

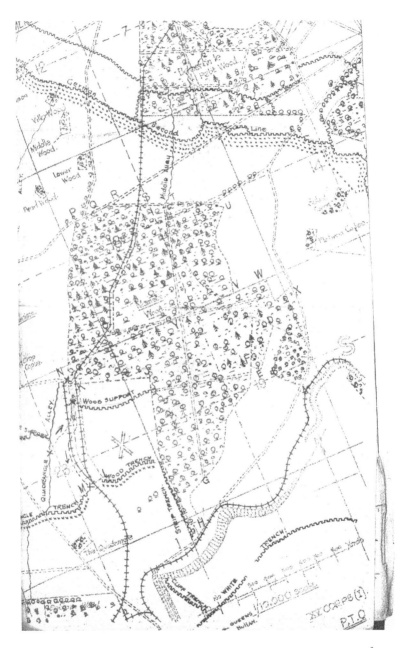

4 A very good hand drawn map of Mametz Wood and the immediate area.[2]

---

[2] TNA: PRO. WO95/2002. War Diary, 7th East Yorks.

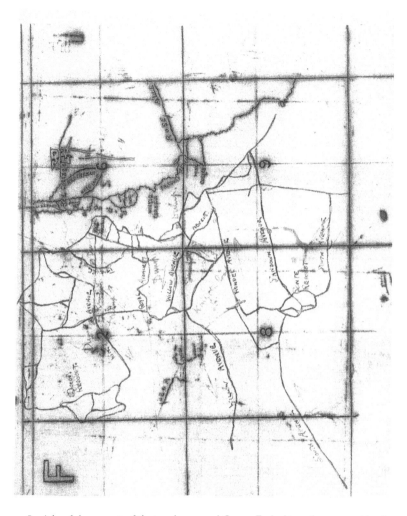

5 A hand drawn map of the trenches around Queens Redoubt on the eastern side of Fricourt village.[3]

---

[3] TNA: PRO. WO95/2002. War Dairy, 7th East Yorks.

The 17th (Northern) Division

On 11 September, 1914, the 17th (Northern) Division was formed. Despite the 'Northern' title the Division was made up of 'Kitchener' volunteers from all walks of life and from all over the British Isles. The infantry battalions were raised in Northumberland, Cumberland, Yorkshire, Lancashire, Nottinghamshire, Derbyshire, Lincolnshire and Dorsetshire. A large number of the men in the Divisional Artillery hailed from Glasgow.

In January 1915, when the Division was in training in Dorsetshire, Major-General T.D. Pilcher arrived to take over. Shortly after returning to Britain from India he had toured the front and made certain recommendations to the Government about the conduct of the war. He had a good deal of military experience and was an expert on German military doctrine. The indirect, heavy machine gun barrage was his idea. Major-General Pilcher was considered to be a rising star.

In the Division's early days everything was in short supply, from trained officers and NCOs to uniforms, tents and blankets. The men in the battalions shared a few ancient drill purpose rifles that were only useful for drill and bayonet practice. Machine gunners trained with dummy machine guns and the artillery had to make do with two old French guns that dated back to 1870. In December 1914 the battalions received a few old Long Lee Enfield rifles and some ammunition; so that a small amount of musketry training could begin. It was sometime before any modern equipment reached the Division. Still, the men of the Division made do and soldiered enthusiastically on with what they had.

Dismissed by the German Press as 'Cannon Fodder', as all Kitchener Divisions were, the 17th Division did its best to learn the ways and different arts of war at Bovington, Purbeck and Larkhill. Just eight months after formation, in July 1915, and still without modern weapons, the 17th Division was declared ready for active service. Almost immediately the 17th Division was designated a Home Defence Division, by a Government fearful of invasion. It seemed that the 17th Division was destined for further training and a posting to the East Coast. As the men looked forward to their first home leave and Major-General Pilcher organised the move to the east a telegram arrived that dramatically changed their orders. The 17th Division was ordered to proceed to France immediately.

By 16 July the entire Division was in France and only thirty miles away from the front. Only now did the men receive ammunition for their modern Short Magazine Lee Enfield rifles which had been issued just before they left Britain. Shortly after their arrival on the Continent the Division moved to the front and as part of the V Corps, their war began in earnest around the Ypres Salient. At the front the weather deteriorated and the men of the Division learned the routine of trench warfare. And in the trenches the inevitable list of casualties began to grow as men succumbed to shot, shell, sickness and trench foot.

Later, in September 1915, the Division played a minor part in the Battle of Loos. In the driving sleet and biting cold of February 1916 they suffered heavy losses in bitter fighting at 'The Bluff'. It was here at 'The 'Bluff' that Captain Mozley of A Company, the 6th Dorsets, began to gain his reputation for being a fine Company Commander, a first rate soldier and where he earned his D.S.O. The Division that went to rest in May 1916 and transferred to XV Corps on the Somme in June 1916 was a hardened and experienced formation well versed in the arts of trench warfare; a far cry from the amateurs that had 'made do' in Dorset in 1915. It was not, perhaps, well versed, despite the training, in the art of offensive operations against siege warfare defences.

The history of the Battle of the Somme and the story of the first day has been ably told many times. Though the bulk of the 17th (Northern) Division was in reserve, the 50th Brigade under Brigadier-General Glasgow was attached to the 21st Division and took part in the fighting, in front of Fricourt village, on the first day. The 10th West Yorks were almost completely wiped out, the 7th Yorks and the 7th East Yorks were severely mauled by German machine guns at Fricourt.

The 17th (Northern) Division went into the front line proper on the evening of 1 July. Along the rest of the line the British attack had stalled, held up by German defences and machine guns. Yet, from 2 July to 6 July, the 17th (Northern) Division actually made progress against a withdrawing enemy.

Prelude : Midnight 4/5 July 1916

From the war diaries of the 10th Lancashire and 9th Northumberland Fusiliers.

At 12.00 midnight of 4/5 July 1916, the mud caked men of the 9th Northumberland Fusiliers waited in what passed for the new British front line. The position that they had taken over was known on the maps as 'The Hedge'. It was nothing more than a series of shell holes, small miserable pits and sections of shallow, narrow trench that had been filled with water by the violent thunderstorm of that afternoon.

From 'The Hedge' the Fusiliers looked up a pock marked slope that was lit in relief by hanging flares and the flashing explosions of shells as the British field guns fired continuously to break the coils of German wire. On the right hand side and to the back of the Hedge stood the eerie remains of 'Bottom Wood' where the broken limbs of splintered trees cast grotesque moving shapes in the light of the flares and exploding shells.

No sniper fire came from the German line; the machine guns that were certain to be there were not firing their usual searching pattern over the British trench and even the German artillery, so busy that afternoon, was now silent. Reconnaissance patrols had reported that the German trench was only lightly held. The 9th Northumberland Fusiliers and the other troops prepared to attack the German trench.

In the Hedge the men noticed that the barrage had increased in tempo and intensity. High explosive shells were now mixed with the shrapnel rounds and threw gouts of mud and earth into the air, making black, gaping fire-edged holes in the darkness. Now was the time. Cautiously and quietly, using the tempestuous barrage as cover, the men climbed from their holes and crept through the mud towards the German wire. When they arrived they lay down and waited for the barrage to lift.

As the barrage stamped up the hill and away from the German trench the officers of the 10th Lancashire Fusiliers gave the order to attack. The left flank rose up and surged forwards through the torn wire and into the German defences. On this flank, alerted at last to the British presence, a German machine gun and a few rifles stabbed fire into the night. One or two men crumpled and fell but, obeying orders, no one stopped to help them. In the middle the

Northumberlands rose and carried steadily on through the wire, as did the Royal Welsh, advancing in a similarly determined fashion on the right flank. Only a few rifles spat defiance from the trench. On the left the Lancashire men were in the German trench and amongst the dazed and bleeding defenders, stabbing, shooting, swearing and shouting. A few moments afterwards the Northumberlands and the Welsh were themselves in the smoking and smashed trench. A few of the German soldiers tried to defend themselves but the British troops put paid to them with their bayonets.

Some German soldiers scrambled over the back of their trench and began labouring through the mud uphill towards their support trench. The Tommies, keen to fight, took up positions on the back of the trench and shot them down in the dark with rifles and Lewis Guns. The remaining few Germans soldiers, seeing the fate of their comrades, wisely threw their hands in the air.

Captain Thacker of the 10th Lancashire Fusiliers reconnoitred his left flank and almost reached the village of Contalmaison with no resistance. He set up a 'stop' or a barricade, manned by a few rifle men and a Lewis Gun team. Then he returned to report how far the left flank extended. The British had now formed a salient in the German line.

With the trench in their hands pity for the casualties of both sides took over and the British helped the injured and bound wounds. Looking around the well made trench they realised that the gunners had done their job extremely well. A majority of the German defenders, from the 1st Battalion, 163rd Regiment, had been unable to defend their trench because they had been killed by the barrage.

This had been a textbook action and had been completely successful. No reserves had been used at all and, when the casualty figures came in to the Company commanders of the Northumberlands, they discovered that in total they had only lost forty men, killed and wounded. A report was duly sent back to Brigade stating that 'Quadrangle Trench', as the British maps named it, was in British hands. This was the new British front line. The 17th (Northern) Division was looking up hill once again and the new German front line was thought to be at the top of the slope. It was known on the map as 'Quadrangle Support Trench'. On the left flank was the fortified village of Contalmaison and on the right loomed the menacing bulk of Mametz Wood.

Congratulations from XV Corps and 17th Division soon arrived at 52nd Brigade Headquarters, situated in the deep, vaulted cellars of the pulverised Fricourt Chateau. Lieutenant-General Horne and Major-General Pilcher were delighted with Brigadier-General Clarke's men. The British army was pushing on. Yet another German position had fallen to the 17th Division of XV Corps in the opening phase of the Somme Campaign.

Chapter One : 6 July 1916

Weather for 6 July: High temperature of 70F. Overcast with intermittent showers.

Early hours of the morning.

In the front line, formerly known by the Germans as the 'Kaisergraben' but now marked on the British maps as Quadrangle Trench, the men of the 9th Northumberland Fusiliers attempted to improve their position while they waited for orders to move forward. Since they had successfully taken the position in the early hours of 5 July they had not moved an inch. Their success, and the failure of the 23rd Division on the left and the 7th Division on the right to capture their objectives, had formed a salient in the German lines. XV Corps Commander Lieutenant-General Horne had sent the Division orders to consolidate their gains.

Therefore, the 17th Division was forced to wait for the others to catch up and for Lieutenant-General Horne to receive his new orders for the next phase of the Battle from his superiors, Generals Haig and Rawlinson. In the line the 38th (Welsh) Division had relieved the 7th Division.

The rain was lashing down as it had been doing for a couple of days and it filled the trenches with deep, clinging mud. Snipers traded shots and the artillery exchanged shells. Bombing parties from both sides met and fought short, sharp skirmishes but twenty four hours after successfully pushing the Germans back the British had still not moved.

The 17th Division History records that "the attack of the three divisions was to be made at 2 am on 7 July, preceded by thirty five minutes of intense bombardment."[4] Three Divisions were not to attack at 2.00 am. The 17th Division was due to make two attacks, one at 2.00 am and another at 8.00 am. The 38th Division was due to attack at 8.30 am and, on the right, the 23rd Division of the III Corps was to attack Contalmaison at the later time of 10.00 am.

---

[4] A. Hilliard Atteridge, *A History Of The 17th (Northern) Division* (Naval and Military Press, 2003), p.127

Brigadier-General H. J. Evans commander of the 115th Infantry Brigade, 38th Division, who were to attack the far eastern edge of Mametz Wood, was extremely unhappy with his orders for 7 July. He wanted to attack at dawn but had been told, by his Division, to wait for an attack on Contalmaison on the left. Lieutenant Wyn Griffith, staff officer to Evans, recorded in his book *Up to Mametz* that he discussed the orders for 7 July with a colleague, asking why the Divisions were not attacking together. Wyn Griffith wondered why the 38th Division was not going to attack early in the morning at the same time as the 17th Division. He reasoned that if both Divisions attacked together, then the Germans would be put under pressure and their artillery fire would be spread thinly. His colleague's reply suggested that such thinking was tantamount to questioning orders; questioning if they should attack Mametz Wood at all.[5]

At his headquarters Lieutenant-General Rawlinson was forming the opinion that the attack on the German second line could go ahead without capturing the wood; it could, he felt, be circumvented and isolated. Haig was firm in his opinion, however, that the wood must fall to the British before the attack on the German second line could begin. Such an obstacle could not be left alone.

12.20 am.

At XV Corps Headquarters in Heilly the staff noted that the wind was increasing, the sky was overcast and some rain was falling. The 17th and 38th Divisions were recorded as consolidating their positions throughout the night. Both Divisions reported that they were under intermittent German shell fire.

Major-General Pilcher had his 17th Division Battle Headquarters in the village of Meaulte, just south of Albert. One of the contributors to Captain Dunn's book *The War The Infantry Knew 1914 – 1919* described it in July 1916. He said that it was a small village, relatively undamaged, but the war had given it a squalid air. Captain Mozley commented that the small, once pretty, gardens were now full of rubbish and dugouts. The main road through Meaulte was choked by vehicles and columns of men going to and from the front, and the fields around the village were thick with tents, men, piles of supplies

---

5 W. Griffith, *Up To Mametz*, (Gliddon Books, 1988), p. 217

and lines of horses. Small wonder then that some of the remaining locals were not particularly pleased with the British presence. Denis Winter, in his book *Death's Men*, quotes a British soldier who said that they (the locals of Meaulte) would have preferred to be under German occupation.[6]

Here at 17th Division Headquarters the staff noted that there was considerable artillery activity in their part of the front, and acknowledged that, on the orders of XV Corps, the battalions were ordered to spend the day making preparations for the forthcoming assault on Quadrangle Support Trench and Mametz Wood. The Division had elements of both 50th and 52nd Brigades in the front line and immediately behind the lines. The battalions of the 51st Brigade were stationed in the rear as the Divisional Reserve.

12.50 am

Because of the coming attacks a certain amount of sideways shuffling to the right was required by the 23rd, 17th and 38th Divisions and all of this redeployment had to be successfully completed by midnight of 6/7 July. Meanwhile Major-General Pilcher began to issue instructions to his Brigades in the field.

Orders were sent out from 17th Division Headquarters to 52nd Brigade instructing them to be prepared to make the attack on Quadrangle Support Trench early on the morning of 7th. The front allotted to them was as follows: "Quadrangle Support Trench from junction with Quadrangle Alley up to Pearl Alley inclusive."[7]

52nd Brigade was detailed to attack early in the morning and 50th Brigade was waiting to attack later in the morning. Orders were sent to Brigadier-General Fell of the 51st Brigade, which was waiting behind the lines in Ville, telling him that his men were to hold themselves in reserve for the coming operations.

2.00 am.

50th Brigade received the warning order from 17th Division headquarters to be ready to take over the frontline trenches between Willow Avenue and Bottom Alley from the 38th Division and to be

---

6 D. Winter, *Death's Men*. (Penguin, 1979), p.143

7. TNA: PRO. WO95/1981. War Diary, 17th Division, July 1916.

ready to co-operate in an attack with the 38th on Mametz Wood. The 6th Dorsets were detailed to relieve a battalion of the 113th Brigade in the front line and officers from the Dorsets were sent forward to reconnoitre the positions that they had to take over.

Sun rose and broke through the rain clouds, lighting up the smoking, mud filled land that had once been a peaceful agricultural region. Fricourt was a smoking and blasted ruin; a village now in name only. The woods that surrounded the ruin; Fricourt Wood, Bottom Wood, Quadrangle Wood, were splintered and broken; the fields were churned up and crossed by trenches and thick coils of wire. Most of the grass was gone, trampled to mud and was replaced by the white rayed shell holes and craters that pock marked the blighted land. And everywhere the eye could see, in the ruins, in the craters, in the trenches, on the road and in the ditches lay pathetic little huddled heaps of rags, some in uniform ranks of platoons and others quite alone. The skin of the unburied dead, flayed by the sun, wind and rain, was going black. As the sun grew hotter swelling had begun and the air, made fetid by the smell of cordite and gas, was tinged with the sweet smell of rotting flesh.

8.00 am.

After a short rest in Ville, 4 km beyond Meaulte, the 51st Brigade Machine Gun Company packed up and began their return journey to the front line.

As the men of the 51st Brigade Machine Gun Company moved out the men of the 50th Machine Gun Company paraded in their sections for work, physical exercises followed by weapon cleaning prior to their move to the front line. As the men began their physical jerks their Commanding Officer and two other Machine gun officers went ahead to reconnoitre the ground around Fricourt so that they could prepare for the attacks.

51st Field Ambulance was based at the File Factory at Meaulte and had elements at the fortified position of Queens Redoubt and A Section at the 'Subway'. The latter was the main forward Dressing Station situated just behind the front line. A message came in from the Subway requesting all cars and three horse drawn wagons be sent forward. [8]

8.55 am.

The 7th East Yorks a situation report to 50th Brigade. They had been in the front line since 6.00 pm the previous evening and at the time of the report they were under 52nd Brigade orders. C Company was in the front line, Quadrangle Trench. The other companies were in support; D Company was in Crucifix Trench, B Company in Railway Alley and A Company was based in Fricourt Wood. The report included the information that Second Lieutenant J. W. Lissett of A Company had been wounded while in Fricourt Wood. XV Corps did later note that the Germans were subjecting this area to a sustained bombardment, particularly the ground around Railway Copse.

In their part of the front line the 9th Northumberland Fusiliers, 52nd Brigade, recorded that the enemy had attempted no counter-attacks upon Quadrangle Trench so far, but seemed content to subject the British positions to intermittent and occasionally severe bombardment.

10.00 am.

XV Corps issued Operation Order No. 15 and maps to the 17th and 38th Divisions, giving the objectives and boundaries for the two attacks on the following day. In the diary entry XV Corps states that the first attack, the attack on Quadrangle Support Trench, was to begin at 2.30 am. Orders were also issued to the Divisional Artillery spelling out their involvement in these operations.

The Divisional artillery was positioned in an arc just behind the lines. Equipped with 18 Pounder 'Quick Fire' field guns the 78th Brigade, R.F.A., was in the centre, grouped around Fricourt. The 78th Brigade's Headquarters was in the ruined village. The similarly equipped 79th Brigade, R.F.A., was at Becordel on the left flank and the 80th Brigade was on the right flank in Carnoy Valley. 81st Brigade, R.F.A., equipped with 4.5-inch field howitzers, was positioned at Bray-sur-Somme. The field guns were employed to

---

[8] The exact location of the 'Subway' has so far not been identified. Subway in military mining language was a tunnel or covered trench.

disperse enemy attacks over the open, to destroy communications and wire cutting. They could also be used for counter battery fire against any enemy batteries within their range as well as the demolition of vulnerable enemy positions. The 4.5-inch field howitzers were used for bombarding weaker enemy positions, the destruction of communication trenches, bombardments of entrenched troops, counter battery fire and to fire gas shells.

The artillery brigades experienced counter battery fire from the German guns and some of the gunners had scant protection from the shrapnel and high explosive shells. Casualties on the gun lines were a daily occurrence. Even at this point the men of the 80th Brigade, R.F.A., had not been issued with steel helmets and were serving the guns wearing their old soft caps. According to Gunner Heraty the infantry had priority where helmets were concerned. The gunners soon began to scavenge among the dead for useable helmets.[9] Lieutenant-Colonel Cardew, the Commanding Officer of the 80th Brigade, noted in his diary that he was quartered in a tent instead of a decent dug out. He recorded in disgust that when they were shelled he had to don his 'tin hat' (he too had obtained a steel helmet) in an attempt to protect himself from the "flying bits."[10]

At around 10.00 am A and C Batteries of 79th Brigade, R.F.A., responded to orders from XV Corps and bombarded Acid Drop Copse and Contalmaison Civilian Cemetery for twenty minutes. Both positions had been reported to be full of enemy troops. 81st Brigade, R.F.A., kept up fire on the German front line. 78th Brigade, R.F.A., bombarded Wood Trench and Wood Support Trench and kept up concentrated fire throughout the day. When they were not bombarding Wood Trench they shelled Quadrangle Support Trench.

B section of the 51st Field Ambulance relieved their A section at Queens Redoubt as tired, hard working medics and bearers rotated their duties.

[9] A. J. Heraty, *A Duration Man, A Staffordshire Soldier in the Great War*, (Churnet Valley Books, 1999), p. 58

[10] Lieutenant-Colonel G. A. Cardew., C.M.G., D.S.O., C. O., 80th Brigade, Royal Field Artillery. (IWM 86/92/1)

10.30 am.

In the rear, at the tent camp near Ville, three battalions of Brigadier-General Fell's 51st Brigade, the 7th Lincolns, the 8th South Staffords and the 10th Notts & Derbys waited in reserve for the coming attacks and prepared for the inevitable call to the front line. The 7th Border Regiment was stationed at Meaulte, near the front line, and was ready to move up to the front when needed.

The 10th Notts & Derbys received orders to be ready to move up to the front line at a moment's notice. Shortly afterwards these orders were rescinded and the battalion was told that no movement was to be made that day, so the 10th Notts & Derbys stood down. The 7th Lincolns recorded the arrival at their Headquarters of Second Lieutenants V. B. Shorter and G. E. Scollick, both formerly of the 9th Battalion, Queens Regiment, and Second Lieutenant H. Ribton-Cook.

11.14 am.

XV Corps issued orders to the artillery for a smoke barrage to be placed on the southern portion of Mametz Wood and Strip Trench to aid the 38th Division's attack at 8.30 am the following morning.

12.35 pm.

XV Corps recorded the situation at the front as unchanged. Wood Trench was reported to be held by the enemy and the enemy guns had shelled the British front line, Quadrangle Trench, that morning.

1.40 pm.

B and C Batteries of 79th Brigade, R. F. A., reported that they bombarded Acid Drop Copse and Contalmaison civilian cemetery for twenty minutes.

Orders for the attacks of the next morning came through to the 17th Divisional Headquarters from XV Corps early in the afternoon and now Major-General Pilcher was able to prepare his operational orders for the Division. A conference for the Division's senior officers was scheduled to be held at his Battle Headquarters in Meaulte later that afternoon.

At about this time in the afternoon, after making no infantry attacks in the morning, the Germans launched a small scale, swift attack, down Pearl Alley communication trench. The German troops got into a small section of Quadrangle Trench and attacked the British 'stop', or barricade, that defended the left hand corner of the British salient at the junction of Shelter Alley. Though the attack was repulsed by the 10th Lancashire Fusiliers, who were holding the far left of the line, the attackers managed to destroy the 'stop' with bombs. Shelter Alley had been consolidated and was at the time a defensive position that covered the left flank of the 17th Division. It would appear that the 23rd Division, who were in the area at this time, had not made contact with the 17th Division.

Shortly after this German bombing attack Lieutenant Clay, of the 10th Lancashire Fusiliers, led a patrol on a reconnaissance up Pearl Alley communication trench. They encountered another enemy patrol on their way to attack the British and a bombing fight ensued. After winning the skirmish Lieutenant Clay and his men established a 'stop' at the junction of Pearl Alley and Quadrangle Trench, blocking the way to any more quick attacks by the Germans. Having encountered Lieutenant Clay's patrol and expecting similar attacks by the British the German infantry set up their own 'stop' further up Pearl Alley.

2.00 pm.

In the space immediately behind the front line the Engineers, Signallers and Pioneers toiled at their allotted tasks. The thunderstorms had ceased for a while and the sun baked the muddy ground. Steam rose from their sodden woollen uniforms as they picked their way through the water logged shell-holes and the dead. The Pioneers and Engineers carried wire or building materials and the Signal men traced severed telephone lines. Occasionally they ducked or dived for cover as shells screamed overhead or landed near them in the mud. Disturbed larks rose into the sunlit, smoky air to sing defiantly above the battlefield where, despite man's best efforts, they managed to cling to life. Sapper F. P. Cook of the 78th Field Company, R.E., remembered that the larks' song seemed to be mocking them.[11]

---

[11] Colonel F.P. Cook. A Sapper in the 78th Field Company, R.E., July 1916. (IWM 81/44/1)

Working between the front line and Meaulte the 17th Signal Company recorded that the heavy rainfall was causing an enormous amount of induction in the telephone lines and maintenance on the lines was extremely labour intensive. They went on to note that the lines that ran to the various battalion headquarters were constantly being cut by shell fire. Though the linesmen were working flat out to mend the telephone lines, the signallers also used carrier pigeons as an alternative communication method with some success.

The 78th Field Company, Royal Engineers who, like other support units, were operating out of the dugouts at Becordel and Queens Redoubt were close to Becourt Wood and just behind the old front line. At this time just, like the few days since its capture, most of the Company were working in Fricourt Wood consolidating what had been gained. The smell of gas and the rotting flesh of unburied corpses made their eyes and noses stream and Sapper F. P. Cook noted that it spoiled the taste of the tobacco that they lit for comfort and to take away the smell.

Others of the 78th Field Company were working in Crucifix Trench wiring and building a machine-gun emplacement that would cover and sweep the entire valley. It would guard against any powerful counter-attack that the enemy may mount in order to recapture their lost ground. The 78th had orders that after the work in Crucifix Trench was complete they were not to go out to work on the night of 6/7 July but remain in their positions at Becordel and Queens Redoubt.

The Divisional pioneers, the 7th Yorks & Lancs were also based in the Queens Redoubt. A and C Companies remained at the Redoubt, resting. B Company was working on the left flank cutting a cable trench from Shelter Wood, along Sunken Road to Lonely Copse. D Company was building a road on the south east edge of Fricourt Wood.

Under orders from the Assistant Director Medical Services the 52nd Field Ambulance handed over the German Prisoners' Hospital at Morlancourt to the 21st Field Ambulance in preparation for the move forward to the front line for the coming attacks. The C.O. of the 52nd and his senior officers had made a personal reconnaissance of the front line Advanced Dressing Stations and Aid Posts the day before so they had a good idea of the terrain that they were moving into.

3.10 pm.

Back at XV Corps headquarters, Lieutenant-General Horne wanted detailed information about the German positions that were soon to be attacked. Therefore 3 Squadron, Royal Flying Corps, were instructed to fly a reconnaissance over Quadrangle Support Trench and Pearl Alley to see how well they were manned. They were also asked to have a general look at Wood Trench, Wood Support and Mametz Wood. 3 Squadron duly complied with the request and sent up a reconnaissance aircraft. Their report was delivered to XV Corps Headquarters about three hours later.

Major George Dutton Walker and Lieutenant R. G. Milward of the 10th Notts & Derbys were sent forward from Ville to reconnoitre the front line prior to the Battalion moving forward. Both men were wounded while they made their reconnaissance in the front line. Both recovered and Lieutenant Milward was back on duty in August when the Division went into Delville Wood. Both of them survived the war.

4.00 pm.

Major-General Pilcher issued Operation Order No. 60 to his Brigadier-Generals, giving instructions to their Brigades for the coming attacks. Shortly afterwards the battalion commanders of 50th and 52nd Brigades were summoned to their respective Brigade Headquarters, for a conference with their Brigadier-Generals, Glasgow and Clarke.

As these meetings began A and B Batteries of 79th Brigade, R. F. A., began to bombard Acid Drop Copse and Contalmaison civilian cemetery.

Brigadier-General Clarke held his meeting in the vaulted cellars of the ruined Fricourt Chateau which, until recently, it had been the local German Headquarters. Like the rest of the village, the building had been pulverised by the British artillery; and only the well constructed cellars remained intact.

Here, as the ground shook to the detonations of the British bombardment, the staff officers of 52nd Brigade discussed the plans for the 2.00 am attack on Quadrangle Support Trench and the two communication trenches. 17th Division's orders informed them that there would be a preliminary bombardment of the enemy positions, lasting thirty five minutes, which would end as the attack began. Two companies of the 9th Battalion Northumberland Fusiliers and three companies of the 10th Battalion Lancashire Fusiliers were detailed to carry out this phase of the operation.

At Meaulte, in 50th Brigade Headquarters, a similar conference was being held. Brigadier-General Glasgow and his senior officers listened as a 17th Division staff officer explained the orders for the next part of the operation, the 8.00 am attack on Mametz Wood. In co-operation with the 38th Division, the 7th East Yorks would attack Mametz Wood from the west out of their positions in Bottom Alley. The 6th Dorsets would attack Mametz Wood from the south out of their positions in Bottom Wood. Support would be given by the 7th Yorks, the Brigade Machine Gun Company and the Trench Mortar battery. There would be a preliminary, twenty minute, bombardment of Mametz Wood beginning at 7.20 am.

It was expected that Quadrangle Support Trench, and therefore the ridge that dominated the left flank of this attack, would be in British hands by 8.00 am. Should Quadrangle Support not be held by 52nd Brigade then Scheme b was to be implemented by the 50th Brigade. They would have to take Quadrangle Support Trench as well as attacking Mametz Wood. It was understood at the time that the 38th Division was going to be attacking at 8.00 am.

With the time of the attacks steadily approaching, the Commanding Officers of both 51st and 53rd Field Ambulance searched the area of Sunken Road and Patch Alley for a dugout to use as an Advanced Dressing Station. They only found one suitable for their purposes and this was already being used as a Regimental Aid post by the medics of the four front line battalions.

The two men visited the medical post at Queens Redoubt on their way back and discovered very few casualties there. When they arrived back at the File Factory, the Divisional Collecting Station near Meaulte, the Commanding Officer of the 51st Field Ambulance met with the Assistant Director Medical Services, who told him about the two attacks that were planned for the next morning. After the briefing the Commanding Officer of the 51st ordered bearers to go forward to Queens Redoubt. The bearers were given orders to work between the front line and the advanced dressing station at the Subway. Major Boyden, R.A.M.C., was placed in command of the doctors and bearers in the front line while Major Kay R.A.M.C., commanded the men at the Subway. The commanding officer of the 51st Field Ambulance assumed command at the File Factory.

6.00 pm.

After the conference at Meaulte ended, 52nd Brigade recorded that only now could definite orders be issued to the attacking battalions. They also recorded that the artillery was extremely active on both sides. The German guns had begun to reply to the British challenge.

6.10 pm.

Lieutenant-General Horne at XV Corps Headquarters received 3 Squadron's reconnaissance report about the Quadrangle Support Trench and Mametz Wood area.

The report said that Quadrangle Support Trench had been badly damaged by the British artillery, though several of the bays still seemed to be intact.

Quadrangle Alley, which ran towards the British front line on the right flank and north towards Mametz Wood, was in good condition. The western portion of Pearl Alley that ran towards the British front line, along which both the British and Germans had sent patrols, was extremely badly damaged some 20 yards either side of the junction with Quadrangle Support Trench. The junction itself was completely flattened by the shelling.

The part of Pearl Alley that ran up towards 'The Cutting' was in bad shape but was quite good after it turned to run north towards the German second line.

Wood Trench was badly knocked about by shell fire, as was the ground on either side of it.

They reported that a new trench had been dug to the North West and that it joined directly onto the road, this was probably a connection to Contalmaison.

Mametz Wood appeared to be in fairly good shape; some trees had been felled near the south eastern and north western edges, though not enough to form any kind of barrier. The crew of the reconnaissance aircraft reported that they did not see any German troops on the ground during their mission. They did mention that there was a heavy barrage going throughout their mission and that movement in the enemy trenches would have been difficult.

So Lieutenant-General Horne read a report that painted a picture of wrecked and largely uninhabited trenches. He had asked for a report about how well the enemy trenches were manned but there were no mentions of machine gun positions, bodies of infantry or field gun batteries in the report. That there were troops in these trenches could not be doubted but how many was still not known. It appeared that the Germans were in retreat and the theory that a certain amount of pressure would break them seemed to being proved correct. Prisoners were telling tales of retreat and chaos behind the German lines, and so far the German trenches had been only lightly held. Perhaps the capture of these next enemy positions would be a formality.

6.30 pm.

The 52nd Field Ambulance, minus the B & C tent subdivisions, began to move out from Queens Redoubt. They were to go to a field adjoining the 53rd Field Ambulance Dressing Station at the Subway just behind the front line. Lieutenant Thomas commanding the B & C tent subdivisions was given orders to report to the 64th Dressing Station at Mericourt L'Abbe behind the lines.

7.30 pm.

If anyone at XV Corps headquarters thought that Quadrangle Support Trench was abandoned they were disabused of the notion when a message was received from the 38th Division. The Welsh reported that Quadrangle Support Trench was full of enemy troops. A further bombardment was ordered to dislodge them.

8.00 pm.

At his headquarters in Ville, Brigadier-General Fell had a visitor; Brigadier-General Gerald Frederick Trotter of the Grenadier Guards had arrived from Amiens with orders to take over the 51st Brigade. General Fell had no idea that he was to be replaced as Major-General Pilcher had not informed him of his impending dismissal. That unpleasant task was Trotter's own.

There is no reason given for the Brigadier-General's replacement in the war diaries of the 17th Division, 51st Brigade or the diaries of any of the Battalions. Nor was it even mentioned. The Divisional history makes only a small comment.

"The 51st Brigade was to be Divisional reserve. It was now under the command of Brigadier-General G.G. Trotter, a Grenadier Guards officer, who had taken over from General Fell…[12]

Perhaps the dismissal was kept a quiet as possible.[13] Only Lieutenant-Colonel Cardew, the C.O. of the 80th Brigade, R.F.A., wrote about it. Fell's own diary makes no mention, it simply ends on 5 July 1916.

Once the uncomfortable business of replacing Fell was done Brigadier-General Trotter found himself taking over a Brigade that was, in sixteen hours, going to be engaged in an operation against the enemy. He did not know his new Brigade or his new staff. He himself admitted that it was not a very good state of affairs. Nevertheless 51st Brigade Headquarters closed down and moved forward to Meaulte leaving Fell to prepare to return to Britain in quiet disgrace.

Up at the front the 51st Brigade Machine Gun Company had arrived from Ville and relieved the 52nd Brigade Machine Gun Company, releasing them to prepare for the coming attacks.

During the course of the day the 52nd Brigade Machine Gun Company had lost two men killed. The deaths of Sergeant Taylor, 3750, and Private Gibbs, 3795, were not recorded by the Company war diary.

The 51st Machine Gun Company placed four guns in Quadrangle Trench with the front line infantry. Eight guns were set up in Railway Alley Trench that ran across a hill at the back of and overlooking Bottom Wood. From here they were to be employed in direct and indirect fire on the German lines; specifically upon Mametz Wood. Four guns and their crews remained in reserve near Headquarters in the ruins of Fricourt Chateau.

Orders for the early attack were issued to the 52nd Brigade Machine Gun Company and the sections prepared for the operation. B

---

[12] A. Hilliard Atteridge, *17th (Northern) Division*, p.127.

[13] See Appendix 02

Section, under Lieutenant Stanbury, was attached to the 10th Lancashire Fusiliers, who were attacking on the left flank. D Section, under Second Lieutenant Mason, was attached to the 9th Northumberland Fusiliers the battalion due to attack in the centre and on the right. C Section was attached to the 9th Duke of Wellingtons who were in support. A Section, under Lieutenant Dawe, was held in reserve. The Company Commander, Major Lintott, established his headquarters at Fricourt Chateau alongside that of 52nd Brigade.

At this time the 50th Brigade Machine Gun Company left Ville for the front.

The 6th Dorsets began to relieve the 14th Royal Welsh Fusiliers. The 6th Dorsets met their guides at the north east corner of Fricourt Wood and started to move into positions immediately behind the front line.

Leading 'A' Company was Captain B. C. Mozley, D.S.O. He was an extremely capable soldier and a veteran of the savage fighting at 'The Bluff' in the Ypres Salient. In his diary he wrote that Lieutenant-Colonel C. A. Rowley, himself, and the other company commanders had gone forward and inspected their new positions at 2.00 am that morning.

'B' and 'D' Companies went into Bottom Wood and 'A' Company moved into Railway Alley Trench just behind them. 'C' Company remained in Fricourt Wood as Battalion reserve. Battalion headquarters was set up in a bay in Sunshade Alley. The positions that they took over were filled with slopping mud that defied any attempts to bale them out. Captain Mozley noted that it was about this time, as the companies took up their allotted positions, that they heard about the forthcoming attack.

8.30 pm.

The 12th Manchesters of the 52nd Brigade had been in and around Lozenge Wood, just alongside Fricourt Farm, all day. Now they were ordered to move backwards and assemble in Fricourt Wood. Their specific task was to act as the Brigade Reserve for the attack on Quadrangle Support Trench the following morning.

As the supporting Battalion the Companies of the 9th Duke of Wellingtons, began to move forward under orders to occupy

Quadrangle Trench as soon as the 9th Northumberland Fusiliers and 10th Lancashire Fusiliers had gone over the top to attack Quadrangle Support Trench and Pearl Alley.

The 7th Yorks, 50th Brigade, were ordered to march in the direction of Fricourt Wood. They had orders to support the 8.00 am attack on Mametz Wood. They bivouacked for the night alongside the Becordel-Fricourt Road.

52nd Field Ambulance arrived at the field adjoining the Subway and the Bearers immediately set up a temporary bivouac. Their orders were to be ready to go wherever they were required. Lieutenant Thomas was by now well on his way to Mericourt L'Abbe. The C. O. of the 52nd Field Ambulance took a tour of his aid posts making certain that they were ready for the casualties that would certainly come their way in the forthcoming attacks.

9.00 pm.

The 50th Brigade Machine Gun Company column arrived at Meaulte from Ville and there they waited for their orders.

Back at the tent camp in Ville orders arrived for the 10th Notts & Derbys. They were to be ready to move at half an hour's notice from 6.00 am the following morning. The C.O., Lieutenant-Colonel Banbury, saw to it that the appropriate orders were issued to the companies to prepare for the move.

9.25 pm.

It was only now that 52nd Brigade headquarters issued detailed orders for the 2.00 am attack to the assault Battalions.

In the front line the 9th Northumberland Fusiliers recorded that the shelling was now intense. They went on to record that forty two other ranks had become casualties throughout the day.

10.00 pm.

German infantry mounted another small scale attack down Pearl Alley on the British left flank and destroyed the 'stop' put in place by Lieutenant Clay at the junction of Pearl Alley and Quadrangle Trench.

Lieutenant-Colonel G. A. Cardew sat down in his tent in Carnoy Valley and began to write his diary for the day. He wanted to go to bed but the Germans were shelling the valley and each salvo seemed to be getting closer; he noted that his batteries were taking casualties on a daily basis. Cardew recorded that the 17th and 38th Divisions were going to attack Mametz Wood in the morning and that his guns were to begin a bombardment of the Wood at 1.15 am.

He had ridden around his gun batteries in the valley during the day and watched them in operation, bombarding German targets. He spoke to the officers in command of the batteries then, after making certain that the ammunition was coming up, he personally issued the orders for the next barrage that night. His guns had fired two, twenty minute bombardments during the day and they were firing another one as he wrote. With his guns firing and the German guns searching for his batteries it seemed unlikely that he would get much sleep. He turned in at 11.15 pm.

11.00 pm.

In anticipation of the coming casualties, Captain Cotter R.A.M.C., of the 51st Field Ambulance, was sent forward to the Subway with six horse drawn ambulance wagons and the bearers of A Section.

11.30 pm

50th Brigade Machine Gun Company arrived at the front. The congested arterial road that ran to and from the front had held them up at Meaulte for two and a half hours. B and C Sections set up their guns in Railway Alley Trench, alongside those of the 51st Machine Gun Company. A Section went into Fricourt and Lozenge Woods and the Section officers and sergeant reported to the Commanding Officer of the 10th Lancashire Fusiliers in his Headquarters in Crucifix Trench. They were instructed to remain where they were and, if the attack on Acid Drop Copse was a success, then they were to 'go over' and take up positions in the copse. D Section remained in reserve at Wicked Corner with orders to go forward and consolidate should the attack succeed. The Machine-gun Company CO made his Headquarters at Fricourt Chateau along with the rest of 52nd Brigade.

Acid Drop Copse had not originally been mentioned as an objective of the 2.00 am attack.

During the night of 6/7 July.

The Germans were also busy preparing for the attack that they knew must come soon. They overlooked the British positions and during the day they had been able to observe the comings and goings of British units. They had also been able to direct artillery fire at the concentrations of British troops. Occasional patrols had met with their British counterparts and on one occasion German troops had managed to get into the British front line. As night fell the Germans relieved the units in their front line.

The 3rd Battalion, 163rd Regiment of the 17th (Reserve) Division took over the front line of Contalmaison Village, Quadrangle Support Trench, Wood Trench and Wood Support Trench from the 190th Regiment. The 163rd Regiment were an experienced unit and had recently had a long spell of rest and recuperation in Corps Reserve near Cambria after serving in the Vimy sector. They had only been on the Somme since 3 July and were fresh. Troops from the Regiment's 1st Battalion had been holding the current British front line, Quadrangle Trench, when it was overrun and captured on the 5 July.

Just two companies, the 9th and 12th, took over Quadrangle Support Trench. The trench was situated just behind the crest of the hill that overlooked the British; it was not on the crest as the British thought. It had been constructed quite recently, was well made and well protected by barbed wire. Like all other trenches in the area it had about three feet of water in the bottom because of the persistent rain. The German Companies were organised into 'Gruppes'; sections of eight men under the command of one NCO. Each Gruppe had a responsibility for two fire bays that commanded a front of about eight yards. The two infantry companies were supported by a Machine Gun Company of four 'Zuge', each with two machine guns and the specialist 71st, Marksman, Machine Gun detachment. This gave the position some twelve heavy machine guns.

Water was brought to the troops along the trenches from the village of Contalmaison. The British shelling made ration carrying an extremely hazardous job, so warm food was not available to the front line troops. The German troops were forced to eat the iron rations that they had carried with them into the line. Despite the lack of warm food and drink the morale of the German troops was high and ammunition for their rifles and hand grenades were in plentiful supply. Information given to British intelligence officers said that the German infantry felt some anger towards their own artillery. It only seemed able to shell the enemy in spasmodic bursts whereas the British seemed to be able to subject the German positions to lengthy bombardments at will and with a degree of precision.[14] The British infantry would have disagreed with this view because to them the German guns seemed to fire lengthy barrages on positions just behind the British front line and hit targets with unerring accuracy.

On the southern edge of Mametz Wood were the 5th, 6th, 7th and 8th Companies of the 2nd Battalion, the Lehr Regiment of the 3rd Guards Division. In reserve behind Contalmaison and Quadrangle Support Trench was the 9th Grenadier Regiment of the Prussian Guard, an elite unit that had recently arrived from a tour of duty on the Russian front. Behind these troops more Regiments were being hurriedly brought up from the reserve.

In the fortified village of Contalmaison, in the well constructed trenches, heavily armed and amply supported, the German troops awaited the inevitable attack. The men of the 163rd Regiment, the 9th Grenadiers and the Lehr Regiment would have been confident in their ability to hold the line against anything that the British could throw at them. They were also capable of mounting a strong counter-attack should one be ordered. Perhaps the only thing that they feared was the British artillery.

As the time of the attacks came ever closer the men in the British front line prepared to do their job. Companies from the 10th Lancashire Fusiliers, the 9th Northumberland Fusiliers the 7th East Yorks and the 6th Dorsets were crammed into the mud filled front line trenches waiting for the time to come. Behind them, in equally bad trenches and mud filled shell holes, were the reserve companies and support troops. The machine guns of the Brigade machine gun companies commenced their indirect fire on the German positions and the British artillery kept up a slow rate of fire. In response the Germans fired back. The rain lashed down again and as far back as Ville the churned up roads and tracks were clogged by columns of men and lines of vehicles. The sheer weight of man power and equipment pressing up to the front line for the next phase of the Somme Campaign was quite staggering.

---

[14] (TNA: PRO. WO157/468. XV Corps Intelligence Summaries.

Chapter Two : 7 July 1916 Midnight to 7.45 am

Weather for the day. A high of 70F, overcast and showery, ½ inch of rain.

Midnight.

In the British front line, standing knee deep in the mud and drenched by the pouring rain, the assault troops of the 9th Northumberland Fusiliers and the 10th Lancashire Fusiliers prepared to attack their objectives. On the right flank the 14th Royal Welsh Fusiliers of the 38th (Welsh) Division made their preparations to attack Mametz Wood at 8.30 am. While on the left flank the men of 24th Brigade of the 23rd Division were making their own preparations to attack Contalmaison at 10.00 am.

In Sunshade Alley, where the 6th Dorsets had their H.Q., Lieutenant-Colonel Rowley and his officers prepared to co-operate with the 38th Division. As they sat and discussed their plans three shells fell out of the wet night sky and detonated within yards of their bay. Lieutenant-Colonel Rowley and his officers decided that it would be prudent to move to a less exposed position.

The Commanding Officer of the 52nd Field Ambulance made a trip around his Aid Posts and Advanced Dressing Stations. Then he visited Brigadier-General Clarke at 52nd Brigade Headquarters in the cellars below the ruins of Fricourt Chateau.

The officers of the assaulting battalions had decided to use the method of attack that had proved so successful on 5 July. Five companies from two Battalions were detailed to attack at 2.00 am. Three from the 10th Lancashire Fusiliers on the left flank; one Company attacking up Pearl Alley towards Acid Drop Copse and the village of Contalmaison; two Companies were to go over no mans land towards Quadrangle Support Trench. One Company of the 9th Northumberland Fusiliers, in touch with the 10th Lancashire Fusiliers, was to attack across no mans land directly towards Quadrangle Support Trench. The other Company was to attack up Quadrangle Alley on the right flank. It was decided that those units out in the open would creep up to the enemy wire under cover of the barrage, as they had successfully done on the morning of 5 July.

The diary of the 9th Northumberlands stated that the dispositions for the attack were to be the same as the successful attack of the morning of 5 July but with B and C Companies leading this time. The first line was made up of fighting patrols from B and C Companies and these included the battalion bombers, the second line consisted of six platoons of B and C Companies, and the third line was made up of D Company who were in support. As the 38th Division were not to attack at 2.00am, D Company was under orders to form a defensive flank in Quadrangle Alley on the extreme right. They were provided with two Stokes guns (trench mortars) and a special unit of the Royal Engineers armed with a *Flammenwerfer*, or a flame thrower. The Flame thrower team had been ordered forward by XV Corps a few days previously.[15] A Company made up the fourth line; they were stationed in the British front line, Quadrangle Trench, as the reserve. Command of the attacking elements of the 10th Northumberland Fusiliers was given to Captain J. S. Allen who had been wounded two days before but who had refused to go back to a dressing station.

The 9th Northumberlands recorded that they were ordered to reach their objective *by 2.00 am.* This appears to be distinct from beginning the attack *at* 2.00 am.

12.15 am.

In Carnoy Valley Lieutenant-Colonel Cardew was woken by an orderly and presented with reams of orders. An inspection of the paper work told Cardew that the 80th Brigade was to begin a barrage at 7.20 am; this was the preliminary barrage for the 8.00 am attack on Mametz Wood. He sent for his adjutant, Lieutenant Dobb, and when he presented himself at the Colonel's tent they set about the task of writing orders for the gun batteries. In the valley, his gunners were preparing for their next barrage that was due to commence at 1.25 am.

---

[15] This was, at the time, a 'hush hush' weapon. There is no mention in any of the war diaries used in the writing of this book of it being used during this phase of the campaign.

1.00 am.

B and C Sections of the 50th Brigade Machine Gun Company finished setting up their weapons in Railway Alley. C Section recorded that their four machine guns were placed some fifteen yards apart. Added to the two Sections of the 51st Brigade Machine Gun Company who were already in the trench there were now sixteen heavy machine guns available for direct and indirect fire in the length of Railway Trench.

In the cellars of Fricourt Chateau the staff of 52nd Brigade recorded that all preliminary movements by the units involved in the 2.00 am attack had been completed by this hour. All was going to plan and was ready for the attack to begin.

Behind the lines, in Becourt Valley, number one section of the 93rd Field Company, Royal Engineers, under the command of Lieutenant Wood paraded ready to go forward. They had orders to follow the attacking infantry and to consolidate Acid Drop Copse once the position was taken.

1.10 am.

As the final touches were being put in place and the units prepared to 'go over the top' the German artillery opened a fierce barrage upon British positions between the British front line and Fricourt. Within moments the telephone lines were severed. Some fifty minutes before the assault went in all telephone communication between the front line, Battalion Headquarters and Brigade Headquarters was lost.

1.25 am.

Following XV Corps orders and using every gun that was available, though ten minutes later than Lieutenant-Colonel Cardew had noted, the British divisional artillery opened fire on their German targets. The field guns of the 78th, 79th, and 80th Brigades, R.F.A., and the 4.5-inch howitzers of the 81st Brigade, R.F.A., began to shell their assigned targets.

1.55 am.

B Section, 50th Brigade Machine Gun Company, began firing three of its four guns, positioned in Railway Alley, over the battlefield, at a target known as the 'Cutting' to the immediate North East of the village of Contalmaison. The intention was to catch any German troops that might be massing just behind the village. The British artillery barrage had by now increased in tempo and ferocity.

2.00 am.

Lieutenant-Colonel Cardew and Lieutenant Dobb finished writing the battery orders for the 7.20 am barrage. The Lieutenant-Colonel treated himself to a cocoa and settled down to sleep.

Working to the timetable the 78th Royal Field Artillery lifted their barrage from Quadrangle Support Trench to the 'Cutting' north of Contalmaison. Their mission was to 'sweep' the roadway east and west of this target. Like the machine guns in Railway Alley, this was an attempt to catch any German troops that might be fleeing from Quadrangle Support Trench or coming up from the German Second Line in support.

After the barrage lifted the 2.00am attack began. XV Corps recorded that 17th Division attacked Pearl Alley, Quadrangle Support, Bottom Alley between Quadrangle Support and Quadrangle Trench in accordance with XV Corps Operation Order No. 15.

Wyn Griffith noted that the Welsh troops on the right of the 17thDivision were subjected to a barrage of gas shells at 2.00 am.

The Germans kept up their barrage on the ground behind the British front line.

The assault companies of 9th Northumberland and 10th Lancashire Fusiliers already out in no mans land rose up out of the mud and began to advance up hill towards the German wire and their objectives. The 10th Lancashire Fusiliers left one company in Shelter Alley Communication Trench, to act as a reserve and to cover the left flank. By now the British front line, the trenches and woods immediately behind were crammed with troops of varying units and arms.

At first all seemed to be going well. As they advanced on the left the 10th Lancashire Fusiliers successfully cut off the German 'stops' in

Pearl Alley by going over the open and getting into the trench behind them. Here they took a number of prisoners. There had been heavy rain and thunderstorms the day before so the ground now being churned up by shellfire made movement extremely difficult and slow. Flares soared overhead lighting up no man's land and now, no doubt able to see good targets and undamaged by the ferocious British barrage, the German gunners of the Machine Gun Company and the specialists of the 71st Sharpshooter Company opened fire from Quadrangle Support Trench. It was also reported that British shells had started to fall short, and were hitting British troops struggling forward in no man's land.

To make matters worse for the attackers there was another menace that they had not planned for. The German trenches were actually packed with infantry. Later it was reasoned that they had been preparing to attack the British at the same moment. It was also possible that the German troops were in position to repel an attack that they knew was due. Now these troops from the 3rd Battalion, 163rd Regiment and the 9th Grenadier Guards began to fire at the attackers coming up the hill towards them. From behind their 'stops' in the two communication trenches they kept up withering fire at the struggling, slipping, British infantry.

The right hand company of the 10th Lancashire Fusiliers, in contact with the 9th Northumberland Fusiliers, were exposed on the muddy glacis and faced by a storm of bullets immediately began to fall back to Quadrangle Trench. The two left hand companies took cover and managed to establish themselves in Pearl Alley and there they grimly held on. In the confusion two small parties of men, some thirty in all, found themselves cut off on the outskirts of Contalmaison and in German territory. To all intents and purposes, for the moment, they vanished.

On the left in Shelter Wood the 9th Duke of Wellington's prepared to move forward along Shelter Alley into the front line once the attacking Companies had gone over the top. Waiting with the 9th Duke of Wellingtons were numbers 9, 10, 11, and 12 guns of C Section, the 52nd Machine Gun Company.

When the attack began two companies of the 9th Duke of Wellingtons went forward, up Shelter Alley and squeezed past the Company of 10th Lancashire Fusiliers that manned the trench covering the left flank. As the infantry went up to the line numbers 9 and 10 guns moved up with them. On the way they had to go through the German barrage which was falling immediately behind the British front line. Number 9 gun and team were hit by a shell and buried. Meanwhile the other two reserve Companies of the 9th Duke of Wellingtons and numbers 11 and 12 gun teams moved to the right along the makeshift line of the Hedge. The troops settled into the line of craters and holes and the machine gunners set up their guns between Shelter Wood and Bottom Wood. They were to remain in this position for most of the day and suffered heavy German bombardment throughout their time in the Hedge. Once it was light much of what the British were doing would be observed by the Germans. The troops in the woods and the Hedge line presented a series of inviting targets.

52nd Machine Gun Company's D section had number 13, 15 and 16 guns with the 9th Northumberland Fusiliers in the front line, Quadrangle Trench. Number 14 gun was with a unit of the 9th Northumberlands at the junction of Bottom Alley and Bottom Wood.

2.25 am.

The three heavy machine guns of B Section, 50th Brigade Machine Gun Company in Railway Alley ceased fire on 'The Cutting'. They had expended 4,500 rounds in half an hour.

3.00 am.

In Pearl Alley two Companies of the 10th Lancashire Fusiliers were holding on to what they had captured. Lieutenant Stanbury had seen that number 5 and 6 guns of B Section, 52nd Machine Gun Company had been set up in the trench to give the Fusiliers support. Then he and Sergeant Smith went forward towards Quadrangle Support Trench as part of the attack. In the fighting that followed they almost made it to Quadrangle Support Trench but Lieutenant Stanbury was severely wounded by a shell fragment in his left leg. Though the Sergeant tried to get the wounded officer back to the British trenches he was unable to do so. Smith was forced to leave Stanbury in a shell hole some twenty yards away from the German line before going back to the British lines to get help.

The 51st Field Ambulance, with units at the Subway, Queens Redoubt and at the File Factory in Meaulte, recorded that the wounded had been coming into them in a steady stream all through the night but at 3.00 am the numbers of wounded increased and the casualties had begun to come in very fast.

Lieutenant-Colonel Cardew was woken by a dispatch rider and given more orders for further bombardments. This time Cardew could not find his adjutant, Lieutenant Dobb.

The 52nd Machine Gun Company diary recorded that Quadrangle Support Trench and the ground in front of it was very heavily shelled by British guns for the hour between 3.00 and 4.00am.

This barrage was probably called for to cover the British troops as they retired but that can have been no consolation to the men like Lieutenant Stanbury, left wounded in front of the German wire.

3.15 am.

A runner of the 9th Northumberland's arrived at Battalion Headquarters and reported that the first wave of infantry had not reached their objectives.

Shortly after the runner arrived a lamp message was flashed back to Battalion Headquarters by A Company who were waiting in reserve in Quadrangle Trench. It said that the attack had been held up by uncut wire.

It was obvious now to the men in the fighting and to those watching from the front line that the attack was gaining no ground and faltering.

3.30 am.

The 12th Manchesters who were waiting in the Fricourt Wood area as the 52nd Brigade reserve, received orders to go forward and relieve the 9th Northumberland Fusiliers in Quadrangle Trench and to send an officer to Brigade Headquarters, at Fricourt Chateau, for further orders. Lieutenant-Colonel Harrison, the C.O., of the Manchesters, detailed Lieutenant Neil Crawhall for the task. The Chateau was situated in a clearing, actually in the Wood itself.

3.45 am.

As the British were falling back, Captain John Stanley Allen of the 9th Northumberland Fusiliers sent another runner back from the front line to his Battalion headquarters. His message to the Lieutenant-Colonel was that the Companies were reorganising in the front line in preparation for a second attack on Quadrangle Support Trench. He also reported the arrival of two Companies of the 9th Duke of Wellington's in the front line.

50th Brigade was informed that 52nd Brigade's attack had failed and that a further attack on Quadrangle Support Trench had been ordered. The 50th Brigade awaited results and continued their preparations for the attack on Mametz Wood at 8.00 am.

The linesmen, supported by the Pioneers, were working very hard to restore communications from the front to Brigade Headquarters in Fricourt Chateau. The heavy rain and the German bombardment hampered their every effort; no matter what they did the appalling conditions ensured that the telephone lines remained cut.

3.50 am.

Major-General Pilcher contacted Lieutenant-General Horne by telephone at XV Corps Headquarters to say that he thought it appeared doubtful whether the attack on Quadrangle Support Trench had succeeded. He added that the telephone lines to the front line had been severed. He was not, therefore, in possession of any up-to-date information.

4.00 am.

It was now daybreak. Second Lieutenant Michell of the 52nd Machine Gun Company was in Quadrangle Trench with his B Section. During the fighting number 6 machine gun of B Section had been blown up by shellfire but numbers 7 and 8 guns were still functioning. Michell heard Sergeant Smith's report that his friend Lieutenant Stanley was laying wounded out in front of the German trench. In hopes that his section officer was still alive, Michell led a party of two, Sergeant Smith and Private E Viccars, out into no mans land to search for Lieutenant Stanbury at the spot reported by Smith. Sadly no trace of the officer could be found. When they returned to their trench they reported that the ground had been heavily shelled and concluded that Stanbury had been buried or killed. Their journey was not wasted because Michell, Smith and Viccars carried a wounded Northumberland Fusilier back to the British lines. Michell was later awarded the Military Cross for his part in this gallant action.

At this time a detachment of the 1st Worcester Regiment of the 23rd Division, III Corps, arrived in the crowded Pearl Alley communication trench in preparation for their attack upon Contalmaison.

The small party of men of the 10th Lancashire Fusiliers 'cut off' and missing since around 2.00 am arrived back in Pearl Alley trench with twenty German prisoners, and the story that the thirty of them had been into Contalmaison. To back up their claims they presented the lock of a machine gun to their officers and claimed that they had destroyed four more machine guns by 'firing into the works' of each weapon. The 10th Lancashire Fusiliers diary makes no mention of this as an organised attack but rather the action of men who had been cut off from their units.

The 17th Division and 52nd Brigade diaries recorded the incident differently. They said that although unable to secure Quadrangle Support Trench the 10th Lancashire Fusiliers established themselves in Pearl Alley and sent a battle patrol into Contalmaison where they destroyed four machine guns and captured twenty prisoners. Instead of being 'cut off' from their unit the men who returned from Contalmaison with prisoners and the lock of a machine gun had become a 'battle patrol'.

On the heels of the missing Fusiliers came the 9th Grenadier Regiment of the Prussian Guard in a serious counter-attack from Contalmaison and Quadrangle Support Trench. Their attack forced the 10th Lancashire Fusiliers to withdraw from Pearl Alley back to the front line, Quadrangle Trench. In the fighting that followed, number 3775 Private Cocks, "did most excellent work" in repelling a German attack with his Lewis gun, after the Fusiliers had withdrawn from the trench.

51st Field Ambulance recorded that, due to casualties among Regimental stretcher bearers from the attacking battalions, RAMC men had to work in front of the Regimental aid posts bringing wounded in from the battlefield. When the counter-attack came the RAMC men were in no mans land and were caught up in the fighting; some of them became casualties themselves. Three men of the bearers were wounded: Private J.T. Barrett, 66328, was hit in the right hand, Private H. Howarth, 100878, was hit in the thigh, and Private H. Tate, 81435, was hit in the chest. Twenty nine year old Private W. Attwell, 78040, was killed by a shell. Other men were slightly wounded and some were buried by shell fire or when the rain drenched trenches collapsed. Some were sent back with "exhaustion and shock". Many men were reported to the commanding officer of the 51st Field Ambulance for meritorious work at this time. The diary does not, at this point, record their names.

17th Division staff reported that the attack was repulsed but heavy fighting continued in no man's land for some time after the German attack. 52nd Brigade recorded that the counter-attack was beaten off by the 10th Lancashire Fusiliers and a company of the 1st Worcesters, 24th Brigade.

The 9th Duke of Wellingtons, holding a portion of the front line, received information that the Germans were counter-attacking and they made ready to repel the attack. They recorded that the attack by the enemy, rather than being repelled, just fizzled out.

The first attack on Quadrangle Support Trench had failed so orders were issued for a second attack. 50th Brigade would attack Mametz Wood and the 23rd Division would attack Contalmaison simultaneously. Preparations for these attacks, said the 52nd Brigade diarist, were difficult.

In fact the situation had descended into chaos. 24th Brigade was attempting to relieve the 10th Lancashires and 9th Duke of Wellingtons in Shelter Alley and Pearl Alley preparatory to their assault on Contalmaison. Time was short and elements of the 52nd Brigade were still fighting the enemy in no mans land. Men from the first attack were crowded into the front line trench and the communication trenches and the German bombardment was heavy.

A second bombardment of Quadrangle Support Trench was ordered.

The 10th Notts & Derbys, back in Ville, were ordered to be ready to move. They had to be in position in the old British front line of 1 July by 9.00 am. Their right flank was to rest on the crossroads facing Fricourt village and here they would link up with the 7th Borders. The Battalion sent gear ahead of the companies and made a dump at the cross roads that consisted of tools, spare Lewis guns, signalling gear and medical supplies.

4.20 am.

An order came into 9th Northumberland Fusiliers Headquarters from 52nd Brigade to send the Battalion second in command, Major G. P.

Westmacott D.S.O., up to Quadrangle Trench to take over operations from Captain Allen. Westmacott was further ordered to reorganise on the line of the front line trench and 52nd Brigade told the 9th Northumberlands that they were to make no further attacks on Quadrangle Support Trench.

4.25 am.

Five minutes later Major Westmacott was sent forward as instructed. When the major arrived in Quadrangle Trench, he immediately sought out Captain Allen. The Captain, who had been wounded for a third time, soon set about telling Major Westmacott what had gone wrong with the attack. Once he had made his report Allen relinquished command and allowed himself to go to a dressing station.

Below are the points that Allen made to Westmacott in his report.

- The assaulting troops had met severe opposition.

- Quadrangle Support Trench was strongly held by enemy troops, possibly preparing for an attack of their own.

- There had been intense machine gun and rifle fire.

- The enemy artillery barrage was opened as soon as the British troops appeared on the skyline, some 300 yards from Quadrangle Support Trench.

- The timing of the attack had been faulty. The attack time had been altered three times between 6.00 pm on the 6 July and 1.00 am on the 7 July each with a variation of 20 minutes.

- The British artillery preparation was inadequate, the heavy artillery being very short.[16]

The report was telling. The British guns had failed to destroy Quadrangle Support Trench and the machine guns stationed there. The barrages had landed short and the attacking troops had been 'sky lined'. Surely this was enough to tell the men in charge that Quadrangle Support Trench was actually behind the crest of the hill, some three hundred yards beyond the crest. The attack time had

---

[16] TNA: PRO. WO95/2013. War Diary, 9th Northumberland Fusiliers, July 1916.

been altered as well, something that was not recorded save by a single mention in the 17th Division diary.

Captain John Stanley Allen was taken back down the line to a dressing station and then onto the File Factory, from there he went to the field hospital at Mericourt L'Abbe and ultimately he arrived in Britain. Allen recovered from his wounds and was sent back to the Battalion.

Captain Mozley and A Company of the 6th Dorsets had been in reserve in Railway Alley. This was on the hill behind the remains of Bottom Wood. He observed that the attack was hampered by the weather conditions. All of the trenches were filled with clogging mud which made movement nearly impossible.

Analysing the failure of the first attack the 17th Division and 52nd Brigade diaries recorded that the enemy were present in great force. The Germans had brought up a large number of fresh troops in preparation for an attack of their own. Therefore the village of Contalmaison was strongly held and owing to the high ground, which was dominated by the village, the attacking British troops suffered heavy casualties. The attack on Quadrangle Support Trench had been over open ground. The troops on the ground reported that Peal Alley was shallow and provided little or no cover from the machine guns in Contalmaison. Perhaps the best that could be said was that the two left hand companies of the 10th Lancashire Fusiliers managed to capture part of Pearl Alley trench and had pushed a battle patrol up towards the village.

4.45 am.

Major-General Pilcher contacted Lieutenant-General Horne at XV Corps headquarters to confirm that the 17th Division's attack had not failed but was indeed *failing*. XV Corps noted that even though events had not gone as planned the 17th Division had managed to occupy Pearl Alley and, despite the fact that they had been forced to withdraw, the Division had taken prisoners.

5.00 a.m.

In the early morning rain D company of the 6th Dorsets moved up from Bottom Wood to the front line in order to support the 7th East Yorks of 50th Brigade. However, when they arrived at Quadrangle

Trench D Company discovered that their help was not required. They handed over their grenades to the 7th East Yorks and returned to their original positions in Bottom Wood.

As D Company moved forward Captain Mozley's A Company moved in two halves along Railway Alley Trench with orders to take over the recently vacated positions in Bottom Wood. They passed through a German barrage but only two men were wounded. Captain Mozley was singularly unimpressed when he saw the new position that his men were taking over; it made an impression in his mind and he wrote about it in his diary. The trench was a shallow ditch that ran along the edge of Bottom Wood and the Wood itself was strewn with dead German soldiers. Mozley noted grimly that it was worse than anything that he had seen at Hooge. They were under constant shell fire and Mozley was amazed that they suffered no casualties. Fortunately for A Company the shells kept landing behind them. He set the men to work improving their position but it was a hopeless task. The rain that lashed down and soaked everyone through soon filled any holes that the men dug in the sodden ground.

A short while later D Company arrived back at Bottom Wood and they found that Captain Mozley's A Company had occupied their positions. Before the officers of both Companies could thin out the over crowded Wood a company of the 7th Borders of 51st Brigade arrived and the wood, not the biggest on the Somme battlefield, was soon heavily congested. Though they were being shelled, the enemy barrage was not heavy enough or accurate enough to cause any casualties.

5.25 am.

XV Corps contacted the 23rd and 38th Divisions and informed them that the attack by 52nd Brigade had indeed failed. Therefore the 17th Division was going to operate 'scheme b'. In accordance with the orders, Pearl Alley, Quadrangle Support and Quadrangle Alley now became extra objectives for 50th Brigade in the 8.00 am attack. The staff at 17th Division headquarters recorded that preparations were 'at once made' for the attack at 8.00 am. Unfortunately the situation was not as clean cut as the staff thought. The front line, Quadrangle Trench, was overcrowded and in chaos.

XV Corps had ordered the 17th Division to hand over their left hand positions in Shelter Alley and the part of Quadrangle Trench that ran north towards Contalmaison to the neighbouring 23rd Division. This was to enable the 23rd Division to make an attack upon Contalmaison village but the hand over proved difficult as 52nd Brigade troops were still fighting with the enemy in that area. Confused, lost, shocked and wounded troops from the failed 2.00 am attack filled the congested trenches. The companies were mixed up and combined with the pouring rain, mud filled the trenches and a constant enemy barrage the officers found organisation difficult. In the confusion there was to be little time to prepare for the next attack.

On the right flank of the 17th Division the 38th Division recorded that they continued preparations for their attack at 8.30 am. In their well prepared positions on the southern edge of Mametz Wood the German troops of the 2nd Battalion, the Lehr Regiment of the 3rd Guards Division waited to receive the Welsh.

5.30 am.

From their positions in Railway Alley, just behind Bottom Wood, C Section of the 50th Machine Gun Company laid down indirect fire on the Western edge of Mametz Wood, Lower Wood and the crossroads on the edge of Mametz Wood. Their fire would also traverse the North edge of Mametz Wood. This indirect fire was designed to disrupt any German movement in or around these positions.

German artillery re-commenced the heavy barrage on the line of Lozenge Wood - Railway Alley.

At the request of the 23rd Division, a battery of French 75's fired a gas barrage at Contalmaison, the first phase of the artillery preparation before the Division's attack.

6.00 am.

The 78th Field Company, Royal Engineers, left their dugouts at Becordel, near Queens Redoubt, and clambered aboard their transport. They had sent their packs into storage and had been preparing to move since the early hours. Their orders were to go forward and begin the work of consolidating the front line and any captured positions.

6.30 am.

The 10th Notts & Derbys, of the 51st Brigade, left Ville-sur-Ancre. With A and D companies leading and B and C following the battalion moved up towards the front line.

The 12th Manchesters of 52nd Brigade arrived in the vicinity of Railway Copse. They had been given orders to move into the front line and relieve the 9th Northumberland Fusiliers. Probably because of the confused situation up at the front, the 12th Manchesters began the process of spreading out and squeezing into the crowded trenches in and around the Hedge and Bottom Wood. Here they remained while Lieutenant-Colonel Harrison, the C.O., awaited the return of Lieutenant Crawhall with orders from Brigadier-General Clarke at 52nd Brigade headquarters. Lieutenant-Colonel Harrison, probably expected that his next orders would be to move into the front line and complete the relief. All the while the German guns kept up the barrage on the British support positions and the 12th Manchesters suffered some casualties.

In Carnoy Valley, after what he called in his diary a 'beastly night', Lieutenant-Colonel Cardew had been woken at 6.15 am. Fifteen minutes later, as he dressed and prepared himself for breakfast, more orders for his brigade arrived at his tent.

23rd Division noted that a barrage of one hundred incendiary shells was fired at Contalmaison; this barrage was later deemed to be a failure.

7.00 am.

In Railway Alley above and behind the 12th Manchesters, C Section, 50th Brigade Machine Gun Company, commenced indirect fire as ordered. They were to sustain their fire for one and a half hours.

A and B companies of the 7th East Yorks, 50th Brigade, received orders that they were not to move from their positions in Fricourt Wood and Railway Alley until 7.30 am.

The 7th East Yorks orders for 'Scheme B' from 50th Brigade were specific. In case the 52nd Brigade's attack on Quadrangle Support failed they had to be prepared to make a bombing attack up Quadrangle Alley and endeavour to capture ground in Quadrangle Support Trench. While the 7th East Yorks were attacking up Quadrangle Alley, elements of the 52nd Brigade would be attacking again up Pearl Alley on the left flank. At the same time the 7th East Yorks were required to make a bombing attack along Wood Trench on their extreme right. 50th Brigade headquarters informed them that they were only required to *prepare* for these attacks. If orders could not be got through to them from Brigade then they were to use their discretion in carrying out these attacks if they saw that the 52nd Brigade attack had failed. If the 52nd Brigade was successful then they would attack Mametz Wood as previously arranged.

The attack had failed. Up at the front the line the fighting had ended for the moment. Having successfully checked the British assault the German infantry withdrew to their positions in Contalmaison and Quadrangle Support Trench and the remaining British troops pulled back from no man's land. There was an expectant pause as both sides watched each other and waited. For a moment the guns stopped firing.

Wyn Griffith serving with the 38th Division on the right flank wrote later that a hush fell over the battlefield at this time, a stillness that, after so much noise, seemed to be full of 'brooding menace.' The pause did not last for long, as the hush was shot through by the chatter of the heavy machine guns of C Section, 50th Machine Gun Company, as they raked Mametz Wood from Railway Alley.

50th Brigade recorded that the counter-attack by the 9th Grenadier Regiment earlier that morning was defeated in part by units of the 23rd Division who had come up to attack Contalmaison. They had taken the German counter-attack in the flank.

7.10 am.

Now that it was abundantly clear that the 52nd Brigade attack had failed. 50th Brigade had to put 'scheme b' into operation. So, despite the orders that they had received ten minutes before, A and B companies of the 7th East Yorks, 50th Brigade, were ordered forward to Bottom Wood. D company were ordered to stay in Crucifix Trench and C Company was already in position in Quadrangle Trench. A and B Companies would be crowded into Bottom Wood with companies from the 6th Dorsets, the 7th Borders and the 12th

Manchesters. Movement through the mass of troops would be difficult, let alone movement over the muddy ground.

7.20 am.

The 79th Royal Field Artillery recorded that the bombardment of Quadrangle Support Trench was restarted; the preliminary bombardment for the 8.00 am attack had commenced.

Heavy artillery under the command of the 23rd Division opened fire on Contalmaison village.

In his position in the Hedge line on the edge of Bottom Wood, Captain Mozley and his men watched the bombardments fall upon Quadrangle Support Trench and Contalmaison, in his diary he described the shell fire as fierce, he also recorded that a smoke barrage was laid down in front of Mametz Wood. Another witness who later wrote about the bombardment was Wyn Griffith of the 38th Division. He watched the shells falling from his position facing Mametz Wood. In his book *Up to Mametz* Griffith remembered that the barrage was so heavy that hill top actually disappeared in smoke and flames and the smoke from the explosions hung in dark clouds against the sky.

7.25 am.

Lieutenant Crawhall returned to the 12th Manchesters headquarters carrying the orders from 52nd Brigade that he had been sent to collect at 3.30 am that morning. Lieutenant Crawhall had been gone for a little under three hours. He had been delayed at Brigade Headquarters waiting for the orders; probably because Brigadier-General Clarke was waiting for reports about the outcome of the fighting. Neil Grant Crawhall who had been attached to the 12th Manchesters from the 2nd East Lancashires went missing in action later that morning in the Manchesters' disastrous attack; it later emerged that he had been killed.

Lieutenant-Colonel Harrison of the 12th Manchesters read the orders and learned that his battalion was to attack Quadrangle Support Trench at 8.00 am after a bombardment starting at 7.30 am. With the bombardment due in five minutes and only thirty five minutes to go before the attack began, Lieutenant-Colonel Harrison knew that there was no time to issue written orders. So he and his adjutant,

Captain Duval, set off on foot to get to their men at the Hedge and personally organise the attack. Lieutenant-Colonel Harrison must have been appalled; his battalion was not in the front line nor was it prepared to attack.

Perhaps Brigadier-General Clarke thought that the 12th Manchesters had completed the relief and were in the line. The orders that Brigadier-General Clarke had sent proved that confusion reigned at Brigade headquarters and that the communications were not working.

Captain Eckhard of the 12th Manchesters wrote about the attack. He mentioned that another battalion was supposed to undertake the attack, but which battalion that was Captain Eckhard did not say. Instead the 12th Manchesters were ordered into the attack. The original plan of attack had been for the Manchesters to creep up behind the cover of the bombardment, and get to within one hundred and fifty yards of the German trench. It took Lieutenant-Colonel Harrison and Captain Duval ten minutes to get to the Bottom Wood area and the bombardment that the 12th Manchesters were meant to follow had already begun.

It does appear that the plan was to have the 9th Duke of Wellingtons attacking on the left, going up Pearl Alley, the 12th Manchesters going up the centre behind the barrage and the 7th East Yorks were to attack up Quadrangle Alley on the right.

7.30 am.

Once Lieutenant-Colonel Harrison had issued his orders the 12th Manchesters had to hastily organise for the attack. They would be hard pressed to attack on time. As Captain Eckhard said later the preparations for the attack would take longer than thirty five minutes. At this moment the barrage was falling with frightening ferocity on the ridge running from Contalmaison that sloped down towards Mametz Wood. The 12th Manchesters should have been getting up behind it. They were nowhere near it; they were behind the British front line.

Lieutenant-Colonel Clive, at the 7th East Yorks headquarters in Railway Copse, received orders from 50th Brigade. The orders, which had been sent out at 7.20 am, stated that if 52nd Brigade's attack *once again* failed the 7th East Yorks were to make a bombing attack up Quadrangle Alley to Quadrangle Support and along Wood

Trench. The battalion officers and men set about preparing for the attack

Each bombing squad was to carry one hundred and sixty bombs, obtained from the dump in Lozenge Wood. The infantry that were to follow the bombers up had to cary two hundred and seventy rounds of small arms ammunition, and as well as wearing standard battle kit they carried two sandbags and two extra bombs. Each company had to make sure that forty tools were also carried into battle. These were to be used to consolidate any captured ground.

It does appear from the orders received by Lieutenant-Colonel Clive that the 7th East Yorks were not due to attack on the right flank of the 12th Manchesters. They were to attack only if the 12th Manchesters attack failed.

7.37 am.

17th Division sent a report to XV Corps Headquarters saying that the Lozenge Wood - Railway Alley area was being heavily shelled. Major-General Pilcher also reported that an enemy counter-attack had been developing on the left of the 17th Division, at the junction of Shelter Alley and Quadrangle Trench.

7.45 am.

This German counter-attack had actually managed to penetrate the British front line and they had gained possession of the junction of Shelter Alley and Quadrangle Trench. The British managed to bring machine gun fire to bear doing the attackers considerable damage. It forced them back from the junction.

If the Germans had held on to the junction any attack up Pearl Alley by the British would be extremely difficult, if not impossible.

Despite the short time available for preparation the Manchesters were nearly ready to advance.

Chapter Three : 7 July 1916 7.50 am to 12 Noon

7.50 am.

Despite the difficulties faced by the 12th Manchesters they managed to launch their attack in the centre from the Ridge behind the Hedge and Bottom Wood. The 12th Manchesters had to go through the troops in front of them and then over the British front line. D and B Companies led the attack, supported by C Company. A Company remained in reserve. The battalion bombers did not go forward with the attack and remained at the battalion headquarters.

Captain Eckhard stated that the 12th Manchesters advanced towards the enemy trench in four lines with the men carrying their rifles at high port as if they were on parade; instead of advancing in short rushes and taking cover. The Lewis gunners advanced with the infantry but they carried their weapons and were not deployed on the flanks. Captain Eckhard believed that the Lewis gunners should have either been deployed on the flanks to return any flank fire or they should not have advanced until the enemy trench had been captured. Even though they had managed to get the attack underway, the 12th Manchesters were well behind the barrage. The barrage had lifted and instead of being within assaulting distance, Captain Eckhard recorded that they were over a quarter of a mile away from their objective. They went into action in the centre believing that a battalion was attacking on their left and another on their right. They attacked up hill, going through their own lines. The rain had made the churned ground into a quagmire and they were in plain view of the German defenders all of the time.

Behind the attacking Manchesters, in Railway Alley Trench, B Section, 50th Brigade Machine Gun Company began indirect fire once again. Three of the Section guns fired over the battlefield, over the heads of the advancing troops, at the 'Cutting'. One gun fired on Pearl Wood, a small copse that lay beyond Mametz Wood.

8.00 am.

79th Royal Field Artillery noted that the infantry assault had begun and therefore the batteries switched their bombardment from Quadrangle Support Trench to Mametz Wood.

In the front line at Quadrangle Trench, Second Lieutenant Mason of the 52nd Machine Gun Company added the eight Lewis guns of the 9th Northumberland Fusiliers to his section.

The two companies of the 9th Duke of Wellingtons in the front line were ordered by 52nd Brigade headquarters to attack up the left flank, along Pearl Alley towards Quadrangle Support Trench. The battalion bombers were to lead the attack, bombing up Pearl Alley as they went. The two companies behind them in the Hedge, Shelter and Bottom Woods were ordered to occupy Quadrangle Trench after the other companies attacked. However, the 9th Duke of Wellingtons had great difficulty moving through the mud and there was a great deal of confusion. The trenches were extremely congested with men from different battalions and the number of wounded was considerable. To make matters worse two of the 9th Duke of Wellingtons company commanders had recently been wounded as they returned from an orders meeting at Battalion Headquarters. When the 9th Duke of Wellingtons began their attack they became mixed up with other units. Like the attack of the 12th Manchesters, the 9th Duke of Wellingtons began their assault behind the scheduled time.

Though they managed to advance and hold a good part of Pearl Alley, the 9th Duke of Wellingtons could not get into Quadrangle Support Trench. As before, the German defence was robust and the wire was intact. Any attempt to attack over the open was met by German rifle and machine gun fire. The 9th Duke of Wellingtons suffered badly. Taking what cover they could, the bombers carried on up Pearl Alley and actually managed to get as far as the Contalmaison Road that ran along the ridge down towards Bottom Wood. Here they met fierce resistance from the German troops in Quadrangle Support Trench but they won the encounter and took nine prisoners. The 9th Duke of Wellingtons established a 'stop' in Pearl Alley, just short of the Contalmaison road, to protect the left flank from assault from Contalmaison.

Despite their position the 9th Duke of Wellingtons could not get into the enemy trench by going over the open, nor could they get into it from Pearl Alley. A report was sent back to battalion Headquarters saying that Pearl Alley was shallow, not continuous and they could not occupy all of it. Furthermore the junction of Quadrangle Trench and Pearl Alley was so badly knocked about by shell fire that it was unrecognisable. To make matters worse they came under fire from British artillery.

A patrol was sent out into Contalmaison and when they returned they reported that they had encountered little opposition in the village itself.

The 1st Worcesters and 2nd East Lancashires of the 23rd Division had attacked Contalmaison at around the same time. They had advanced to the north edge of the village when their attack had been held up by machine guns firing from Peake Wood; outside the village. A number of men from these two units joined the 9th Duke of Wellingtons in Pearl Alley. The ranking officers of the three units hastily conferred and, armed with the knowledge that Contalmaison was not strongly held, if held at all, they planned a joint attack on the village from their position. Something may have been salvaged from the situation had the attack taken place but the 23rd Division men were ordered to withdraw and the impromptu attack was called off. A chance to take Contalmaison had gone.

Orders were sent forward from battalion headquarters to the men at the 'stop' in Pearl Alley telling them to move forward and take Acid Drop Copse, a position that lay behind Quadrangle Support Trench. The bombers tried to comply, but again they ran into heavy opposition from the defenders of Quadrangle Support Trench. This time the British were beaten back. The 'stop' was proving to be a nuisance and the Germans had no intention of allowing the British garrison to remain there. Their artillery began an extremely violent bombardment that wreaked havoc in Pearl Alley and casualties were high among the British troops in the congested position. Lieutenant D. H. Fletcher of the 9th Duke of Wellingtons was hit just above the right eye by a piece of shrapnel. He was lucky that it did not penetrate his brain. Lieutenant Fletcher was taken to a Regimental Aid Post where emergency surgery took place to remove the remains of his right eye.

Under heavy shell fire from both sides and machine gun fire from Quadrangle Support Trench, the men realised that the position had become untenable. They withdrew, leaving their dead like flotsam and jetsam marking a high tide mark, and the Germans re-occupied Contalmaison.

What happened to the 12th Manchesters was recorded by Captain Eckhard, a survivor of the doomed assault. The advancing parade ground lines of Manchesters were simply cut to pieces. Going steadily uphill across no mans land; the ranks were torn apart by both British and German barrages. Demonstrating how hopeless the task was, Eckhard reported that the German defenders of Quadrangle Support Trench actually stood calmly on their own parapet, took aim and shot the Manchesters down. To make matters even worse they came under machine gun fire from both left and right flanks. The flank machine gun fire was murderous and they could not advance through it. Their own Lewis gunners, who could have returned fire, had no opportunity to do so, they had been cut down with the rest.

Eckhard said that they had attacked believing that the flanks were to be secured by two other battalions. The 9th Duke of Wellingtons had tried their best on the left but, as has been seen, they had been forced to retire. The situation on the right was completely confused: there was no sign of the 7th East Yorks. Yet, despite their losses, there were reports that small units of the 12th Manchesters had actually reached Acid Drop Copse, which was behind Quadrangle Support Trench.

Unsupported, facing determined opposition, and with so many casualties, the 12th Manchesters could not hope to carry on the attack. They too were forced to retire.

When the Battalion had gone into the line it had a trench strength of eight hundred and forty NCOs, Other Ranks and twenty two officers. Five hundred and ninety men became casualties and out of the sixteen officers who advanced only three returned. Around 193 men and 8 officers had died, the rest were wounded.

A XV Corps Forward Observation Officer watched the attacks and sent back a report to XV Corps Headquarters. He said that British infantry were actually in Acid Drop Copse at 8.05am. Then, at 8.10am, they were advancing on Pearl Wood and by 8.20am they were retiring from Acid Drop Copse.

It is not known which troops these were. They may have been from either 9th Duke of Wellingtons attack or the 12th Manchesters. The 12th Manchesters did get a small party into Acid Drop Copse. Pearl Wood was just over one kilometre beyond Contalmaison civilian cemetery and in front of the German second line. Neither the 9th Duke of Wellingtons nor the 12th Manchesters reported getting that far forward. At the time Pearl Wood was under machine gun fire from B Section, 50th Brigade Machine Gun Company, sited in Railway Alley. A possible explanation is that British troops *did* get that far forward but did not live to tell the tale.

What had happened on the right flank? The 7th East Yorks had obeyed orders and watched events unfold. They did not attack but waited for orders from 50th Brigade to launch an attack up Quadrangle Alley.

8.20 am.

At 50th Brigade Headquarters they thought that the situation at 8.00 am was 'involved', although it looked as if a successful attack up Quadrangle Alley towards the right hand end of Quadrangle Support Trench would cut off the remains of the German 9th Grenadiers. So they ordered the 7th East Yorks to launch an attack, spearheaded by bombers, to take and secure the junction of Quadrangle Alley and Quadrangle Support Trench. The attack was to begin immediately. Major King, commanding the companies of the 7th East Yorks in the front line had sent a reconnaissance party up Quadrangle Alley sometime before the orders arrived.

8.23 am.

The 7th East Yorks were ready and got their attack underway within three minutes of receiving their orders, but it was too late to support the 9th Duke of Wellingtons and the 12th Manchesters.

Immediately that the 7th East Yorks reached the junction they were engaged by German bombers, machine guns and enfilading rifle fire. Unable to go forward and take the junction, they were forced to fall back. A 'stop' was set up at a point some fifty yards away from the junction.

The 17th Division diary recorded that the 9th Duke of Wellingtons and the 12th Manchesters had attacked as ordered. The 12th Manchesters advanced over the open ground both battalions were met by heavy rifle and machine gun fire. Though small parties made it through to Acid Drop Copse casualties were high and they "failed to make good their objective."[17] It was also recorded that the attack by the 7th East Yorks was driven back by machine gun fire from

---

[17] TNA: PRO. WO95/1981. War Diary, 17th Division, July 1916.

Mametz Wood and from the north. The enemy were reported to be in Strip Trench and the western edge of Mametz Wood. 52nd Brigade noted that the 12th Manchesters "got into one of our own barrages, put down by a neighbouring Division."[18]

Scheme b, such as it was, had failed and with heavy losses. Neither 52nd Brigade nor 17th Division recorded that the attack by the 12th Manchesters was launched from behind the British front line. It stood little chance of success.

Major-General Pilcher had called forward his reserve Brigade. Units of the 51st Brigade were beginning to get into position in preparation for going into the front line. The 7th Lincolns were ordered to rendezvous in original front line trenches of 1 July and await orders. The 8th South Staffords were reported to be in the reserve trenches at Fricourt.

B Section, 50th Brigade Machine Gun Company, in Railway Alley, ceased firing on the 'Cutting' and Pearl Wood.

8.30 am.

79th Royal Field Artillery batteries, firing barrages across Mametz Wood, lifted their fire.

The 78th Royal Field Artillery recorded, erroneously, that the attack continued successfully and that Contalmaison and the north western corner of Mametz Wood were captured.[19]

38th (Welsh) Division began their attack on Mametz Wood. In the front line, on the right of the 7th East Yorks, two companies of the 6th Dorsets were waiting to go forward and support the 8.30 am attack on Mametz Wood. The assault upon the Wood was the main attack of the day and its capture was seen as vital by General Haig if not by Lieutenant-General Horne or Major-General Pilcher. But the assault was not unfolding. The 38th Division got held up at the north

---

[18] TNA: PRO. WO95/2009. 52nd Brigade, War Diary, July 1916.

[19] It must be said that they were only recording what they were told by their Forward Observation Officers and by other units. The field was shrouded in the fog of battle and, the events of 1 July notwithstanding, the British Army at the time was not seeing these opening days of the Somme Campaign as the disaster that it is now considered or perceived by many to be.

eastern edge of Caterpillar Wood and the 6th Dorsets would have to wait until 6.00 pm for any progress.

C Section, 50th Brigade Machine Gun Company, ceased their indirect fire against Mametz and Lower Woods. They reported that each gun had expended 2,000 rounds of ammunition during the action. They had been heavily shelled as the German guns sought to knock out the heavy machine guns and seven men of the section had consequently been wounded by shrapnel. During the barrage the Section Sergeant did sterling work and kept the guns firing. The machine gunners were heavily shelled throughout the day.

8.40 am.

Despite the shelling, B Section, 50th Brigade Machine Gun Company opened fire with three guns on the northern edge of Mametz Wood.

The 79th Royal Field Artillery received a report stating that British infantry had been seen advancing on the South Western side of Contalmaison; these must have been 23rd Division troops.

52nd Brigade recorded that after the failure of the 8.00 am attack they were to maintain their positions all day. Small groups of men were still out in no man's land and there was sporadic fighting during the day. Grenade fighting in the communication trenches, Pearl Alley and Quadrangle Alley was constant without any change in the situation. The shelling and rain was heavy.

So, as sporadic fighting continued in no man's land, the sides took stock of the situation. The 17th Division had put in two attacks against Quadrangle Support Trench and both had been repulsed. The main attack on Mametz Wood had not materialised. On the left the 23rd Division had failed to take Contalmaison village and on the right the 38th Division was nowhere to be seen. The German forces had defended their positions very well. While Contalmaison and Mametz Wood remained in their hands and support was given in terms of artillery and re-supply they could hold off the British for quite some time.

9.00 am.

A and D companies of the 10th Notts & Derbys were now in position in the old British front line trenches facing Fricourt. These trenches were dug deeply into the chalk and gave the sodden soldiers some shelter from the incessant rain. B and C companies spread out behind them in support. Upon their arrival a message was received saying that the attack by 52nd Brigade had been a failure and therefore the attack was being renewed at 8.00 am. This news was a little late...

Half an hour after beginning their assault the left hand attacking battalion of the 38th Division had become 'hung up' by machine gun fire at the south east corner of Mametz Wood.

In his tent in Carnoy Valley Lieutenant-Colonel Cardew noted in his diary that the morning was damp and cold and bemoaned the fact that he was extremely tired and sleepy after a bad night. His batteries were firing as he wrote and the noise, he noted, was awful. His brigade had just been informed that the 8.00 am attack had failed. He also recorded that a telephone wire had been run from the valley forward to Pommiers Redoubt and that he was now receiving messages from Preston, an 80th Brigade officer, who was stationed there. Pommiers Redoubt was a former German strong point built astride the road from Mametz to Montauban. With a good view of the current battlefield it was now being used as Brigade headquarters for units of 38th Division and as an artillery forward observation post.

9.15 am.

Lieutenant-General Horne was becoming impatient with the situation at the front; he wanted to begin the bombardment of the German second line as soon as possible. Major-General Pilcher was therefore ordered to advance his Division on the left and the right flanks and "clear up the situation in Quadrangle Support Trench as early as possible so that the heavy artillery barrage could be adjusted properly."[20] Lieutenant-General Horne ordered the 17th Division to advance its left hand units along Pearl Alley and get in touch with III Corps who were reported to be in and around the village of Contalmaison. On the right the 17th Division was to push along Wood Trench and Wood Support Trench and on towards Mametz Wood.

---

[20] TNA: PRO WO95/921. War Diary, XV Corps, July 1916

In Railway Alley B Section, 50th Brigade Machine Gun Company, ceased fire on the north edge of Mametz Wood. They recorded that they had used up some 3,000 rounds of ammunition.

9.40 am.

The 10th Notts & Derbys received orders to move forward to the area around Lonely Copse.

10.00 am.

Lieutenant-Colonel Wade of the 10th Lancashire Fusiliers visited his men in Quadrangle Trench. He found that they were mixed up with men from the 9th Duke of Wellingtons, 12th Manchesters and 9th Northumberland Fusiliers. The 9th Northumberland Fusiliers were ordered to move to the right to try and ease the congestion in the trench.

Acting upon XV Corps orders to clear the situation up Major-General Pilcher got in touch with the 50th Brigade and ordered them to comply. Shortly afterwards a message arrived at the 7th East Yorks battalion headquarters, from 50th Brigade, ordering an attack across the open. They had to push on to their objective quickly.

Lieutenant-Colonel Clive, commanding officer of the 7th East Yorks was not at all keen on the idea of attacking up the glacis in broad daylight; he was only too aware what had happened to the battalions that had tried this in daylight at 8.00 am, and at 2.00 am under the cover of darkness. Fortunately, the Linesmen had succeeded in repairing a telephone line that ran from the front to Brigade Headquarters at Fricourt Chateau, so he telephoned Brigadier-General Glasgow and discussed the situation. As a consequence, the Brigadier-General agreed that these orders were to be modified. Making another assault upon Quadrangle Support Trench dependant upon the outcome of further bombing attacks.

Perhaps Brigadier-General Glasgow was still painfully aware of the dreadful slaughter done by the German machine guns to the 10th West Yorks on 1 July. Maybe he had no desire to repeat such a disaster.

The 6th Dorsets' headquarters moved from near Sunshade Alley and into Bottom Wood. Thanks to the pouring rain the shell holes and narrow trenches were still full of mud and water. The men had given up trying to improve them and bale them out; they had been fighting a losing battle. To add to their misery they were still being shelled as the German gunners tried to suppress the heavy machine guns in Railway Alley and disrupt reinforcements. Despite the shelling, casualties among the Dorsets were surprisingly few.

The 7th Borders, 51st Brigade, marched up from the cemetery at Fricourt to join the 6th Dorsets in Bottom Wood, where they were heavily shelled in the same barrage. They were to remain here until called forward later that night.

News arrived at the 12th Manchesters Headquarters 'of the complete failure' of their attack upon Quadrangle Support Trench. Only now did Lieutenant-Colonel Harrison learn how his men had suffered in the attack.

After inspecting the Fricourt, Mametz, and Contalmaison Road the Commanding Officer of 78th Field Company, Royal Engineers sent a preliminary report into 17th Division Headquarters about its condition. He stated that further inspection was required, but with masterful understatement, he remarked that the current situation did not permit this.

79th Royal Field Artillery lifted their barrage from Mametz Wood and then commenced shelling the German second line.

10.10 am.

38th Division reported to XV Corps that their left hand battalion had been held up by machine gun fire since 9.00 am near the south east corner of Mametz Wood. 38th Division asked for further bombardment of the wood, but Lieutenant-General Horne told Major-General Phillips that they must use their own Divisional artillery as they could obtain direct observation of the targets. Lieutenant-General Horne then informed Major-General Phillips that the situation on the left, the 17th Division area, was improving and the pressure on his Division would be eased during the course of the morning. Major-General Phillips was asked to keep Corps informed of the situation so that heavy artillery fire could be adjusted accordingly.

10.15 am.

A note arrived at the 7th East Yorks headquarters in Railway Copse. It was from Major King who was with the companies in the front line. It was about their previous bombing attack. In this he said that the bombers had penetrated up Quadrangle Alley as far as the junction with Quadrangle Support Trench but they had been unable to dislodge the defenders. Major King and his men were holding their positions and he reported that the Germans were still holding Quadrangle Support Trench and a strip of wood alongside the railway. Major King requested instructions from his commanding officer.

The former is all that the 7th East Yorks battalion diary records, but there is more to King's note. Major Hughes-Onslow, second in command of the 6th Dorsets, intercepted Major King's message and sent a copy of it to his own Headquarters. The full message said that the 12th Manchesters could not be found and that their wounded claimed that the battalion had been wiped out.

The war diary of the 7th East Yorks recorded that four officers, Captain Dring, Lieutenant Ashington, Second Lieutenant Topping and Second Lieutenant Jackson, had been wounded and an estimated sixteen other ranks had been killed in the attack up Quadrangle Alley at 8.23 am. In fact it was an over estimation; they lost eight men killed that day.

10.20 am.

XV Corps informed Major-General Phillips at 38th Division headquarters that the heavy guns would now bombard the eastern part of Mametz Wood at 10.45 am and continue until 11.15 am. If they wanted more smoke then they were to employ the special party that they had with them.

10.25 am.

No doubt trying to obey Major-General Pilcher's orders, Brigadier-General Glasgow of 50th Brigade sent orders to Lieutenant-Colonel Rowley at the 6th Dorsets headquarters in Bottom Wood. The Brigadier-General wanted the 6th Dorsets to try to get in touch with 7th East Yorks and to go forward and occupy the southern side of Mametz Wood. Brigadier-General Glasgow also informed

Lieutenant-Colonel Rowley that the 7th Yorks were moving up to Railway Alley with their headquarters, "Where yours are now."[21]

Brigadier-General Glasgow seemed to think that the 6th Dorsets had their Headquarters in Railway Alley. Evidently Brigadier-General Glasgow was not aware that the 6th Dorsets headquarters had moved.

10.26 am.

Lieutenant-Colonel Rowley wasted no time and sent a message to Major Denzil Hughes-Onslow, D.S.O., who was commanding the 6th Dorset Companies in the front line. The Lieutenant-Colonel told Major Hughes-Onslow that they had been ordered to push forward by Brigade and that they were to support the 7th East Yorks in Mametz Wood. The battalion had also to occupy Wood Trench and Wood Support Trench if they had not already been occupied. A single platoon of C Company was being sent to Railway Alley. At the end of the message Rowley added that Acid Drop Copse had been captured. It had not been.

10.35 am.

Behind the lines Brigadier-General Trotter was preparing to take over part of the line and was getting his battalions into position. The 10th Notts & Derbys were in position as ordered. Battalion Headquarters was established and the companies had been put into disused trenches near Well Lane and Lonely Trench.

11.00 am.

As part of the 51st Brigade preparations the 7th Lincolns moved up to Willow Trench and then began to insert men into Quadrangle Trench, the front line.

11.13 am.

Despite his orders to go forward with urgency and speed nothing seemed to be happening. So Lieutenant-General Horne kept up the pressure on Major-General Pilcher. He sent instructions to the 17th

21 TNA: PRO. WO95/1998. War Diary, 50th Brigade, July 1916.

Division reminding Major-General Pilcher that they had to keep on pushing up Pearl Alley and keep in touch with the 23rd Division on the left. Major-General Pilcher was also ordered to make all ground his Division could in the centre, to keep pushing the right into Mametz Wood and to work on to the original objective; the central ride of the wood, where they were to link up with the 38th Division.

Lieutenant-General Horne explained to Major-General Pilcher that he wanted the 17th Division to take the pressure off the struggling 38th Division who, he said, were some two hundred yards away from Mametz Wood and waiting for a fresh bombardment before attacking again. Lieutenant-General Horne had promised Major-General Phillips of the 38th Division that success on the left would ease the pressure on his struggling troops. He was now trying to make his promise come true.

In response to the instructions Major-General Pilcher telephoned XV Corps and said that the 51st Brigade had already been ordered to pass through to the front and take over from the 52nd Brigade. One battalion of the 51st Brigade was already at Lonely Copse and moving forward; another was going to be inserted from the south of Fricourt Wood at Willow Trench. Major-General Pilcher explained his proposals for action and then gave Lieutenant-General Horne the good news that it was 'believed' that they now held Acid Drop Copse.

Lieutenant-General Horne must have welcomed this news; at last there seemed to be movement on the front. In truth it masked the fact that nothing had been gained.

11.15 am.

Further good news arrived at 17th Division headquarters. The 23rd Division of III Corps had captured the village of Contalmaison.

The 23rd Division had indeed managed to get two companies of the 1st Worcesters and a number of the 2nd East Lancs into the village but they had not captured it as had been claimed. The Germans had mounted a spirited counter-attack.

At XV Corps headquarters Horne was probably extremely pleased with the turn of events. Things were apparently looking up. Acid Drop Copse had been captured and now the 23rd Division had taken the fortified village of Contalmaison. It seemed that German defences were crumbling and now, perhaps, the pressure on the 38th Division would be eased. If his Divisions obeyed orders and kept pushing forwards, then Quadrangle Support Trench and Mametz Wood were bound to fall into British hands. Lieutenant-General Horne would then have something positive to report to Lieutenant-General Rawlinson.

11.20 am.

In the 51st Brigade the forward momentum was kept up and the 10th Notts & Derbys were ordered into the front line. Their orders from Brigadier-General Trotter at 51st Brigade were to move into Quadrangle Trench and be ready to relieve the 52nd Brigade. Brigadier-General Trotter made it quite plain to Lieutenant-Colonel Banbury that his men were not to commit themselves to any attack without orders. Brigadier-General Trotter was keen to know exactly where his battalions were and, probably well aware of the unreliable nature of the telephone, he ordered Lieutenant-Colonel Banbury to report his next position by bearer.

Accordingly the companies moved out of their positions near Well Lane and Lonely Trench, and made their way through the rain and German barrage with orders to reorganise south west of the Hedge between Bottom and Shelter Woods. C and D companies moved off first, as they were to go into the front line.

Before 12.00 noon.

The Germans had no intention of giving Contalmaison up and fighting in the village intensified. The 1st Worcesters and 2nd East Lancs were hard pressed to defend themselves against the German counter-attacks. Slowly but surely they were pushed back as their ammunition and stock of bombs rapidly dwindled.

12.00 noon.

Surviving elements of the 1st Worcesters and the 2nd East Lancs were pushed back into Quadrangle Trench where they became mixed up with the 10th Lancashire Fusiliers and the 9th Duke of Wellingtons of the 52nd Brigade.

Making the most of the British retreat the Germans launched a series of ferocious bombing attacks from Contalmaison concentrating, as they had done before, upon the junction of Pearl Alley and Quadrangle Trench. The British responded by sending all available bombers to the junction where a savage bombing fight began. The British bombers prevailed and the Germans, apparently showing no interest in pushing the British out of Quadrangle Trench, did not renew the contest.

Lieutenant-Colonel Wade, commanding officer of the 10th Lancashire Fusiliers, was actually in the front line and in an effort to bring about some cohesion he took charge of the mixed up units in the left hand section of Quadrangle Trench.

Also in the trench was Lieutenant Pratt of the 9th Royal Welsh Fusiliers. He reported to Lieutenant-Colonel Wade and informed him that two companies of his battalion had also assaulted Contalmaison and at that moment they were under attack on the north western edge of the village. The 9th Royal Welsh Fusiliers belonged to the 58th Brigade of the 19th (Western) Division which was operating on the left flank of the 23rd Division. The two companies of which Lieutenant Pratt talked had been sent out to protect the extreme right of a 19th Division attack. Their presence served to demonstrate the level of confusion and chaos in the front line.

Lieutenant-Colonel Wade wasted no time and organised the men under his command into a relief force. He sent a mixed force of the reserve company of the 10th Lancashire Fusiliers, men from the 9th Duke of Wellingtons, and men from the 1st Worcesters forward to help and re-enforce the 9th Royal Welsh Fusiliers.

This mixed force experienced great difficulty and were unable to get to the Welsh troops in the village. The ground was extremely difficult to cross and the German infantry brought heavy fire to bear. The situation was made even worse for the British because all of the time that they tried to get into the village, they were shelled by British artillery. Contalmaison remained firmly in German hands.

Now that reports from the fighting units were filtering back to 52nd Brigade Headquarters the reasons for failure of the attacks upon Quadrangle Support Trench were being discussed. Some very important pieces of information concerning Quadrangle Support Trench had come to light.

Brigadier-General Clarke and his staff at 52nd Brigade headquarters now realised that mistakes had been made. They now knew that

Quadrangle Support Trench lay, not at the crest of the glacis, but actually over the crest on the reverse slope. It was invisible to attacking troops until they were nearly on it. The key to capturing the objective was perhaps the one thing the Germans feared the most, the British artillery. When the infantry attacked, instead of taking a pulverised trench and dealing with a few shocked and dazed soldiers, as had happened on the night of the 4/5 July, the German defenders had not suffered at all and were ready to defend their position with vigour. The guns had missed; the bombardments had fallen short, landing on the crest where the trench was thought to be.

Brigadier-General Trotter arrived at Fricourt Chateau and opened 51st Brigade headquarters in the cellars.

Numbers 2, 3 and 4 Sections of 93rd Field Company, Royal Engineers, stood by in the remains of Fricourt village to build strong points in Quadrangle Trench, should Quadrangle Support Trench be taken.

17th Division made a brief note that the 23rd Division, III Corps, had been driven out of Contalmaison Village and that the Germans held the position once more.

Chapter Four : 7 July 1916 12.15 pm to 4.30 pm

12.15 pm.

The 10th Notts & Derbys arrived at their rendezvous having moved on from Lonely Copse. Lieutenant-Colonel Banbury, set up his headquarters in a shell hole 400 yards north of Fricourt Wood, just behind the Hedge and between Shelter and Bottom Woods

12.20 pm.

Once battalion headquarters was set up and the companies had reported to him, Lieutenant-Colonel Banbury sent a situation report to Brigadier-General Trotter. C and D companies had entered Quadrangle Trench and A and B companies were held back near headquarters as a reserve. C and D companies had reported that the front line was congested and occupied by the ragged and disorganised remains of three other battalions of the 52nd Brigade along with remnants of the neighbouring 23rd Division. Two companies were all that that the 10th Notts & Derbys could get into the trench. It was also reported that there were units from the 52nd Brigade in the dug outs in Railway Alley and Crucifix Trench. Lieutenant-Colonel Banbury passed on the message that the situation in the front line was confused.

This was, perhaps, unfair to Lieutenant-Colonel Wade who had done sterling work organising and successfully defending the front line with his scratch force. The officers of the 10th Notts & Derbys could be forgiven though; at that moment they were not quite prepared for the confusion.

Lieutenant-Colonel Banbury reported to Brigadier-General Trotter that he had met with Lieutenant-Colonel Harrison of the 12th Manchesters some twenty minutes before the situation report was sent. Lieutenant-Colonel Harrison had told Lieutenant-Colonel Banbury that he was on his way to the front line with orders to organise the elements of the 52nd Brigade for a new assault upon Quadrangle Support Trench at 5.00 in the afternoon.

If anyone was fully aware of the mistakes that had been made that morning it would be Lieutenant-Colonel Harrison. No doubt he had personally briefed Brigadier-General Clarke about the events of the morning; perhaps bringing Captain Eckhard's report about the disastrous attack by the 12th Manchesters to the General's attention.

Lieutenant-Colonel Banbury's adjutant, 'George Jimmy'[22] Partridge had been in the front line and he had been informed by an officer of the 52nd Brigade that Quadrangle Support Trench was in British hands. Lieutenant-Colonel Banbury treated this statement with caution and told Brigadier-General Trotter that he had not yet verified the man's statement.

The German barrage, said Lieutenant-Colonel Banbury, continued to be heavy in vicinity of Railway Copse to the north.

After his meeting with Lieutenant-Colonel Banbury, Lieutenant-Colonel Harrison made his way towards the front line. He did not arrive because on the way forward Harrison was shot in the neck. He was incredibly lucky because the bullet passed through his neck, and missed his vital arteries and spinal cord. A stretcher bearer was called for and the wounds were dressed immediately. Harrison was able to walk and felt it was his duty to report to headquarters before he presented himself a dressing station. He set off on foot, walking through the barrage to Bottom Wood and then on to Fricourt Chateau where he reported in person to Brigadier-General Clarke.[23]

With Lieutenant-Colonel Harrison wounded Lieutenant-Colonel H. Bryan of the 9th Northumberland Fusiliers was now placed in command of the 52nd Brigade troops in the front line. Lieutenant-Colonel Bryan called a meeting that included Lieutenant-Colonel Clive of the 7th East Yorks (50th Brigade), and Captain Duval, now the senior officer of the 12th Manchesters. Between them they swiftly concluded that the third attack could not go ahead and must be cancelled. Lieutenant-Colonel Bryan duly reported their decision to Brigadier-General Clarke at 52nd Brigade Headquarters. Their

---

[22] Captain George Partridge was known as 'George Jimmy' to his fellow officers and had been since he joined the battalion in 1914. He was well liked and known to be a kind and decent man.

[23] What happened to Lieutenant-Colonel Harrison is in no doubt but when and in what circumstances is. The Divisional history states that he was wounded superintending the withdrawal of his men after their disastrous attack. The 10th Notts & Derbys and the 12th Manchesters diaries state that he was wounded going forward to prepare for another attack. The 10th Notts & Derbys say that he went forward sometime between 12 noon and 12.30 pm and the Manchesters said that it was 2.30 pm.

analysis of the situation and their recommendation was going to be ignored by their superiors.

12.25 pm.

Rumours from the front had by this time spread to the Divisional Artillery. The gunners received the news that Contalmaison had been occupied by III Corps and that the 17th Division had captured Acid Drop Copse, Contalmaison civilian cemetery and Quadrangle Support Trench. Now, perhaps, the gunnery officers turned their thoughts to the next target; the German second line. The rumours were unfounded.

12.30 pm.

Those in and near the front line were far more aware of the truth. In the pouring rain elements of Brigadier-General Trotter's 51st Brigade moved into position. When the 8th South Staffords arrived at Lonely Copse, despite the optimistic news that was circulating in the rear, they received the unpleasant information that the last attack upon Quadrangle Support Trench had failed and that the Germans still held the trench.

Responding to the rumours of success numbers 1, 3 and 4 Sections of the 93rd Field Company, Royal Engineers were ordered forward to consolidate Quadrangle Support Trench. C Company of the Pioneer battalion, the 7th Yorks & Lancs, were also ordered forward from Queens Redoubt to work with the Engineers. When the Engineers and Pioneers arrived they soon discovered that the Germans were still holding the trench so no work could be done. Two men of the 93rd Field Company were reported as wounded at this time.

As the number of casualties mounted the 51st Field Ambulance had commandeered any road transport that they could in order to get the wounded away from the front as quickly as possible. At 12.30 pm two motor buses reported for duty at the Subway and these along with the Lorries, horse drawn carts and ambulances took stretcher cases, threading through congested and ruined roads, to the 64th Field Ambulance at Mericourt L'Abbe. They carried sitting cases to the 36th Casualty Clearing Station at Heilly or the 34th Casualty Clearing Station at Vecquemont.

12.33 pm.

Lieutenant-Colonel Rowley, commanding officer of the 6th Dorsets, sent a situation report to Brigadier-General Glasgow at 50th Brigade Headquarters. Along with the report he attached a copy of Major King's message about the attack by the 7th East Yorks at 8.23 am.

Demonstrating that he was following the orders that he had received at 10.25 am Lieutenant-Colonel Rowley informed Brigadier-General Glasgow that he had sent one company to try and occupy Wood Trench and Wood Support if at all possible; the company also had orders to give assistance to the 7th East Yorks. Lieutenant-Colonel Rowley reported that his battalion headquarters was now in a dugout in Bottom Wood. He had one company in Railway Alley Trench and two companies were stationed in Bottom Wood and in the trench, the Hedge, running along northern edge of the wood. He told the Brigadier-General that it was advisable to have no less than two Companies in Bottom Wood in case of a counter-attack.

Lieutenant-Colonel Rowley also stated that the enemy was maintaining a very heavy barrage on the front line and communication trenches with shells of all sorts. Quadrangle Support Trench had not been taken and he reported that he was unable to get in touch with 52nd Brigade H.Q. There was no sign, he added, of the 38th Division on the right flank.

It was Captain Mozley's A Company that Rowley had sent up to the front line and Captain Mozley wrote about it in his diary; though it was the conditions on the ground that struck the Captain, not higher strategy. He did not, for instance, mention any orders from Lieutenant-Colonel Rowley for the occupation of Wood or Wood Support Trenches, only that he was to support the 7th East Yorks.

He received his orders to go up to the front line and support the 7th East Yorks in the early afternoon. So he led his men out of their positions in Bottom Wood up the communication trench, Bottom Alley, towards the front line. The going was heavy; the narrow trench was filled with deep mud and was overcrowded. Captain Mozley's men had to squeeze slowly past troops going to and from the front and often they had to wait as stretcher cases were carried painfully down the line.

It took the leading portion of the company a great deal of time to reach the front line and when they did arrive there Captain Mozley could find no one who knew why they had been sent forward. He found the 7th East Yorks and quickly realised that they had, at some point, attacked Quadrangle Support Trench. He asked if they were expecting his company for support but the answer they gave was negative. He did discover from them that Quadrangle Support Trench was still in German hands and that they were apparently holding it in great strength.

Captain Mozley went further along the trench to the left asking if any one was expecting his company. Despite Lieutenant-Colonel Rowley's claim that he could not get in touch with 52nd Brigade H.Q., Captain Mozley met some 52nd Brigade troops. Various units from the 52nd Brigade were in the front line and as he went along the trench they all said that his men had been sent to relieve them. Captain Mozley did not believe them and made his way back to his company.

He and his men waited in the front line for a short time while Captain Mozley made up his mind what to do. In the meantime the Germans began to shell Quadrangle Trench. Not all of his company had managed to get into the front line; many of them were still in the overcrowded Bottom Alley communication trench. It did not take Captain Mozley long to decide that, like the day before, he should take his men away from the front line and return to his original positions. Just before he left he was struck by the pathetic figure of a man, sitting on a fire step in Quadrangle Trench. Unlike everyone else he had no steel helmet and nor did he have any equipment with him, he was dressed only in a Tommy's great coat and was nursing a bad thigh wound. No one seemed to be attending to him and Captain Mozley wanted to help but his own stretcher bearers were at the rear of his company and still trying to get up the communication trench. Much later it occurred to Mozley that the wounded man had probably been a German soldier.

12.35 pm.

Very shortly after Lieutenant-Colonel Rowley sent in his report Lieutenant-Colonel Clive of the 7th East Yorks submitted his own situation report to Brigadier-General Glasgow.

He reported that two companies were position in Quadrangle Trench. They had a 'stop' in Quadrangle Alley, about 50 yards from the junction with Quadrangle Support Trench, but they were unable to make any progress there. His men had made contact with the 38th

Division; Lieutenant-Colonel Clive reported that one platoon of the South Wales Borderers were holding a portion of Quadrangle Trench, beyond the junction with Quadrangle Alley and that they had their right flank on the railway.

He informed Brigadier-General Glasgow that all of the company officers in the front line were wounded, many other ranks were wounded and about sixteen men had been killed. He told the Brigadier-General that Wood Trench and all of Mametz Wood was now occupied by the Germans and even as he made the report the Germans were attempting a counter-attack by bombs. Lieutenant-Colonel Clive put in an urgent request for more bombs to be sent up to his men in the front line.

XV Corps received an encouraging report from the 21st Divisional Artillery saying that British infantry were advancing on Quadrangle Support Trench and attacking Wood Support Trench. The Germans were shelling the North West corner of Mametz Wood.

Who was attacking Quadrangle Support Trench at this point and had British infantry actually got as far as the North West Corner of Mametz Wood as the Forward Observation Officer had reported earlier on in the day? This report must refer to one of the earlier attacks on Quadrangle Support Trench.

1.00 pm.

The attacks, sniping, bombing fights and constant shelling was causing casualties all of the time. Consequently the R.A.M.C were crying out for any kind of vehicle to carry the flow of wounded men away from the battlefield. The 23rd Division History recorded that an aid station that had been set up in the rubble of Fricourt village. The wounded were tended in tents and under tarpaulins stretched from a bank. Neither tents nor tarpaulins were shelter from the shells that were bursting all around them.

Captain Dougal of the 52nd Field Ambulance marched B subdivision Bearers to the Aid Post in Sunken Road at the junction with Patch Alley, to assist the 51st Field Ambulance Bearers. Patch Alley was on the left flank just behind Birch Tree Wood on the left hand side of what was, and still is, a sunken road.

Captain J. R. Mitchell and Lieutenant Thomas assisted the 53rd Field Ambulance Advanced Dressing Station at the Subway.

Two sections of the 78th Field Company, Royal Engineers, along with D Company of the Pioneer Battalion, the 7th Yorks & Lancs, were ordered forward to consolidate Strip Trench, Wood Trench, and Quadrangle Trench and to join Quadrangle Alley to the latter point. Sections 3 & 4 Royal Engineers were allotted this work. Work instructions were issued for the building and wiring of strong points in all of those trenches. Sections 3 & 4 and the Company of Pioneers were ordered to proceed to Lozenge Wood to collect building materials from the dump and to await developments.

This work could not be carried out. Strip and Wood Trenches were still in German hands and any attempt, at this point, to join Quadrangle Trench to Wood trench would be almost impossible. All that the Engineers and Pioneers could do was add to the congestion on the roads and in the mud filled trenches.

XV Corps informed the 38th Division that the 17th Division had cleared Wood Trench and were pushing north up a strip of wood that protruded from Mametz Wood and terminated in the gap between Quadrangle Trench and Wood Trench. The 17th Division could not advance over the open ground between Wood Trench and Wood Support because of machine gun fire from the east. In response the 38th Division reported back to Corps that patrols had gone into Mametz Wood near Strip Trench but no report had yet been forthcoming. Corps ordered them to push on.

In fact the information about Wood Trench was erroneous. Wood Trench had not been cleared at all; Lieutenant-Colonel Clive had informed Brigadier-General Glasgow of this only twenty five minutes before. Captain Mozley's Dorsetshire men, who apparently had orders to occupy the trench, had not attempted to occupy the trench. Unable to find anyone who knew about their arrival they had returned to their support positions.

Evidently Brigadier-General Glasgow had passed Lieutenant-Colonel Rowley's situation report on to Division and somewhere in the process the translation had altered from "try and occupy Wood Trench" to "occupy Wood Trench." Perhaps someone at 17th Division had painted a far more optimistic picture for Lieutenant-General Horne than was the case. Or maybe Lieutenant-General Horne was trying to spur Major-General Phillips of the 38th Division on. A third alternative is that Lieutenant-General Horne genuinely believed that Wood Trench had been occupied as per instructions issued in the morning. He had been receiving positive reports and it seemed that his command was gaining the upper hand and advancing. The report from the 21st Divisional Artillery did seem to paint this picture.

The problem was that the 17th and 38th Divisions were not advancing and the objectives were not yet taken. However, Lieutenant-General Horne repeated the optimistic view in his situation report to Lieutenant-General Rawlinson. After lunch General Haig visited General Rawlinson at Fourth Army headquarters and directed him to take Mametz Wood and push on to Pozieres.

1.05 pm.

XV Corps telephoned an optimistic situation report through to Fourth Army Headquarters.

The night attack got forward on the left, but not on the right; the left was then counter-attacked and driven back. At 7.00 am the Germans developed a strong counter-attack which succeeded in capturing junction of Shelter Alley and Quadrangle Trench. The attack on the right was driven off with heavy loss to the enemy. Then the British bombardment started, and the attack went forward at 8.00 am. The fighting in that portion of the area had been extremely confused, and it was difficult to ascertain where the boundary of the exhausted 52nd Brigade, which had been fighting all night, actually was. The 51st Brigade was now passing through the 52nd Brigade, as far as could be made out, but its present position on the left was not known. 50th Brigade on the right had cleared Wood Trench and was advancing up the strip of wood which runs due south to the main wood. There was a report, at present unconfirmed, that British infantry were in the North West corner of Mametz Wood, which the Germans were shelling. The 38th Division had, under instructions from XV Corps, ordered patrols to push forward through the most southerly portion of the wood and join hands with the remainder of the 17th Division because the 50th Brigade could not make a direct advance on Wood Support on account of flanking machine gun fire.

1.30 pm.

D Company of the 7th Yorks & Lancs, the Pioneers, left Queens Redoubt at Becourt to work on the consolidation of Quadrangle Trench with 78th Field Company, Royal Engineers. Their instructions were to put strong points into the trench and to put out barbed wire. At around this time Queens Redoubt was shelled, fourteen men were wounded and two, Private Ernest Gardner and Private J.W. Taylor were killed. These two men were buried, side by side, on the same day in the small cemetery next to the Redoubt. It is now known as Norfolk Cemetery, Becordel-Becourt.

The Pioneers recorded that they received the following message from the 17th Divisional Commanding Officer, Major-General Pilcher.

The Divisional Commander wishes to express his appreciation of the way in which communication has been maintained during the past week and to thank all ranks concerned for their hard work. He is particularly pleased to hear of the way in which the forward cable laying was carried out today by the signal coy and PIONEERS, despite considerable difficulties and heavy shellfire. [24]

2.00 pm.

Brigadier-General Glasgow at 50th Brigade headquarters wanted to know if the 6th Dorsets had actually got into Wood Trench. He sent a message to Lieutenant-Colonel Rowley demanding that if he did not know the answer then he had better find out. The information was urgently required, said the Brigadier-General, as the entire artillery programme depended on it. Not to mention the fact that XV Corps Commander Lieutenant-General Horne and now Lieutenant-General Rawlinson had been told that Wood Trench had indeed been cleared by Brigadier-General Glasgow's Brigade.

A Section, 50th Machine Gun Company received orders to remain in Lozenge Wood for the afternoon as the attack upon Quadrangle Support had been a failure. While they waited two high explosive shells landed on their dump destroying a gun, a tripod and all gun gear.

Nineteen year old, 3514, Private Charles Edward Reynolds, a member of the 50th Machine Gun Company, was killed in action on this day. When he was killed has not been recorded, it may well have been when the dump was hit.

---

[24] TNA: PRO WO95:1995. 7th Yorks & Lancs (Pioneers). July 1916.

The 52nd Machine Gun Company recorded that the 52nd Brigade was to be relieved and units began withdrawing from the front line to Fricourt.

The Commanding Officer of the 52nd Field Ambulance was ordered by the Assistant Director Medical Services, to take over the collection of wounded from the battle area. Bearer divisions of 51st, 53rd and 54th Field Ambulances, the latter at Carcaillot Farm on the outskirts of Meaulte, were placed at his disposal.

Consequently the headquarters of the 52nd Field Ambulance moved to the Aid Post dug out at the junction of Patch Alley and Sunken Road and Aid Posts were set up in Railway Copse.

Lieutenant-General Horne received the truthful news that the 38th Division had not actually been able to put patrols into the Mametz Wood even though the Division previously stated that it had.

At 2.00 pm the 6th Dorsets had reported to 50th Brigade that the enemy were holding Quadrangle Support Trench at its junction with Quadrangle Alley. They were also holding the railway line between Quadrangle Support and Quadrangle Trenches, Wood Trench and Wood Support Trench.

2.10 pm.

The truth was beginning to dawn at XV Corps headquarters. The report that Lieutenant-General Horne had sent to General Rawlinson now looked as if it was wrong. 17th Division was not advancing up the strip of wood protruding from Mametz Wood and the 38th Division had no patrols in Mametz Wood. Lieutenant-General Horne swiftly issued orders to remedy the situation and to make certain that his Divisions would do what he had already told his superior officer they *had* done.

Both 17th and 38th Divisions were informed by XV Corps that a fresh bombardment of enemy positions would take place at 4.30 pm and would last for half an hour. At 5.00 pm the 38th Division were to attack Mametz Wood and the 17th Division were to attack the strip of wood projecting southerly from Mametz, Quadrangle Support and Pearl Alley. The Divisions were to notify Corps the areas they wanted bombarding by 3.30 pm. The recommendation made by three front line officers, Lieutenant-Colonels Bryan and

Clive and Captain Duval, that the 5.00 pm should not take place was ignored.

2.30 pm.

Lieutenant-General Horne and Major-General Pilcher wanted movement and progress up at the front. Therefore long orders were issued by Brigadier-General Glasgow at 50th Brigade headquarters to the 6th Dorsets and the 7th East Yorks for an attack.

Brigadier-General Glasgow told his battalion commanders that to enable the battalions to advance a re-bombardment had been arranged by XV Corps. Wood Support and the Northern side of clearing would be shelled but not the southern part of the junction of Wood Support Trench and Quadrangle Alley. Wood trench would also come in for the attention of the guns, as would the Eastern edge of the clearing as far south as situation of the 38th Division allowed. At this point no one in the 17th Division seemed to know where the 38th Division actually was.

The battalions were told that zero hour for the forthcoming attack would not be before 4.30 pm. The new bombardment would begin thirty minutes before zero hour.

The 6th Dorsets were told that their objective was Wood Trench, if they did not already hold it. Wood Support trench and the Northern edge of the clearing. The left flank of the 6th Dorsets was to join up with the 7th East Yorks along the line of the railway.

The 7th East Yorks were to seize the line of the railway as soon as bombardment stopped and from that line help the 6th Dorsets advance. They were told that the time of zero hour would be sent to them later. The 7th Yorks were to move in and take over line now held by the 6th Dorsets as they advanced. The battalions were instructed to acknowledge the receipt of these orders. There had to be no doubt that the instructions had been received.

3.00 pm.

The German guns, some of them 15 cm howitzers, continued to pound the ground between Fricourt and Bottom Woods. It was here that along with many other units of all three brigades that the 10th Notts & Derbys had their headquarters and their reserves, A and B companies.

The barrage was taking a toll on the waiting troops and the 10th Notts & Derbys suffered many casualties. Both companies were forced to move to the right, taking up positions in shell holes and trenches near the already over crowded Bottom Wood.

Second in command of the 10th Notts & Derbys, Major J. Hall-Brown was killed by the shelling. Captain N. H. Pratt, of B Company and Lieutenant W. H. Nelson were wounded and were taken to the 64th Field Ambulance at Mericourt L'Abbe. Both men died the next day of their wounds. It is also possible that Sergeants Morris D.C.M., and Nowell and Privates Longdon and Robinson were also killed at this time.

The hospital at Heilly was alongside the railway and the tents stood in long rows, each with a red cross painted on the roof to guard against air attack. Despite the heavy rain the sultry weather made the tents unbearably hot for the casualties who lay within them.

3.05 pm.

Lieutenant Colonel Clive of the 7th East Yorks received the long and detailed orders from Brigadier-General Glasgow at 50th Brigade headquarters concerning the forthcoming bombardment and attack. He forwarded the orders to Major King commanding the 7th East Yorks in the front line.

D Battery of 79th Royal Field Artillery received orders to shell part of Quadrangle Support Trench, Quadrangle Alley and the western edge of Mametz Wood.

3.10 pm.

The 7th East Yorks received a message from 50th Brigade stating that zero hour for the new attack would be 5.00 pm. The new bombardment was to begin at 4.30 pm. They were also told that one battalion of the 51st Brigade would assault Quadrangle Support Trench on the left flank. Lieutenant-Colonel Clive sent this information on to Major King.

3.20 pm.

XV Corps Headquarters received a report from a Forward Observation Officer saying that Contalmaison village was indeed in German hands.

Because of their losses in the continuous and heavy fighting, Major-General Pilcher finally decided to pull the 52nd Division out of the line and replace them completely with the 51st Brigade who had, for a few hours now, been in the process of getting into position.

3.30 pm.

113th Brigade, of 38th Division, recorded that the two patrols that had been sent out earlier on (the time was not recorded) to reconnoitre Strip Trench returned to their positions. This was presumably Cliff Trench and the patrols were presumably from the 15th Royal Welsh Fusiliers. They reported that Strip Trench was strongly held. An attack was prepared.

Earlier that day, once again the time was not given, 113th Brigade had noted that they had received orders to make a reconnaissance of Strip Wood where Strip Trench was located. They had also been instructed to "demonstrate in south of Strip Wood to keep attention from attack by 17th Division in direction of Wood Trench."[25]

4.00 pm.

Even though Major-General Pilcher was preparing the orders to pull the 52nd Brigade out of the fighting Brigadier-General Clark's men were still in the thick of it. The 9th Duke of Wellingtons recorded that at around 4.00 pm a German counter-attack seemed to be developing and was suspected to be imminent. An ad hoc force of men from every available unit were organised to meet the expected attack. A defensive flank was built up in Shelter Alley, made up of a concentration Lewis Gun teams and bombers. The straight forward relief system which the Divisions and Brigades had become accustomed to since summer 1915 were now impossible under offensive operation conditions.

---

25 TNA:PRO WO95/2552. 113th Infantry Brigade. July 1916.

The 52nd Brigade recorded that at about this time they were notified of their relief by the 51st Brigade. Therefore the units of the 52nd Brigade began to make preparations for the move back to Meaulte.

Second Lieutenant Jones of the 52nd Machine Gun Company led their transport column into the rubble of Fricourt village where the weary men of the machine gun sections were waiting. They loaded their equipment onto the wagons and then returned by sections to temporary billets in the fetid dugouts of Meaulte village.

51st Field Ambulance recorded that at 4.00 pm it began to rain very heavily and the rain continued all afternoon, evening and night. The weather conditions continued to make the bearers' work much more difficult.

4.05 pm.

There was confusion at XV Corps and 17th Division headquarters. XV Corps recorded that 17th Division had reported that it could not discover whether Quadrangle Support Trench was in British hands or not.

Yet why was there confusion? The units in the front line knew very well that Quadrangle Support Trench was definitely not in British hands. Reports of its status had been sent back to the Brigades by the battalions throughout the morning and afternoon. An hour earlier, at 3.00 pm, the 79th Royal Field Artillery had been ordered to shell the trench. At 2.00 pm a report had been sent in to 50th Brigade stating that the trench was held by the Germans. Lieutenant-Colonels Rowley and Clive had reported it as occupied by the enemy at around 12.30 pm. At roughly the same time the 8th South Staffords had been informed that it was in enemy hands. And there had been no new attacks against the trench since the morning.

Major-General Phillips of the 38th Division joined in the debate and telephoned Lieutenant-General Horne. Major-General Phillips was also uncertain about the situation in Quadrangle Support Trench. After much talking on the telephone with his two subordinates Lieutenant-General Horne reluctantly concluded that the best course of action would be to postpone the forthcoming attack until the situation was clarified. However, he ordered that all arrangements had to be made by 6.30 pm for the next assaults upon Quadrangle Support Trench and the strip of wood that jutted out towards the

British front line. He told Major-General Phillips that his Division must attack at 6.30 pm

Brigadier-General Clark, still at his post in 52nd Brigade headquarters below Fricourt Chateau, contacted XV Corps headquarters by telephone and Lieutenant-General Horne confirmed the cancellation of the forthcoming attack. Brigadier-General Clark was told that the reason for cancellation was the confusion over the actual situation in Quadrangle Support Trench.

In the front line positions occupied by Major King and elements of the 7th East Yorks they unaware that the attack had been delayed by their superiors. They continued their preparations for the attack and the rain showers became incessant rain.

4.10 pm.

An attempt was made to clear up the situation and get a clearer picture of just what was going on in Quadrangle Support Trench; XV Corps headquarters ordered an air reconnaissance.

In accordance with their orders Captain Cecil Lewis of No. 3 Squadron R.F.C and his observer Pip flew over the Fricourt section of the battlefield in their Moraine Parasol aircraft. Lewis says in his book *Sagittarius Rising* that they dropped down to 800 ft to get a look at a party of men down seen moving around in Quadrangle Support Trench. The infantry men ducked down into cover as the aircraft flew over but Lewis recognised them as Germans because of the colour of their uniforms and the shape of their helmets. Lewis and Pip returned with the news. There was no doubt now; the British did not hold Quadrangle Support Trench. After the flight Lewis recorded in his log that XV Corps acted upon their information and Quadrangle Support Trench was bombarded for two hours.[26]

4.15 pm.

All elements of 52nd Brigade were now withdrawing. The 9th Northumberlands, 12th Manchesters, and 9th Duke of Wellingtons began to move out of their positions in the front line.

---

[26] C. Lewis, *Sagittarius Rising*, (Originally published by Peter Davis, 1936. Reprinted by Greenhill Books, 1993), p. 125

4.20 pm.

At 7th East Yorks Battalion headquarters Lieutenant-Colonel Clive received orders from 50th Brigade stating that the 5.00 pm attack was to be postponed until further notice. Lieutenant-Colonel Clive set about telephoning these orders through to the men in the front line. Unfortunately Major King was out of telephone contact and Lieutenant-Colonel Clive was unable to get through to him.

Unaware of the changed orders Major King carried on with his preparation for the attack. There had not been time to get fresh troops from D Company into the line so Major King intended to use B Company for the attack. Because all of B Company's officers were wounded Major King planned to lead the attack personally.

Back at battalion headquarters, unable to get through to Major King on the telephone, Lieutenant-Colonel Clive realised that he had to send runners out to find the Major and his men. The runners set out and found that the communication trenches were blocked with troops and deep mud. Therefore they had no other choice than to leave the trenches and go over the open ground to reach the 7th East Yorks B Company.

Meanwhile, in the front line, B Company was involved in a fire fight with German troops who were holding Wood Trench. The trench was almost a continuation of Quadrangle Trench and Major King's men brought a Lewis Gun to bear doing a good deal of damage to the German troops who were crowded into the trench.

4.25 pm.

XV Corps informed 17th Division that the hour of bombardment would be given as soon as the situation in Quadrangle Support Trench was clear. Two hours notice would be given before the hour for the bombardment was to be fixed.

17th Division noted the arrival of XV Corps orders for the next attack and   issued orders for the complete withdrawal of 52nd Brigade and their replacement by the 51st Brigade.

4.30 pm.

The eight Lewis gun teams of the 9th Northumberland Fusiliers ceased their temporary secondment to Second Lieutenant Mason's D

Section of the 52nd Brigade Machine Gun Company and left the front line.

B Section, 50th Brigade Machine Gun Company opened fire with three guns from Railway Alley on the northern edge of Mametz Wood. One gun concentrated upon Pearl Wood, while C Section fired at the western edge of Mametz Wood and at the ground between Mametz Wood and the German second line.

Chapter Five : 7 July 1916 4.35 pm to 11.30 pm

4.35 pm.

In the front line Major King received the 50th Brigade orders, forwarded from 7th East Yorks' Headquarters, concerning the bombardment that would proceed the coming attack. Five minutes later Major King received zero hour for the joint attack. He and his men were to attack at 5.00 pm. He was still unaware that the attack had been cancelled.

4.50 pm.

17th Division issued Operation Order No. 61. 50th Brigade was to capture Wood Trench and the strip of Mametz Wood along the Railway. They were also to take Wood Support Trench and Quadrangle Alley. 51st Brigade was ordered to capture Quadrangle Support Trench. The attack was to take place at an hour to be named later but would not sooner than 6.30 pm. By this time all arrangements for the attacks had to be completed.

4.58 pm.

With barely two minutes to spare Lieutenant-Colonel Clive's runners finally reached Major King's position where he and his men were ready to 'go over the top'. The news of the cancellation dramatically halted what would have only been a disastrous, lone attack.

5.00 pm.

The 10th Notts & Derbys were ordered to relieve all units of 52nd Brigade in Quadrangle Trench. As the 10th Notts & Derbys went into the front line the severely mauled 10th Lancashire Fusiliers withdrew and immediately headed for temporary billets in Meaulte. Brigadier-General Trotter issued orders that once the relief was complete the 10th Notts & Derbys were to clear up the situation in Pearl Alley and prepare for an attack upon Quadrangle Support Trench.

Once the relief of the 10th Lancashire Fusiliers was complete the Notts & Derbys duly sent a patrol up Pearl Alley. They soon discovered that it was still in German hands. They returned to report this fact and, to complicate matters further, they reported that the left portion of Quadrangle Trench, where it turned up northwards, was little more than a shallow ditch. Anyone in that part of the trench was in full view of Contalmaison and it was well known that German snipers were active in the village. A bombing squad was sent up Pearl Alley and they cleared it of German troops almost as far as the civilian cemetery.

10th Notts & Derby Battalion headquarters had moved forward now to a dugout in Railway Copse. The diary recorded that the rain had stopped but that the ground was difficult to move over because of the mud.

C Section, 50th Brigade Machine Gun Company reported that they had lost one machine gun. It had been put out of action by a direct hit from high explosive shell during the constant German barrage that was falling on Shelter Wood, Railway Alley and Bottom Wood.

79th Royal Field Artillery received the rather late news that British troops had been forced to evacuate Contalmaison village.

5.30 pm.

B Section, 50th Brigade Machine Gun Company, ceased firing on Mametz Wood and Pearl Wood. The three guns firing on Mametz Wood reported that they had used 4,000 rounds. The single gun firing on Pearl Wood had expended 1,250 rounds.

Nearby in the same trench C Section ceased firing at the western edge of Mametz Wood and the ground up to the German second line. After firing ceased C section packed up and withdrew to Fricourt Wood.

6.00 pm.

50th Brigade sent a message to the 6th Dorsets and 7th East Yorks. It said that in the event of attack being ordered for that evening the 7th East Yorks would be responsible for bombing up Quadrangle Alley and up Railway Strip to their junctions with Mametz Wood. This was in addition to the task already allotted to them at 2.30 pm; the capture the line of the Railway that ran between Quadrangle and Wood Trenches.

The 6th Dorsets were given the objectives of Wood Trench and Wood Support.

The bombardment would fall on Wood Trench, Wood Support Trench, and the edges of the big clearing and Railway Strip down to a point two hundred yards north of Wood Trench. Quadrangle Alley would be shelled up to the junction with Quadrangle Support Trench.

6.10 pm.

By now Lieutenant-General Horne was in possession of Captain Lewis' aerial reconnaissance report. It was now clear to him that Quadrangle Support Trench was not in British hands so orders were issued for the 17th Division to renew the attack. 17th Division was informed that the bombardment was scheduled to begin at 7.30 pm, lift at 8.00 pm and that III Corps would attack Contalmaison village at the same time.

17th Division recorded the receipt of the orders from XV Corps and began sending the necessary orders out to the 50th and 51st Brigades. Despite being told by XV Corps that elements of III Corps would attack Contalmaison the 17th Division diarist recorded that there was to be no advance by the Divisions on either flank. These were the 23rd Division of III Corps on the left and the 38th Division of XV Corps on the right.

50th Brigade was ordered to make the bombing attack up the strip of wood that protruded from Mametz Wood. 51st Brigade was ordered by Major-General Pilcher to take Acid Drop Copse in addition to their main objective of Quadrangle Support Trench. In turn the Brigades began to send out orders to their battalions in the line.

In the 6th Dorsets headquarters Lieutenant-Colonel Rowley received his orders from 50th Brigade. He was told that the attack was to take place at 8.00 pm and that the preliminary bombardment would begin at 7.30 pm. His men were ordered to bomb up Railway Strip and then along Wood Support Trench the latter of which, Brigade informed him, was now only thinly held by the enemy. Lieutenant-Colonel Rowley was told that the 38th Division had actually got troops into Wood Trench on the right. He was asked to make sure that they were there. Then he was given the information that III Corps, on the left, was also going to be attacking at the same time as the 17th Division. Lieutenant-Colonel Rowley acknowledged the receipt of his orders and set about implementing them.

6.15 pm.

Finally relieved by elements of the 51st Brigade the 9th Duke of Wellingtons withdrew from the front line to Fricourt where they had hot tea. After their welcome mugs of tea they marched away to billets in Meaulte. They had lost, wounded or killed, fourteen officers and 251 other ranks.

6.25 pm.

The 7th East Yorks received almost identical orders to those issued to the 6th Dorsets. Lieutenant-Colonel Clive was informed of the start time for the preliminary bombardment and the time for the start of the attack. 50th Brigade also informed him that the 38th Division were in Wood Trench. Despite the fact that two hours earlier Major King's B Company had been involved in a fire fight with German troops in Wood Trench. He was also told that III Corps, on the left, was going to attack at the same time, 8.00 pm.

6.30 pm

The 15th Royal Welsh Fusiliers, 113th Brigade, recorded that they launched a minor attack upon Strip Trench from Cliff Trench. Thirty bombers supported by two companies began their advance down hill from their positions. They were exposed and soon came under heavy machine gun fire. It was quickly realised that the Germans were alert and had many machine guns in their positions. The 15th Royal Welsh Fusiliers were forced to withdraw leaving eleven dead men behind them.

6.40 pm.

Lieutenant-Colonel Rowley of the 6th Dorsets responded to his orders from Brigade by sending a situation report to Brigadier-General Glasgow. The report may not have made comfortable reading.

He told Brigadier-General Glasgow that the Germans were keeping up the pressure on the British and more bombs were urgently needed in the front line. The 7th East Yorks were hard put to it to maintain themselves in the front line even with the help of one company of the 6th Dorsets. Brigade was told that the 6th Dorsets had observed many German troops in Mametz Wood throughout the day and German machine guns had been spotted in Mametz Wood, Wood Support Trench and in Strip Trench.

Lieutenant-Colonel Rowley reported that he had one company in the front line, Quadrangle Trench. Two companies were in Bottom Wood along with one company of the 7th Borders. He had one company in position in Railway Alley. He reported that the shelling had been very heavy in all parts of the line and the 6th Dorsets had many casualties.

The strain was beginning to show... As was Lieutenant-General Horne's increasing impatience.

Lieutenant-General Horne personally telephoned Major-General Phillips at 38th Division headquarters, ordered him to withdraw his men and re-organise the battalions engaged at the south east corner of Mametz Wood. Lieutenant-General Horne ordered the 38th Division to make adequate arrangements for holding the line that night and to prepare a raid on Strip Trench that night. This raid would then be supported and developed during daylight.

These orders by Lieutenant-General Horne made certain that there would be no attack made by the 38th Division on the right flank at 8.00 pm that evening.

6.45 pm.

At his headquarters in the dugout in Railway Copse Lieutenant-Colonel Banbury of the 10th Notts & Derbys received his orders from 51st Brigade. His men were ordered to launch an attack on and capture Quadrangle Support Trench at 8.00 pm that evening. He was informed that there would be 30-minute preliminary barrage starting at 7.30 pm. His headquarters were some way behind his troops on the left flank of the front line. With three quarters of an hour to go before the barrage began Lieutenant-Colonel Banbury realised that there was not enough time for *complete orders* to be written and to be sent out to all of the units concerned before the attack commenced. Although he had a little more time in which to prepare Lieutenant-Colonel Banbury and his men were in a similar situation to that of Lieutenant-Colonel Harrison and the 12th Manchesters earlier on that morning.

6.50 pm.

German artillery fire was reported to be heavy on the British front line, Quadrangle Trench, and immediately behind in the Bottom and Shelter Woods area. XV Corps, no doubt having received the report by the 6th Dorsets, noted that the enemy appeared to be in strong numbers in Mametz Wood.

7.00 pm.

The 7th Lincolns left Quadrangle Trench and returned to positions in the original front line behind Fricourt.

52nd Brigade Machine Gun Company recorded that their last gun teams were finally relieved in the front line. The relief had taken from 2.00 pm. Their casualties for the day's work were twenty-two men. One killed, three missing and eighteen wounded. This figure was later revised to three killed and nineteen men wounded.

52nd Brigade Machine Gun Company took no further part in the action against Quadrangle Support Trench. They went to the rear any way that they could; on foot, cycle or by lorry. Their priority once they were out of the line and had rested was to reorganise and refit.

The 52nd Field Ambulance Bearers took over the left hand side of the battlefield clearing the casualties via a post in Shelter Wood. The casualties were then sent on to the 53rd Field Ambulance which was operating in the Red Cottage dugout in the remains of Fricourt village. Ambulances picked up the seriously wounded here. The 64th Field Ambulance Bearers worked on the right, clearing their casualties via Railway Copse to Fricourt Wood and then on to Rose Cottage in Fricourt and from here they were picked up by ambulances and taken to the rear. Captain Dougal was in charge of a bearer division of the 52nd Field Ambulance; with Captain G.C. Bury and Lieutenant G. T. Baker in charge of subdivisions. It was recorded that such was the steady stream of casualties the bearers worked all night.

7.20 pm.

50th Brigade sent a message to the 6th Dorsets and the 7th East Yorks.

On reaching their objectives the units were ordered to consolidate and hold on to what they captured during the night. Strong patrols were to be sent out to gain touch with units in either flank and to gain ground to the front. Reconnaissance had to be maintained during the night to take advantage of any possible withdrawal by the enemy.

7.30 pm.

The 8th South Staffords were ordered to provide a bomb carrying party for the 10th Notts & Derbys stationed in Quadrangle Trench. The remains of the 12th Manchesters were finally relieved by 51st Brigade. That night the 12th Manchesters returned to Meaulte. Back in Fricourt Wood C Section, 50th Brigade Machine Gun Company, opened fire on the western edge of Mametz Wood. The machine gun that had been destroyed by shelling had now been replaced by one from D Section which was acting as the reserve at Wicked Corner. C section was to remain in position in Fricourt Wood overnight.

7.40 pm.

In Railway Alley B Section, 50th Brigade Machine Gun Company, commenced firing on the northern edge of Mametz Wood with three guns. As before one gun opened fire upon Pearl Wood.

Captain B. C. Mozley noted in his diary that he reported to Lieutenant-Colonel Rowley's headquarters in Bottom Wood and discovered for the first time that the battalion should have attacked at 5.00 pm but the attack had been cancelled. With the British barrage already in progress Captain Mozley was informed of the orders for the attack on Wood Trench at 8.00 pm. During the time of Mozley's visit to headquarters B Company and a single platoon of D Company were preparing to attack.

It was around this time that the 6th Dorsets recorded that they were told by Brigade that their attack upon Wood Trench was to coincide with an attack by the 38th Division on Strip Trench. The 38th Division attack had been ordered by Horne at 6.40 pm.

8.00 pm.

The attack began. There was confusion from the beginning and the attack once again failed, according to the 10th Notts & Derbys, in a very short time. The attacking units went forward having been told that there would be a corresponding attack by III Corps on the left and that the 38th Division was in Wood Trench and would make an attack on Strip Trench on the right. There were no attacks made on either flank; the 17th Division attacked with both flanks 'in the air.'[27]

In appalling conditions and heavy rain the men climbed from their trenches to begin the uphill attack through the deep cloying mud. The bombers of all three battalions led the assault. B Company and a single platoon of D Company of the 6th Dorsets, 50th Brigade, attacked on the right flank towards Wood trench; the 7th East Yorks, 50th Brigade, attacked in the centre up Quadrangle Alley towards the junction of Quadrangle Support Trench. C and D companies of the 10th Notts & Derbys, 51st Brigade, attacked on the left up Pearl Alley and over the open towards Quadrangle Support Trench.

The story for all three attacking units was the same. As soon as they began the attack they were subjected to a ferocious German bombardment and fierce machine gun and rifle fire from their objectives and the two flanks. The British barrage appeared to have had no effect upon the defenders of Quadrangle Support Trench. Private Eric H. Harlow, of the 10th Notts & Derbys wrote in his diary that the shelling was heavy and that the attackers were enfiladed by machine guns sited in Contalmaison and Mametz Wood. There were, Private Harlow wrote, many casualties.

Lieutenant Hoyte, serving on the 51st Brigade Staff as the Bombing Officer and formerly a member of the 10th Notts & Derbys, wrote later that the German barrage made the British advance, over heavy ground, difficult. He also noted that the enfilading fire that the 10th Notts & Derbys experienced from Contalmaison was murderous.

The German artillery barrage severed the telephone lines and communications were severed with the advancing troops. The 10th Notts & Derbys managed to get to within forty yards of Quadrangle Support Trench but there they were halted and could get no further forward. Both Companies had casualties and D Company lost its

---

[27] A common phrase of the time meaning an unsupported attack, with no allies on either flank.

110

popular company commander. Captain John Wilfred Fisher D.S.O., affectionately known as 'Fishcakes' to his friends, in this attack.

Private John R. Osborne, 11323, of Lincolnshire and formerly of the 2nd Notts & Derbys may have also died and disappeared in this attack. Many of the casualties suffered by the battalions on this and many other days have no known graves. Most of them appear on Thiepval Memorial, a testament to the mud, the fury of the barrage and the fact that no one could get into no man's land to retrieve the bodies.[28]

In the centre the 7th East Yorks suffered the same fate as the 10th Notts & Derbys at the hands of the German machine gunners, riflemen and gunners. Their attack stalled.

On the right flank the 6th Dorsets were hit from three sides and their attack was halted. Second Lieutenant Albertanson managed to struggle back to the British front line with only three survivors. He was in time to prevent another company being sent to their deaths. Lieutenant-Colonel Rowley seeing the futility of the attack and that there was no apparent co-operation from the 38th Division on his right flank, ordered his men to retire.

Captain Mozley's A Company had taken up positions in Bottom Wood in support of the attack. He wrote in his diary that the expected attack by the 38th Division did not happen and that the 6th Dorsets, advancing over open ground, came under fire from the very beginning. Some of the fire came from Mametz Wood on their right and that, wrote Captain Mozley, was receiving no attention at all. The 6th Dorsets suffered heavy losses and when it was obvious that the attack had once again failed A Company returned, wet and weary, to Railway Alley. Captain Mozley noticed that one of his officers, and a personal friend, thirty year old Lieutenant Gerald Louis Davidson M.C., was so fatigued that he could not even speak.

The 113th Brigade, of the 38th (Welsh) Division commanded by Brigadier-General Price Davies, was on the right of the 6th Dorsets. Price Davies stated that he had never heard about the attack by the 17th Division. He himself was with the 15th Royal Welsh in Cliff

---

[28] Private Osborne is not a relation of the author but at the time when the research for this book began he was thought to be. This is of no matter, when the family visit the Somme we will always place a cross at Thiepval Memorial for him because without him this book would never have been written. More details of his service have emerged and have been recorded in Appendix 01

Trench when the attack began. He claimed that his forward posts were some hundred yards away from Mametz Wood and while he was visiting one of these posts he saw infantry, whom he thought were the 6th Dorsets, attacking the wood from the east, firing rifle grenades as they advanced on the strip of wood that jutted out towards his position. He tried to get covering fire going but the Lewis gun in his position jammed and the attack 'fizzled out.' He stated that had they known about the attack then they could have provided heavy covering fire. He also said that the 115th Brigade was attacking Mametz Wood, at the same time, from the east.

8.15 pm.

The 10th Notts & Derbys war diary recorded that after only fifteen minutes their attack was abandoned. The diary recorded that the withdrawal was undertaken in "excellent style" and that the men were wet and cold when they returned to Quadrangle Trench. The ground was heavy and both flanks were recorded as being 'in the air'; in other words, unsupported.

The diary of the 10th Notts & Derbys stated that the time allowed for actually organising this attack was not sufficient. Orders from 51st Brigade had arrived three quarters of an hour before the barrage commenced and full advantage could not be taken of the barrage. Consequently the attack was "ragged".[29]

51st Brigade noted, somewhat briefly, that the attack failed due to the "hostile barrage".[30]

8.20 pm.

In Railway Alley B Section, 50th Brigade Machine Gun Company, ceased firing upon the Northern edge of Mametz Wood having expended 5,000 rounds of ammunition. The single gun team firing on Pearl Wood also ceased fire and reported using 1,750 rounds of ammunition and having one soldier wounded (presumably by the German shelling). A Section, in Lozenge Wood was ordered to join D Section in reserve at Wicked Corner.

---

[29] TNA: PRO. WO95/2008. War Diary, 10th Notts & Derbys, July 1916.

[30] TNA: PRO. WO95/2005. War Diary, 51st Brigade, July 1916.

The company of 7th Borders stationed in Bottom Wood were ordered forward to the front line to relieve the 10th Notts & Derbys. In turn the 7th Lincolns were ordered forward from their positions in the original front line in Fricourt village in order to take up the positions vacated by the 7th Borders in Bottom Wood.

9.00 pm.

Lieutenant-Colonel Banbury received orders to the effect that the 7th Borders would relieve his men in the front line. Once the relief had been completed the battalion was to proceed to Willow Trench and Red Cottage at Fricourt and take up positions there. As ordered the 7th Borders moved up from Bottom Wood to relieve the 10th Notts & Derbys in Quadrangle Trench.

9.10 pm.

Major-General Phillips of 38th Division telephoned Lieutenant-General Horne to ask about the strength of the forthcoming raid that had been ordered on Strip Trench. Perhaps Major-General Phillips did not know that the 17th Division had expected his troops to attack an hour and ten minutes ago. At this point Major-General Phillips was informed by Lieutenant-General Horne that the 17th Division had actually taken Quadrangle Support Trench and Acid Drop Copse. It was important, Major-General Phillips was told, that elements of 113th Brigade establish themselves, by the raid, in Mametz Wood that night.

No news had yet come from the front line. Even the 17th Division did not know that the troops had suffered yet another reverse at the hands of the defenders of Contalmaison, Quadrangle Support Trench, Wood Trench and Mametz Wood.

9.50 pm.

Sporadic fighting was still going on around the Wood Trench area. At his headquarters in Bottom Wood Lieutenant-Colonel Rowley of the 6th Dorsets sent a situation report to 50th Brigade Headquarters under Fricourt Chateau. The news that he sent was grim. Rowley informed his Brigadier-General that the Germans are still holding the South Eastern corner of Mametz Wood and they had a machine gun set up there. Five of platoons of the Dorsets attempted to advance towards Wood Trench but were mown down by machine gun fire from two directions. According to the report of one man who came back, the whole of the leading company was shot down.

The situation in Wood Trench was not at present clear. Rowley reported that about ten men had been seen through glasses outside the trench, and later a bomb was seen to burst in the trench. He told Brigadier-General Glasgow that as soon as he could ascertain the situation at Wood Trench a further report would be sent.

50th Brigade wasted no time in sending Lieutenant-Colonel Rowley's situation report back to 17th Division headquarters in Meaulte. Major-General Pilcher was informed that the attack on Wood Trench had not succeeded because the infantry had been held up by uncut wire in front of the enemy trench. The 6th Dorsets, he was told, were still engaged in a bombing fight with the enemy in Wood Trench and along the strip of wood by the railway. The situation at the junction of Quadrangle Trench and Quadrangle Alley was uncertain.

Later the area around Wood Trench came under intense bombardment from British Artillery and the 6th Dorsets found that it was difficult to send out patrols to carry out reconnaissance.

9.55 pm.

17th Division received the unwelcome news that the attack by the 10th Notts & Derbys on Quadrangle Support had been halted forty yards from their objective. They had experienced heavy rifle fire, machine gun fire and a punishing enemy barrage. This message of the failure was delayed because communications had been disrupted by the shelling.

Lieutenant-Colonel Cardew returned to his headquarters in Carnoy valley after a trip to the observation post at Pommiers Redoubt. Cardew had been soaked by rain and perspiration and was covered in mud. He later noted, somewhat ruefully, that he had no dry clothes to change into because nothing could dry in the conditions. He would have to wear the same muddy, sodden, clothes the next day. He was pleased with one of his batteries though, they had done some good shooting and the battery commander knew that his guns had knocked out a machine gun and killed many of the enemy.

10.30 pm.

78th Field Company, Royal Engineers, recorded that the situation at the front was not yet clear. Their Commanding Officer arranged with Brigadier-General Glasgow to go forward and assist the infantry consolidating the positions around Bottom Wood and Quadrangle Alley.

10.50 pm.

Brigadier-General Glasgow of 50th Brigade sent out orders to his battalions in the field. The 7th East Yorks and the 6th Dorsets were to consolidate and reorganise on the line they currently held. The 7th Yorks were to hold the line of Bottom Alley from its junction with Quadrangle Trench to Bottom Wood then along the North Eastern edge of Bottom Wood. The officer commanding the Field Company (the Pioneers) was ordered to report to the commander of the 7th Yorks, Lieutenant-Colonel Fife, at 11.30 pm to arrange for the construction of strong points in these positions. The 7th Yorks also had orders to get in touch with the 38th Division on right flank.

The 51st Field Ambulance recorded that they had dealt with six hundred and ninety casualties in twenty four hours. The bearers had worked hard all night, all through the day and again into the night to clear the front of casualties. They had managed to do their job well and had kept the Advanced Dressing Stations free of congestion at all times.

10.52 pm.

17th Division sent a situation report to XV Corps. Major-General Pilcher said that nothing more could be done this night and he told Lieutenant-General Horne that the day's operations had been made "extremely difficult by the state of the ground owing to heavy rain."[31]

XV Corps noted that the failure of the 8.00 pm attack by the 17th Division. Quadrangle Support Trench was still in enemy hands, the bombing attack on Wood Trench had failed and the attack over the open had been held up by uncut wire. XV Corps did acknowledge

---

31 TNA: PRO. WO95/1981. War Diary, 17th Division War Diary, July 1916.

that the 8.00 pm attack by III Corps did not go ahead and that the ground was in a bad state because of the afternoon's heavy rain.

Lieutenant-General Horne had to now inform Lieutenant-General Rawlinson, Fourth Army Commander.

11.00 pm.

Consolidation work was underway. Number 2 Section of the 78th Field Company, Royal Engineers, was ordered to join number 1 section at Fricourt and to be in ready for any work which might be required. Numbers 3 and 4 sections, who with the company of Pioneers were standing by in Lozenge Wood, were ordered to proceed to the south-west corner of Bottom Wood where their commanding officer would meet them.

Numbers 1 and 2 Sections duly arrived at Fricourt village and met up with their commanding officer. Then he set out to take the two sections forward to Bottom Wood. At Lozenge Wood the company of Pioneers, not certain of finding their way to Bottom Wood, tacked on to numbers 3 and 4 sections as they left to rendezvous with their commanding officer. This made a very long line of men, all loaded with tools and materials. The delivery of these much needed materials was slowed down and the work delayed.

11.30 pm.

79th Brigade, R. F. A., commenced night firing at the German second line. They used one battery at a time.

The night of 7/8 July.

German had suffered casualties as well, caused in the main by the British artillery. Such were the losses to the German units that re-enforcements were desperately needed. On the morning of 7 July the 183rd, 184th Regiments and the 122nd Wuttemburg Regiment had been on their way to bolster the German defences around Contalmaison, Quadrangle Support Trench and Mametz Wood. On the way up to the front the 184th had been diverted to the front near Le Sars. The 122nd Regiment were caught by British shellfire and suffered high casualties. Five officers and two hundred and twenty other ranks were killed and wounded in the barrage. The relief was not as substantial as planned by the German staff.

During the night the German 183rd Infantry Regiment took over the line between Ovillers and Contalmaison from the shattered 9th Grenadiers. A much depleted 122nd (Reserve) Infantry Regiment went into the line, taking over Contalmaison and Quadrangle Support Trench down to the South West Corner of Mametz Wood from the battered 163rd Regiment. The 5th, 6th, 7th and 8th Companies of the 2nd Battalion Lehr Regiment were not relieved at this point and were forced to maintain their positions in Mametz Wood and Flat Iron Copse. Those who saw the corpses in the Wood after this phase of the battle reported that the men of the 2nd Battalion Lehr Regiment were big and well built men, much bigger than the British who lay among them.

At his Headquarters in Querrieux, Lieutenant-General Rawlinson sat down to write his journal. He wrote of the XV Corps situation that day

A day of heavy fighting without very much success. We took Contalmaison in the morning but failed to get into Mametz Wood. Prisoners tell us the Boche are in a state of chaos but their machine gunners seem to go on fighting all right. In the pm we lost Contalmaison without sufficient excuse I think as it is reported we were shelled out. I have ordered both attacks to be renewed. It is raining hard tonight. We must go on pressing the Boche now they are getting tired; as fresh troops may be brought up...[32]

One can sense the tiredness and disappointment in Lieutenant-General Rawlinson's tone. Also it is evident why the attacks were to be pushed on apace. He believed that the Germans were on the point of cracking, if more pressure could be brought to bear then his men would take these trenches and his army would be clear to assault the German second line. He feared that if they did not act swiftly then the Germans would bring up fresh reinforcements. Such a situation would delay the capture of these trenches and Mametz Wood and ultimately delay the assault on German second line.

From his Headquarters behind the lines General Haig sent a message to XV Corps.

The Commander in Chief wishes the following wire from his Majesty the King circulated to all ranks, begins- 'Please convey to the Army under your

---

[32] In Colin Hughes, *Mametz – Lloyd George's Welsh Army at the Battle of the Somme* (Orion Press, 1990), p. 94

command my sincere congratulations on the results achieved in the recent fighting. I am proud of my troops; none could have fought more bravely.[33]

It was signed George R.I.

Rain was falling hard on the exhausted troops who were working to consolidate the mud filled trenches and shell holes of the front line.

---

[33] TNA:PRO. WO95/921. War Diary, XV Corps, July 1916.

Chapter Six : 8 July 1916

The night had been quiet as neither side launched any significant attacks. Both the Germans and British were content to consolidate, reinforce and wait for the events of the new day to unfold. 17th Division recorded that the 38th Division was still held up near Caterpillar Wood on the right. The 23rd Division had been driven back to the line of Peake Wood, Birch Tree Wood, Shelter Wood and Shelter Alley. The 17th Division held the salient from the junction of Pearl Alley along Quadrangle Trench to the junction with Bottom Alley. 'Stops' had been put in place in Pearl Alley and Quadrangle Alley, both some two hundred yards from their respective junctions with Quadrangle Trench.

During the night the 12th Manchesters had returned to Meaulte. The battalion had suffered eight officers wounded including the Battalion commander and two majors, seven officers killed and five hundred and thirty nine Other Ranks killed or wounded. At some point during the day Major P. M. Magnay arrived and took over the remains of the battalion from the adjutant, Captain Duval. Later on they marched to Ville, with other units of the 52nd Brigade, to begin the task of refitting. Packs and stores were brought back from Morlancourt Chateau where they had remained since July 1st. Many of the packs would go unclaimed.

12.10 am.

At XV Corps headquarters in Heilly, Lieutenant-General Horne was annoyed that there was little information forthcoming about the failure of 17th Division's 8.00 pm attack. It was noted at XV Corps that the attack on the right, on Wood Trench, had been repulsed by machine gun fire from the southern point of Mametz Wood.

Meanwhile fresh troops of the German 122nd Regiment settled down to defend Contalmaison, Quadrangle Support Trench, Wood Trench, Wood Support Trench and the South Western portion of Mametz Wood. Like the units that they had just relieved the junior officers in the front line had the responsibility for making tactical decisions. They could decide if their men should attack or retire, always with an eye for minimising their own casualties. If a position was untenable they were empowered to evacuate it if necessary.

12.15 am.

XV Corps gave the 17th and 38th Divisions orders for patrolling that night. The 17th Division began to prepare for another attack later in the day.

12.30 am.

The 7th East Yorks and 6th Dorsets were ordered by 50th Brigade to withdraw from the front line.

The 7th Yorks were detailed to take over positions from them on the right from the northern edge of Bottom Wood to the Railway, then the front line between the junctions of Quadrangle Alley and Wood Trench.

The 7th East Yorks were to withdraw to Railway Copse and Railway Alley behind and to the west of Bottom Wood. The 6th Dorsets were ordered to withdraw to the right hand portion of Railway Alley, to posts 2 and 12 and to Sunshade Alley. The withdrawing units were ordered to replenish their stores at a big mined dump at post 12. They were urged to complete these moves as soon as possible.

1.00 am.

Half an hour later and the 7th Yorks had successfully relieved the 6th Dorsets. The 6th Dorset's A & C Companies returned to Railway Alley, D Company to posts 12 and 5, B Company, now down to sixty six other ranks after the attack at 8.00 pm the previous evening, went to Sunshade Alley. Lieutenant-Colonel Rowley set up his headquarters in Railway Copse.

1.05 am.

It was time to prepare to try again and 17th Division received a telegram from XV Corps ordering that a bombing attack upon Quadrangle Support Trench should be organised. Major-General Pilcher duly ordered the 51st Brigade to organise the bombing attack from Pearl Alley. Brigadier-General Trotter was informed by Division that the 50th Brigade was going to attack Quadrangle Support Trench with bombs from Quadrangle Alley.

1.22 am.

Brigadier-General Glasgow sent orders to the 7th Yorks for the bombing attack on Quadrangle Support Trench. He informed them that zero hour would be 6.00 am. They were told that the 51st Brigade was to co-operate on the left and that there would be an artillery bombardment laid down on the German communication trenches behind Quadrangle Support Trench.

1.30 am.

In preparation for the forthcoming bombing attack a carrying party of the 8th South Staffords took more bombs up to the front line.

2.00 am.

The 7th Borders finally managed to complete the difficult change over with the 10th Notts & Derbys and the latter moved back to Fricourt as ordered. A, C and D companies took up positions near Fricourt Trench, B company moved into Lonely Trench and Lieutenant-Colonel Banbury set up his Battalion headquarters under a crucifix in the centre of the rubble of Fricourt village.

The 7th Borders were not particularly pleased with their positions or the conditions in which they found themselves. They took over during a heavy German barrage and the trenches were full of rain water, sometimes waist deep. The mud was ankle deep, stuck like glue and impeded movement.

2.30 am.

B Section, 50th Brigade Machine Gun Company, received orders to report, with four guns, to Lieutenant-Colonel Fife of the 7th Yorks who was at his headquarters in Bottom Wood. As men of the 6th Dorsets and the 7th East Yorks filed past them to take up residence in Railway Alley, B Section handed over their machine gun positions to A Section who had come up to relieve them.

2.45 am.

50th and 51st Brigades issued orders for the bombing attack upon Quadrangle Support Trench. The attack, with 21st Divisional artillery co-operation, was to begin at 6.00 am. Instead of attacking over the open, the 7th Borders would advance on the left up Pearl Alley towards the junction with Quadrangle Support Trench. The 7th Yorks would assault on the right; going up Quadrangle Alley towards the junction with Quadrangle Support Trench. Their plan was that they were to bomb along Quadrangle Support Trench and meet in the middle. At some point, after these orders were issued, the start time for the attack was changed to 7.00 am.

While preparations were underway for the next attack numbers 3 and 4 Sections of the 78th Field Company, Royal Engineers arrived at Bottom Wood to rendezvous with their commanding officer. They were at the head of a long, unwieldy column of men that had set out from Lozenge Wood. Despite trailing behind the Engineers for fear of getting lost most of the Pioneers had not yet managed to get to the wood.

As it was the Engineers had arrived too late to be of any real use. They had been ordered to go from Lozenge Wood to Bottom Wood some three and three quarter hours ago and Lozenge Wood was actually only about half a mile away. No wiring could be done as the materials being brought up from Lozenge Wood failed to arrive. Some work was carried out; trenches were dug on the north side of Bottom Wood. Number 2 Section and one platoon of Pioneers repaired the Trench railway.

The commander of the 78th Field Company must have been furious that things had not gone as planned. He had personally suggested to Brigadier-General Glasgow that his men support the infantry. The night was pitch-black, it was pouring with rain, the ground was filthy, movement was difficult; and the German gunners were busy. The Engineers blamed the trailing column of hapless Pioneers for the delay.

3.00 am.

In their trenches near Fricourt the 10th Notts & Derbys were issued with rations and a tot of rum each. After this they settled down to sleep in the deep, chalk trenches and there they remained, out of the rain, for the rest of the day.

At the File Factory near Meaulte the 51st Field Ambulance recorded a lull in casualties arriving from the front line. This lull was to continue until early evening. Captains Barclay and Walker returned to the File Factory from Queens Redoubt after being relieved by

Captains Lewis and Forman. Though the rain did stop at dawn, it was only a short respite because the rains came down on and off all day and the men and patients were plastered with mud.

The 7th Lincolns recorded that they remained in and around Bottom Wood in positions that they had taken up the day before.

3.30 am.

79th Royal Field Artillery ceased firing at the German second line. The 81st Brigade, Royal Field Artillery recorded that they made preparations for the bombardment of Mametz Wood.

4.15 am.

B Section, 50th Brigade Machine Gun Company, arrived in Bottom Wood and reported to Lieutenant-Colonel Fife of the 7th Yorks as ordered. It had taken one and three quarter hours to move the Section and four guns from Railway Alley.

4.30 am.

D Battery, 79th Royal Field Artillery was ordered to shell Quadrangle Alley up to the junction with Quadrangle Support Trench. They had orders to destroy the trench if at all possible.

6.30 am.

XV Corps recorded that there was no change on the 17th Division front and no headway had been made against Quadrangle Support Trench. At this point, however, the expected attack had not gone in.

The 38th Division reported to XV Corps Headquarters that the 113th Brigade was preparing to make an attack on Strip Trench with one battalion. Orders had been issued by the Division at 4.45 am. The diary of the 113th Brigade makes no mention of this and nor does the diary of the battalion in the line; the 16th Royal Welsh Fusiliers. They only made one reference to 8 July, "Quiet."[34]

Lieutenant-General Horne had sent orders for a raid on Strip Trench at 6.40 pm on the previous day and Major-General Pilcher had

---

[34] TNA: PRO. WO95/2556. War Diary, 16th Royal Welsh Fusiliers, July 1916.

expected the raid to go in at the same time his men attacked at 8.00 pm that evening.

7.00 am.

The 79th Royal Field Artillery was ordered to block Quadrangle Alley to aid the bombing attack upon Quadrangle Support Trench.

At 7.00 am, not 6.30 am, the attack began. The plan was for the 7th Borders to advance up Pearl Alley and then attack Quadrangle Support Trench from the left. The 7th Yorks were to advance up Quadrangle Alley and attack Quadrangle Support Trench from the right. The principle weapon of this attack was to be the bomb. Both units were to bomb along Quadrangle Support Trench until they met up in the middle.

The 7th Borders advanced as ordered pushing out a further bombing attack to cover their left flank. The men on the left reached the south western outskirts of Contalmaison and established a post there. The main bombing attack got as far as the junction of Pearl Alley and Quadrangle Support Trench but a fierce and accurate German barrage halted their progress. Here they came under fire from Contalmaison and Quadrangle Support Trench and were forced to face both ways in order to try and return fire.

On the right the story was no better. B Company of the 7th Yorks began moving up the communication trench, the mud was over the men's knees and soon they became exhausted. They advanced about one hundred yards up Quadrangle Alley to where the trench became shallow. Here they were held up by machine gun and rifle fire.

Though the 7th Yorks continued to try and break through both 50th and 51st Brigades were informed of the failure. Both the 7th Borders and the 7th Yorks reported that the mud was four feet deep in places. Reports came in later to say that Pearl Alley was enfiladed from the dominating heights of Contalmaison. A new attack was ordered.

8.00 am to 9.00 am.

C Section, 50th Brigade Machine Gun Company, reported that the German artillery was firing registering rounds at them. One high explosive shell landed on the corner of Fricourt Wood and another on Railway Alley. The German gunners were evidently trying to find the irritating machine guns; which may well mean that their indirect fire was having some effect.

During the hour between 8.00 am and 9.00 am the Commanding Officer of the 50th Brigade Machine Gun Company paid C Section a visit. As the shelling grew worse and got closer to the machine guns C Section was ordered to withdraw from Railway Alley and relocate to Willow Trench. During the move C Section's sergeant and two number ones were mentioned as showing "great willingness and coolness in their work under shell fire."[35]

As the rain stopped Captain Mozley and his exhausted, soaked men tried to make the best of things in Railway Alley. He wrote in his diary that the sun came out and as the morning went on it grew stronger and hotter. He and his men had a liberal rum issue but the one thing that they craved, sleep, was denied by the German gunners. Mozley noted that the Germans concentrated their fire on Railway Alley, Fricourt Wood and the communication trenches. Lieutenant-Colonel Rowley had set up his headquarters in Railway Copse and was undergoing great deal of shelling. The runners, Captain Mozley said, lived in the barrages but they did excellent work getting messages to and from the companies regardless of the danger.

Captain Mozley and his men were gleefully entertained when a shell scored a direct hit on an ammunition and Verey Light dump near Fricourt Wood. The resulting explosions and pyrotechnics were worthy of a firework display.

10.00 am.

The German artillery were still barraging Railway Alley two hours later and had managed to destroy one Lewis gun and parts that belonged to the 7th East Yorks.

The exhausted bearers of the 64th Field Ambulance were relieved and sent back to Carcaillot Farm.

XV Corps sent orders to 17th Division saying that they should prepare for an attack up Pearl Alley, then from Contalmaison civilian cemetery on Quadrangle Support Trench. An attack was ordered up

---

[35] TNA: PRO. WO95/2004. War Diary, 50th Brigade Machine Gun Corps, July 1916.

Quadrangle Alley on the right. The plan was the same as before; to attack up the communication trenches and then advance from left and right bombing along Quadrangle Support Trench and meet in the middle.

10.30 am.

52nd Field Ambulance officers returned with b subdivision having cleared Aid Posts at Railway Copse. A and C Sections were relieved by fifty bearers of the 50th Field Ambulance and thirty six bearers of the 51st Field Ambulance. The latter had been sent out under Captain Barclay to collect wounded that had been reported lying in front of Railway Copse. The heavy German barrage was causing many casualties. A and C Sections of the 52nd Field Ambulance returned to the Subway.

10.35 am.

At XV Corps Headquarters Lieutenant-General Horne decided to halt the battalion attack by the 113th Brigade on Strip Trench. He telephoned Major-General Phillips at 38th Division to tell him that he did not want such an attack. He told Major-General Phillips, bluntly, that he wanted a reconnaissance only.

11.00 am.

A telegram arrived at 17th Division headquarters from XV Corps saying that the Division was expected to mount an attack that afternoon. 17th Division was informed, once again, that III Corps would also attack on the left.

11.30 am.

A, B, and C batteries of 79th Royal Field Artillery were ordered to keep up desultory fire of sixty rounds per battery, per hour, on the western edge of Mametz Wood. B battery also fired on parties of troops observed entering Contalmaison.

12.00 noon.

The 7th East Yorks counted their losses. One officer and six other ranks were dead; six officers and eighty-three other ranks were injured and forty-nine men were missing.

C Section, 50th Brigade Machine Gun Company, now successfully set up in Willow Trench, commenced indirect fire at Mametz Wood. This fire was kept up at regular intervals until 6.00 pm.

The 7th Yorks gave up their attempt to break through in Quadrangle Alley. 50th Brigade recorded that the joint attack, with 51st Brigade, at 7.00 am had now failed. The mud and the foul state of the trenches were blamed for the failure.

Both the 50th and 51st Brigades sent reports to 17th Division saying that it was apparent that no further progress could be made in the attacks on Quadrangle Support Trench. Division recorded this as the fourth attack on the trench.

Sometime during the day General Haig gave General Rawlinson orders to capture Mametz Wood and Contalmaison before any attempt was made to attack the German second line. He later noted in his diary that the fighting in Mametz Wood proved that German morale was still high.[36]

12.15 pm.

52nd Field Ambulance headquarters received a message from the A.D.M.S (Assistant Director Medical Services). In it he said that the D. M. S. (Director Medical Services) at XV Corps had received a report that there were 7th Borders wounded in Quadrangle Trench.

12.50 pm to 1.00 pm.

17th Division received a message from XV Corps saying that III Corps would not now attack as they had previously been told. The 17th Division was informed that they should carry out their own independent attack. They could fix their own hour of attack upon their allotted objectives and there would be a bombardment of

---

[36] D. Haig, in G. Sheffield and J. Bourne ed, *Douglas Haig War Diaries and Letters 1914-1918* (BCA 2005), p. 201

twenty five minutes upon the enemy positions prior to the attack. 17th Division fixed the time of attack for 5.50 pm that afternoon.

In Carnoy valley Lieutenant-Colonel Cardew had returned to 80th Brigade Artillery headquarters from a trip around his batteries. The valley was packed with soldiers, horses and wagons, they were being shelled most of the time but Cardew noted that the shells were falling in an area away from the troops and doing no damage.

His own guns were firing practically all day and all night now. He recorded that the gunners were sticking it very well and he heard no complaints from them even though they were getting very little sleep and were wet most of the time. But, said the Lieutenant-Colonel, their lot was nothing to that of the infantry. He noted that the ground conditions were bad; during his visit to 'A' battery he had watched wagons being pulled by struggling teams of fourteen horses. He opted to remain at his headquarters for the afternoon; he noted that it had begun to rain hard once again.

1.30 pm.

Responding to the report from the A.D.M.S concerning wounded in the front line the commanding officer of the 52nd Field Ambulance went forward with Lieutenant Gush R.A.M.C and a party of bearers to get them out of Quadrangle Trench. They reported that the conditions were appalling. It was very heavy going in the trenches owing to the rain and the bearers were compelled to walk over the open rather than travel through the crowded and flooded trenches.

Once they found the wounded men they had to get them away. The best route that they could find was via Railway Copse communication trench and then along the north and west sides of Fricourt Wood to the Advanced Dressing Station in Fricourt.

1.40 pm.

Earlier in the day, after his telephone call to Major-General Phillips, Lieutenant-General Horne paid a personal visit to 38th Division Headquarters to discuss the situation and to give verbal instructions. On his return to his headquarters he sent orders to Major-General Phillips for an attack on the southern salient of Mametz Wood. He made it clear that he wanted the attack to take place that night and that the gains that were made were to be exploited the next day, 9 July.

2.00 pm.

At this point Brigadier-General Glasgow issued orders for the next attack. He informed the units involved that they would be notified about the zero hour later, though it was likely to be 5.00 pm. The 51st Brigade was going to attack Quadrangle Support on the left. He also told them that while the Brigade was attacking Wood Trench the 38th Division would be making an attack upon Strip Trench on the right.

But as has been seen the 38th Division had been ordered, by Lieutenant-General Horne in person, to put in an attack on the southern salient of Mametz Wood (Strip Trench) that night not at 5.00 pm that afternoon. Perhaps Brigadier-General Glasgow was in possession of misinformation.

The 6th Dorsets were to attack the west end of Wood Trench from the east end of Quadrangle Trench. The Field Artillery was to cut the wire at the west end of Wood Trench in the afternoon, to allow the infantry through. The time of this bombardment would be wired through to the 6th Dorsets. To avoid casualties they would have to clear their troops out of the eastern end of Quadrangle Trench before the bombardment began. Also, before the bombardment, the 7th Yorks would have to withdraw their 'stop' in Quadrangle Alley to a point some 200 yards south of the junction with Quadrangle Support Trench. This would again avoid British casualties from the shellfire and facilitate the British advance up the trench.

The 7th Yorks were told that as soon as barrage lifted their bombers were to advance up Quadrangle Alley and establish stops in Quadrangle Support Trench and in Quadrangle Alley north of the junction. They were ordered to hold and defend the junction of Quadrangle Support Trench and Quadrangle Alley. Both the 6th Dorsets and the 7th Yorks were ordered to begin making their preparations for the attack straight away. Actual details of the bombardment would follow and Brigadier-General Glasgow stressed that as far as possible the attack was to be a bombing attack.

93rd Field Company, Royal Engineers marched to Meaulte and took over the billets from the 77th Field Company, Royal Engineers. It was reported that one mule was wounded by shell fire in the process.

79th Royal Field Artillery ceased desultory fire on the Western edge of Mametz Wood.

2.06 pm.

The 7th East Yorks recorded that their effective trench strength was down to fifteen officers and four hundred and forty four other ranks.

2.40 pm.

The 7th Yorks received their orders for their part in forthcoming bombing attack. They were told that zero for their bombing attack was to be 5.40 pm. The time was then written down in the same message as 'five fifty pm today'.[37] This was not the same zero, they were informed, as the time fixed for the attack on Wood Trench by the 6th Dorsets. They would be notified of that time later.

At zero hour the bombers were to rush up to the junction of Quadrangle Alley with Quadrangle Support Trench to a point some one hundred yards west of their 'stop'. They were then to advance to a point two hundred yards north of their 'stop'.

At thirty minutes after zero hour they were to begin to work North West to join up with elements of the 51st Brigade who would be working south east along Quadrangle Support Trench from Pearl Alley.

The 7th Yorks were left in no doubt that it was essential that an effective 'stop' be made at junction of Quadrangle Support Trench and Quadrangle Alley. Also this was the only attack that the 7th Yorks were to make that evening. After the attack had been delivered they were responsible for holding their present line throughout the night. It seemed no reinforcements were available as they were to hold the line with the remainder of the battalion and the machine guns that were attached to them. This message was repeated to the 6th Dorsets and the 7th East Yorks.

---

[37] TNA: PRO. WO95/2004. War Diary, 7th Yorks, July 1916.

2.45 pm.

17th Division issued Operation Order No. 63 giving instructions for a further bombing attack on Quadrangle Support to be made simultaneously by the 50th and 51st Brigades.

3.30 pm.

C Company of the 6th Dorsets moved into Quadrangle Trench in preparation for a bombing attack on Wood Trench. They were given the zero hour of 5.00 pm, and they noted that their assault was to be made in conjunction with an attack by the 38th Division.

38th Division did appear to have orders for a 5.00 pm attack. Their attack was to be at 2.00 am.

As C Company of the 6th Dorsets moved forwards for the assault A Company moved and took over their positions in Bottom Wood again. Captain Mozley recorded in his diary that his company passed through the usual German barrage as they moved up and got through unscathed. They suffered casualties once they were in Bottom Wood. Twelve men were wounded, two seriously.

The 6th Dorsets diary entry of 3.30 pm records these two short sentences. "Attack postponed till 9 pm." Followed by "Attack postponed till 2 am."[38] An attempt has been made to hide these words as both entries have been blacked out by a heavy black pen or pencil, and in one case typed over using the '=' key but they are still readable.

3.40 pm.

Lieutenant-Colonel Rowley sent his orders for the coming attack out to the commanders of A and C Companies.

The attack would begin after artillery preparation, which would include cutting the wire in front of Wood Trench, heavy shelling of the trench itself, and the belt of trees that protruded out of the wood towards the British front line. The company commanders were told that the 38th Division were to be attack Strip Trench and the wood nearby at the same time. C Company was to attack Wood Trench with bombing squads and if they got a footing in Wood Trench then

---

[38] TNA: PRO. WO95/2000. War Diary, 6th Dorsets, July 1916.

A Company would support them from the east end of Quadrangle Trench. A Company was instructed to detach a strong patrol to occupy the southern end of belt of trees. Lieutenant-Colonel Rowley recommended that they should get themselves about twenty yards inside the wood where an enemy machine gun was suspected. Should the attack be successful then the trench had to be consolidated at once and touch gained with 38th Division on the right. The company officers were told that the probable hour of attack was to be 5.00 pm but the time would be sent to them. Lieutenant-Colonel Rowley did point out that it was possible that the battalion might not receive the zero hour in time to let the front line troops know, so they had to watch the bombardment. The 51st Brigade was to attack Quadrangle Support Trench at the same time.

Lieutenant-Colonel Rowley had already despatched his second in command, Major Hughes-Onslow to direct operations in the front line. Major Hughes-Onslow was on his way to Quadrangle Trench as the orders were being written.

A Company was ordered to send two platoons forward to support C Company in Quadrangle Trench at once. Two platoons were to remain in Bottom Wood. D Company was instructed to move up to Railway Alley. During the bombardment Quadrangle Trench should be cleared to avoid casualties.

The information concerning the 38th Division attack was out of date; they were not going to attack at 5.00 pm. The battalion attack by the 38th Division had been cancelled by Lieutenant-General Horne at 10.35 that morning. He had personally ordered a reconnaissance be launched at Strip Trench at 2.00 am the following morning. It would seem that 50th Brigade did not know this at the time.

3.45 pm.

That state of affairs did not last long. 17th Division issued the further orders to 50th Brigade for a joint attack with 38th Division on Mametz Wood at 2.00 am the following morning. The 38th Division would attack the tongue of Wood that jutted out south from the main body of the wood and contained Strip Trench. They were to go as far north as Wood Trench. The 6th Dorsets were to bomb down Wood Trench at same time towards its junction with Strip Trench.

Quadrangle Trench and Wood Trench were not actually connected so the 50th Brigade troops, the 6th Dorsets, were ordered to advance on Wood Trench after dark and gain a footing at the western end of the trench.

4.45 pm.

The 9th Northumberland Fusiliers paraded and marched to Ville-Sous-Corbie where they went into billets to undertake "interior economy reorganisation."[39]

At some point during the day, their diary does not record the time; the 10th Lancashire Fusiliers arrived at Ville-sur-Ancre beyond Albert. They took no further part in the attacks upon Quadrangle Support Trench. The 10th Lancashire Fusiliers had lost seventy six men killed in the assaults on 7 July and a further three men had died of their wounds on that day. All told the battalion had lost 108 and men killed since 1 July 1916. This was not, however, the highest loss suffered by a 17th Division battalion during this phase of the Somme Campaign. That dubious honour fell to the 10th West Yorks.

Back in Meaulte the 9th Duke of Wellingtons scraped the mud from their uniforms and kit and as things dried they collected their stores and ascertained what was deficient. In the Regimental Aid Post, among the wounded and dying that had been hauled from the battlefield, Lieutenant D. H. Fletcher underwent the first 'plastic' operation on his right eye socket. He was recorded by the Medical Officer who tended him at the time as doing well.

5.00 pm.

53rd Field Ambulance bearers cleared the Aid Posts in preparation for the inevitable casualties that were due to arrive from the coming attack.

5.30 pm.

79th Royal Field Artillery was ordered to commence a half hour barrage, using all batteries, of Acid Drop Copse, Quadrangle Alley and Mametz Wood.

---

[39] TNA: PRO. WO95/2013. War Diary, 9th Northumberland Fusiliers, July 1916.

50th Brigade issued further orders for the operations that night. The eight-inch howitzers of the Siege Artillery would begin a barrage at 8.30 pm that evening and continue until 8.50 pm. Then the barrage would creep steadily eastwards reaching junction at the eastern end of Wood Trench at 9.10 pm. A barrage was to be maintained on Wood Support Trench and on the east end of Wood Trench. Mametz Wood would also be shelled in the north and south of this area.

As soon as heavy guns lifted their barrage at 8.50 pm, the 6th Dorsets were to rush the western end of Wood Trench with a bombing and Lewis gun party and establish a 'stop' at this end of the trench. Behind this 'stop' the men would then dig to join the trench to Quadrangle Trench.

At 2.00 am the 6th Dorsets were then to push onwards and occupy Wood Trench to its junction with Strip Trench joining there with the 38th Division who, the 6th Dorsets were told, were to attack at the same time. The line of Wood Trench, now added to the British front line would then be consolidated and held.

The 6th Dorsets were ordered by Brigade to send a Liaison Officer to report to the 38th Division who were supposed to be in or by Dantzig Alley just east of Mametz. The Liaison Officer was to explain the 6th Dorsets' orders to the 38th Division and to get details of their proposed attack.

After his tea, at his headquarters in Carnoy Valley, Lieutenant-Colonel Cardew went over to Pommiers Redoubt. From there he watched the battle for a while but later wrote in his diary that not much was going on. From there he went around his batteries and to his delight one of his men gave him a hair cut.

5.50 pm.

The 17th Division attack on Quadrangle Support Trench went ahead, preceded by an artillery barrage.

As the barrage lifted B Company supported by the bombers of D Company of the 7th Yorks and led by Lieutenant H. K. C. Hare began their attack on the right flank up Quadrangle Alley. Lieutenant Hare had orders to set up two 'stops', one in Quadrangle Support Trench and the other in Quadrangle Alley north of its junction with Quadrangle Support Trench. Lieutenant Hare and his men expected to join up in Quadrangle Support Trench with the 7th Borders who were at that moment carrying out a simultaneous bombing attack upon the left flank.

The 7th Borders did manage to get troops up the pulverised remains of Pearl Alley and into Quadrangle Support Trench. Once there they found that the trench was empty. The German defenders had evacuated their position and withdrawn to a depression behind the trench where they were immune to the British machine gun fire. The 7th Borders were not able to occupy the position as they very soon came under fire from Contalmaison on their left flank.

On the right the 7th Yorks found that rapid movement up the mud filled morass of Quadrangle Alley was impossible and their attack stalled once again.

51st Brigade recorded that the 7th Borders bombing attack went in as ordered but they were outflanked by enemy fire from the direction of Contalmaison. 50th Brigade recorded that an attack on the junctions had been delivered and again the attack by the 7th Yorks had failed.

C Section, 50th Brigade Machine Gun Company, concentrated its fire on the junction of Wood Trench and Strip Trench in anticipation of the Dorsets assault, later that evening.

The batteries of 79th Royal Field Artillery, barraged the Western edge of Mametz Wood.

6.00 pm.

52nd Field Ambulance recorded that the British barrage was heavy, and lasted for a half an hour finishing at 6.00 pm. It was then followed by an attack.

XV Corps noted that the 17th Division attack on Quadrangle Support Trench had not progressed very far. 17th Division reported to XV Corps that in an attempt to get closer to the enemy position, they intended to dig a trench that night across the ground between Pearl Alley and Quadrangle Alley, parallel to Quadrangle Support Trench. This plan was not put into operation.

6.20 pm.

C Section 50th Brigade Machine Gun Company ceased firing at the junction of Wood and Strip Trenches. They were praised by the Dorsets Commanding Officer, Lieutenant-Colonel Rowley, for firing with good effect. C Section had suffered two men wounded in the action.

6.40 pm.

17th Division received a report stating that the 7th Borders had succeeded in getting troops into Quadrangle Support Trench but the situation was vague.

7.20 pm.

The 7th Yorks recorded that the recent attack had failed. They noted that the attack had failed for the same reasons as the 7.00 am attack. Rapid advance was impossible because of the mud and the communication trench, Quadrangle Alley, had been destroyed by British artillery. The trench gave no cover to the attacking infantry from the German machine guns that enfiladed them.

7th Lincolns recorded that they relieved the 7th Borders in Quadrangle Trench on this night. Second Lieutenant A. W. S. Cowie was killed in the process of the relief.

8.00 pm.

Captain Dougal and one bearer of the 52nd Field Ambulance went up to the front line. Three casualties in the front line had reportedly died of their wounds and needed to be cleared away for burial.

Captain Mozley wrote in his diary that C Company of the 6th Dorsets had moved into the British front line. At this time they received their orders to launch a bombing attack on the western end of Wood Trench. They would have to cross the space in between the ends of the two trenches and get into Wood Trench then capture and hold the Western end. The trench was to be re-bombarded and captured the next day.

8.30 pm.

XV Corps recorded that the British heavy artillery side stepped Wood Trench and bombarded the junction of Wood Trench and Quadrangle Support Trench. Consequently the 6th Dorsets were able to get one Company of men, C Company, into Wood Trench.

8.50 pm.

After the heavy guns lifted their barrage from the western end of Wood Trench the 6th Dorsets attacked, their diary records that a bombing squad, and a Lewis gun team under the command of Lance Corporal Routcliff, rushed over the open between the east end of Quadrangle Trench and Wood Trench. Their objective was to make a stop at the west end of wood trench. Captain Mozley wrote that the plan more than succeeded. Routcliff and his men got into Wood Trench and encountered little opposition. The enterprising Routcliff led his men well down Wood Trench, and captured over half of it. They erected a 'stop' at the far end of the trench. The 6th Dorsets were now some seventy yards away from Mametz Wood and ahead of the attack schedule.

At the same time the patrol, led by Second Lieutenant Moss advanced into the south end of the belt of trees. Meanwhile two platoons of Captain Mozley's A Company began to dig a trench from the eastern end of Quadrangle Trench to join up with the western end of Wood Trench. Captain Mozley recorded that though the work was hard and the men encountered chalk all the way they worked well and as swiftly as they could.

Now the that 6th Dorsets had succeeded in their part of the plan they waited for the 2.00 am attack by 38th Division on the Southern end of Mametz Wood.

17th Division recorded that after dark the 6th Dorsets of 50th Brigade got men into the west end of Wood Trench as planned.

9. 00 pm.

It was becoming apparent to the 17th Division that no progress was being made against Quadrangle Support Trench by either 50th or 51st Brigades. The 5.50 pm attack was recorded as the fifth attack on Quadrangle Support Trench. In accordance with orders from XV

Corps, preparations were underway for a joint attack with the 38th Division on Mametz Wood at 2.00 am the following morning.

9.15 pm.

Captain Mozley's two platoons completed the work of connecting Quadrangle Trench to Wood Trench. C Company began to consolidate their gains made in Wood Trench. They were counter-attacked by the Germans twice during the night. The first of which was repulsed, Lewis guns dispersed the second before it could develop.

10.00 pm.

The remaining two platoons of the Captain Mozley's A Company moved into the east end of Quadrangle Trench to assist C Company while D Company moved from Posts 12 and 5 into Railway Alley. B Company, it must be remembered, was reduced to sixty six men.

A Section, 50th Brigade Machine Gun Company, moved up to relieve B Section in Bottom Wood. The relief was completed by dawn.

D Section of the 50th Machine Gun Company had remained in reserve all day but its men were employed taking ammunition up to the other Sections engaged in the fighting. They were kept in touch with the other Sections by runner and it was noted that no gun was out of touch during this period. A simple statement but in a situation where, by the nature of terrain and the shelling, communications of all sorts were poor, it speaks of a great achievement.

10.30 pm.

At his headquarters in Carnoy Valley Lieutenant-Colonel Cardew sat down to make his regular diary entry. Nearby his guns began some extra bombardments but Cardew noted that they were not part of a bigger show that had been going on for some time. The 81st Brigade, R. F. A., and the 78th Brigade, R. F. A., were bombarding the German Second line.

The events of the previous day had left him in a reflective mood. He recognised that the 17th Division had not done as well as had been expected on 7 July. He knew a Brigade had been unable to go forward but he had been unable to find out which one it was. Also the 38th Division had been held up and had suffered a huge amount of casualties. Lieutenant-Colonel Cardew was in no doubt as to the reason for the failure to capture the objectives; the weather. It had been raining hard for quite some time and the roads and tracks were in an awful state. He was of the opinion that the offensive should be halted to wait for drier weather. Despite the rain of the afternoon it was fine now and he was optimistic that it was going to dry up soon.

He was proud that XV Corps had taken most of the prisoners to fall into the hands of the Fourth Army. He wrote that he had heard that the 38th Division were going to attack again in the morning. He also recorded that a Corporal from the Bedfords, who been in a post in Caterpillar Wood, had told him that troops of the 38th Division had refused to go forward at the south eastern end of Mametz Wood. No other information about this event seemed to have been forthcoming.

11.00 pm.

79th Royal Field Artillery commenced night firing at the road leading into Contalmaison. They used one battery at a time; firing for two hours and using fifty rounds an hour.

11.50 pm.

The 7th Yorks began construction work on emplacements for Stokes Mortar guns in Quadrangle Alley in anticipation of a renewed attack.

12 midnight.

Lieutenant-Colonel Rowley sent a situation report in to 50th Brigade headquarters. He reported that he had C Company and a half of A Company plus bombing squads on duty in Wood Trench. Half of A Company were working on the connecting trench between Quadrangle Trench and Wood Trench and D Company, was in support of the working party, and were posted in Bottom Wood. The remains of the 'cut up' company, B Company, were employed carrying rations and supplying a reserve of three hundred bombs to the Companies in the line. Major Hughes-Onslow was in command of Wood Trench.

52nd Field Ambulance recorded that the 7th Yorks had casualties in Quadrangle Trench and Bottom Wood. Bearers were sent out to collect them.

Unspecified Time.

78th Field Company Royal Engineers sent in a report of the work that they had managed to complete so far in the Bottom Wood area. No.4 Section and two platoons of Pioneers had worked hard. Twelve bays and machine-gun emplacements had been completed and wired and barbed wire had been laid out north-east as far as the railway. One hundred yards of wire had been laid on the north edge of Bottom Wood. This had to be done and the 78th Field Company Commander was able to detail Numbers 1 and 3 sections for the work. The Pioneers dug one hundred yards of new trench to join with Railway Alley and laid one hundred yards of wire along its length.

During the day General Haig wrote a letter to his wife. In it he said

> *The troops are fighting very well and the battle is developing slowly but steadily in our favour. In another fortnight, with Divine Help, I hope that some decisive results may be obtained. In the meantime we must be patient and determined.* [40]

The night of 8th July.

There were no reinforcements for the German units holding the line. The 183rd Regiment held the line from Ovillers to Contalmaison; the 122nd Wuttemburg Regiment remained in the line from Contalmaison, including Quadrangle Support Trench, to the South Western Corner of Mametz Wood. The 2nd Battalion, the Lehr Regiment still held the southern edge of Mametz Wood and Flat Iron Copse. Behind them, in reserve in the second line, were the 1st Battalion, the Lehr Regiment, the 3rd Battalion, the Grenadier Regiment and the 2nd Battalion, the 122nd Wuttemburg Regiment.

The men in Quadrangle Support Trench had successfully held on against the two more British attacks. The officers and NCOs had used the terrain and the weather conditions to their advantage yet

---

[40] Haig, in Sheffield and Bourne ed, *Douglas Haig War Diaries and Letters 1914-1918*, p. 201

they were puzzled as to why the British had not made more concerted attacks and in greater numbers. Still, they were greatly troubled by the British guns. To the German soldiers the British gunners seemed to have an inexhaustible supply of shells and an uncanny knack for causing mayhem in the rear positions. The rear trenches and dug outs were in a dreadful state thanks to the attention of the British guns.

Chapter Seven : 9 July 1916 Midnight to 2.00 pm

12.00 midnight.

Over in Carnoy Valley Lieutenant-Colonel Cardew was having a rough time of it, the German artillery was shelling his headquarters once again. At midnight he was forced to leave the dubious protection of his tent and go in search of a better and safer billet. He went down into the telephone dug out and found, as he later noted in his diary, the others there. Who the others were he did not say but it would be safe to assume the other members of his headquarters staff. It would seem that there was no room for the Lieutenant-Colonel so he walked around in the open, as the shells fell all around him, searching for another dug out.

His search was fairly short because by 12.45 am he was back in his tent again, though he had identified one place where he may be safe. He wrote that fifteen minutes later bits began hitting his tent so he turned out again and headed for the bomb store. Here he sat for the next hour, surrounded by bombs, as the shells fell all around. Lieutenant-Colonel Cardew recorded that during the bombardment the water-cart was perforated, the horse team that pulled it were killed and a shell smashed the telephone cart.

12.40 am.

17th Division reported to XV Corps that the 6th Dorsets held all of Wood Trench. XV Corps noted that at this time the 17th Division held Wood Trench, Quadrangle Alley up to its junction with Quadrangle Support Trench, Quadrangle Trench and Pearl Alley up to the civilian cemetery.

The 52nd Brigade was now out of the line and, for a while, out of the fighting. In their billets at Ville-Sous-Corbie the 9th Northumberland Fusiliers received this special order from their Brigade Commander, Brigadier-General J. Clarke.

The Brigadier-General commanding desires to place on record his appreciation of and gratitude for, the magnificent conduct of all ranks and units of the Brigade during the operations of the past week.

The traditions of the famous Regiments to which the New Army Battalions comprising the Brigade belong were most nobly and worthily maintained. He congratulates the 9th Northumberland Fusiliers and 10th Lancashire

Fusiliers on the successful attack which resulted in the capture of Quadrangle Trench. Nothing could have exceeded the gallantry of the 9th Duke of Wellington's Regiment and 12th Manchester Regiment in this attack in broad daylight over the open on the Quadrangle Support Trench. The co-operation of the Brigade Machine Gun Company and Brigade Trench Mortar Battery with the infantry was carried out with marked success.

Whilst deploring the loss of many brave and fearless officers and men, the Brigadier desires to remind all ranks that the initiative so necessary for success on war remains with us, and so the great sacrifices have not been made altogether in vain. [41]

None of the other 52nd Brigade formations made any mention of this message.

The 12th Manchesters began a period of refitting at Ville. The 9th Duke of Wellingtons moved to billets in Ville-sur-Ancre near Albert.

Unspecified time.

The 7th Yorks & Lancs, the Pioneers, recorded their dispositions for the day as follows. D Company was detailed to work with one section of the 77th Field Company Royal Engineers. They were to have made a strong point at the Junction of Quadrangle Trench and Pearl Alley but the situation at the front meant that they were unable to get to their work. B Company was also unable to get to their work. A Company worked throughout the day in Railway Alley servicing the trench and putting in fire steps, or in the language of the time they were to 'reverse the trench'. Like most of the trenches now occupied by the Division the trench had been dug by the Germans and the fire steps faced the wrong way. They also built two small strong points in the trench and laid barbed wire along its front. The Pioneers worked on the road from Fricourt Farm to Crucifix Trench seeing to it that it was repaired; a bridge was put in Lozenge Alley. Seven men were wounded in the course of the day's work.

Alongside the Engineers and Pioneers the 17th Signal Company continued to work on the communication lines where it was practicable. Rain water was causing induction in the telephone lines

---

[41] TNA: PRO. WO95/2013. 9th Northumberland Fusiliers, July 1916.

so the Linesmen had a number of small poles made which they then placed in the cable trenches to raise the telephone lines up and out of the water.

The remains of the 10th West Yorks, the battalion with the worst casualties of 50th Brigade, were still based in Fricourt and continued to support the other units of their Brigade. They were employed taking rations, ammunition and building materials up to the front line. During the day Second Lieutenant Bacon and five other ranks were wounded while carrying out one of these tasks.

The 81st Royal Field Artillery continued to bombard the enemy positions as they had the day before. The 78th Royal Field Artillery barraged the German second line and searched Villa Wood, Middle Wood, Lower Wood and the north western side of Mametz Wood.

2.00 am.

50th Brigade recorded that the 6th Dorsets were to attack Mametz Wood in conjunction with the 38th Division at this hour. However the 6th Dorsets watched for the 38th Division attack on Strip Trench and noted that the long awaited attack did not materialise. Like the day before the German artillery continued to maintain a heavy barrage on the areas immediately to the rear of the British front line where many troops were massed, namely Bottom Wood, Railway Alley and the 6th Dorsets H.Q.

Despite the artillery fire runners continued to operate; taking messages to and fro. The Linesmen of the 17th Signal Company were kept very busy all day and night repairing severed telephone lines.

A Section, 50th Brigade Machine Gun Company, completed the relief of B Section in Bottom Wood. B Section then moved to Wicked Corner and remained there in reserve.

52nd Field Ambulance recorded that all bearers under Captains Dougal and Bury went out to the aid station at Railway Copse.

3.35 am.

Under cover of darkness the 7th Yorks launched a bombing attack up Quadrangle Alley. Like the attacks before it this isolated assault was doomed to failure. Struggling through the mud the British soldiers could not get past the machine gunners and bombers who manned the German stop. This latest failure was reported to 17th Division headquarters. Around this time, on the left, the 7th Borders were relieved in the front line by the 7th Lincolns. The 7th Borders went into positions in the Hedge and Bottom Wood.

51st Field Ambulance recorded that the stream of wounded was steady during the night but the morning was quiet.

4.00 am.

Back in his tent, Lieutenant-Colonel Cardew noted that after all the 'excitement' of the hostile bombardment he was in no mood for sleep. Even so he did try.

4.10 am.

Two hours and ten minutes after the 38th Division operation against Strip Trench was supposed to have begun Major-General Phillips telephoned XV Corps headquarters to explain why it had not happened. He told Lieutenant-General Horne that the orders for the attack had not reached the infantry in the front line in time for the attack to go ahead. His men would therefore operate 'Scheme b' and attack later.

This was not a situation that Lieutenant-General Horne could countenance. The 38th Division had failed to carry out his own explicit orders and his superiors would soon want an explanation from him. The capture of Mametz Wood, Quadrangle Support Trench and Contalmaison were considered essential before the next phase of the battle could begin; namely the attack upon the German second line.

Meanwhile in the front line, sometime in the early morning, and the diary does not record when, 'A' Company of the 6th Dorsets, posted in the eastern end of Quadrangle Trench, salvaged three Lewis guns, a most welcome addition to their fire power. A little while later they observed parties of German troops moving towards Contalmaison. The 6th Dorsets opened fire on them with their Lewis guns.

17th Division headquarters received a message at around this time stating that the attack by the 38th Division had been cancelled. It had been rescheduled to go in at 4.00 pm that afternoon.

5.00 am.

50th Brigade was informed that the 38th Division was going to attack at 4.00 pm that afternoon.

6.00 am.

Lieutenant-Colonel Rowley sent a situation report to Brigadier-General Glasgow at 50th Brigade headquarters. The 6th Dorsets now held Wood Trench to a 'stop' some seventy yards away from Mametz Wood. From here the 6th Dorsets had been able to find out that the junction of Wood Trench and Strip Trench was held in some force by the enemy. They had waited in vain for the 38th Division to put in an appearance but they did not show. Wood Trench had now been connected to Quadrangle Trench by a communication trench which was dug to a depth of five feet. 6th Dorset casualties had been heavy.

His companies were positioned as follows. C Company was in Wood Trench; A Company had withdrawn from Quadrangle Trench and was now in Railway Alley, D Company was at Post Number Five in Sunshade Alley, Fricourt. The remains of B Company, now down to some fifty men, were in Willow Trench.

Major-General Pilcher telephoned a report to Lieutenant-General Horne saying that the 6th Dorsets had been trying to attack up Wood Trench with bombers to try and gain contact with the 38th Division. Lieutenant-General Horne noted that the rest of the 17th Division's front remained unaltered.

6.20 am.

There now followed a busy twenty minutes. Lieutenant-General Horne sent situation reports to Lieutenant-General Rawlinson at Fourth Army Headquarters. These were based upon the telephone reports that he had recently received from the 17th and 38th Divisions.

6.30 am.

Ten minutes later he sent a separate message to Fourth Army. In this message he informed Lieutenant-General Rawlinson that an investigation was already underway into the reasons why the 38th Division did not attack as ordered.

52nd Field Ambulance recorded that few casualties were coming in. Captain Bury returned and reported that Quadrangle, Wood, Strip Trenches, and the edge of Mametz Wood also Bottom Wood and Aid Posts had been cleared of casualties by the 52nd Field Ambulance bearers. At the time Strip Trench or at least its junction with Wood Trench was reported to be still in German hands. The 7th Yorks Aid Post was reported to be in Bottom Wood but Captain Bury and his bearers failed to find it. They did find the 7th Yorks battalion headquarters and the 7th Yorks wounded were being cleared through the aid post in Railway Copse. From there they were being directed to the Advanced Dressing Stations.

6.40 am.

Lieutenant-General Horne had finally lost patience with Major-General Phillips. He ordered the 38th Divisional Commander to report to XV Corps Headquarters. Major-General Phillips was going to be dismissed; he had held things up for far too long.

7.30 am.

Lieutenant-Colonel Cardew was roused from his bed after a badly disturbed night. He had not slept and noted in his diary that he was half dead through a lack of sleep.

52nd Field Ambulance headquarters received a note from Captain Dougal reporting that all was well, and that most of the old casualties who lay out in front of Quadrangle Trench had been retrieved. Captain Dougal reported that the bearer squads were being reassembled at Railway Copse. Once they had gathered together they would begin to clear the whole length of Quadrangle Trench of any wounded men.

8.00 am.

XV Corps informed the 17th Division that they would be relieved in the front line by the 21st Division on the night of 10 July.

8.20 am.

XV Corps telephoned instructions through to 17th Division for their next attack on Quadrangle Support Trench. It was impressed upon the 17th Division staff that the capture of Quadrangle Support Trench was now considered 'essential'. The coming assault on the German second line was very much in the minds of Lieutenant-Generals Rawlinson and Horne.

The new attack was arranged for 12.15 pm in the afternoon. Major-General Pilcher informed both 50th and 51st Brigades that they would co-operate by once more bombing up Pearl Alley and Quadrangle Alley.

8.55 am.

17th Division telephoned a situation report through to XV Corps headquarters reporting that the Division held the junction of Quadrangle Support Trench and Pearl Alley. Also, having consolidated Wood Trench, it was now fully connected to Quadrangle Trench.

9.00 am.

XV Corps ordered the Special Section of the Royal Engineers to report to 50th Brigade Headquarters in Fricourt. These men operated two portable flame throwers. No mention was made of their use.

9.20 am.

Lieutenant-General Rawlinson at Fourth Army headquarters sent out orders directing that the artillery would start shelling the wire in front of the second German line as soon as possible. This would be prior to the assault on the second line. A programme for the initial bombardment of the second line was also issued to the batteries. Lieutenant-General Rawlinson anticipated that Contalmaison, Quadrangle Support Trench and Mametz Wood would soon fall and the attack upon the second line could begin in earnest.

10.00 am.

The 8th South Staffords moved up to relieve the 7th Borders. They recorded that the Germans were shelling Bottom Wood and the

Hedge as they took over the positions. The 7th Borders moved into saps in the village of Fricourt.

The commanding officer of 50th Brigade Machine Gun Company visited D Section which was waiting in reserve at Wicked Corner.

Meanwhile A Section, of the same Machine Gun Company, opened fire from Bottom Wood on enemy troops seen moving about in Strip Trench.

The 4.5-inch Howitzers of the 81st Royal Field Artillery based at Bray-sur-Somme fired upon German troops who had been observed moving around in Quadrangle Support Trench.

10.15 am.

In their positions in the deep trenches at Fricourt the 10th Notts & Derbys received their orders. They were to stand by from 12 noon to relieve a battalion in the front line.

10.20 am.

By now Major-General Phillips had been informed by Lieutenant-General Horne that he no longer commanded the 38th Division and had been dismissed. Major-General C. G. Blackader was on his way to take over the 38th Division. Fourth Army headquarters had contacted XV Corps headquarters and suggested that Major-General Sir Herbert Watts of the 7th Division should temporarily take over the Welsh Division. Watts' division had earned high praise for the capture of Mametz Village and had just gone out of the line for a brief rest. Such a suggestion could not be ignored; Major-General Watts would command the Division in the short term. According to the 38th Divisional History Major-General Blackader took over the 38th Division later in July 1916 and commanded it until May 1918.

Lieutenant-Colonel Cardew began his morning rounds visiting the batteries of the 80th Brigade, R.F.A.

11.10 am.

Very shortly after being recommended for the post of 38th Divisional Commander, Major-General Watts arrived in person at XV Corps Headquarters. He had orders to review the situation on the 38th Division front and within the Division itself. He was to report to

XV Corps which troops he proposed to retain, if any. He was to push along all arrangements for attacking and taking Mametz Wood. He had been told that the capture of the Wood must be taken. Watts brought his senior staff officers, Colonel's Bonham Carter and Wingfield with him as well as his signals officer, Captain O'Connor and the 7th Divisional Signal Company.

At around this time XV Corps sent an aerial reconnaissance report to the 17th Division relating to the 8.00 pm attack of the previous day. Lieutenant-General Horne pointed out the failings of the previous attack as he saw them. Then he once again took the opportunity to impress upon Major-General Pilcher of the great importance of success in the forthcoming attack on Quadrangle Support Trench.

11.40 am.

A message to Lieutenant-Colonel Rowley at the Dorsets' battalion Headquarters was sent from C Company in Wood Trench. It referred to a German attack on their position.

Early in the morning some of the men, including the Company Sergeant Major, stated that they saw a force of about forty Germans attacking Wood Trench from the direction of Wood Support trench on the left. C Company at once opened fire with their rifles and machine guns. After the attack was repulsed the Machine Gun Sergeant reported that he saw the Germans fetching their wounded in. Captain O'Hanlon the company commander had to report that all he saw of the attack and aftermath were 'trees and thistles'. He saw no attack at all.[42]

Captain Mozley and his A Company were stationed in Railway Alley immediately behind Bottom Wood, snatching what rest they could. He wrote in his diary that orders arrived for his company to prepare to move forward and relieve C Company in Wood Trench that evening. In preparation for the move forward he sent two trusted NCOs forward to Wood Trench, via Bottom Alley to learn the lie of the land and to take over the trench equipment and tools from C Company.

---

[42] O'Hanlon made no mention of this incident in his History of the 6th Battalion.

11.50 am.

III Corps telephoned XV Corps to say that the 23rd Division was going to co- operate with the 17th Division attack upon Quadrangle Support Trench by assaulting Contalmaison at the same time. The hour of this joint attack was to be arranged directly with the 17th Division.

11.53 am.

Despite the continuous German barrage of the area the 8th South Staffords completed the relief of the 7th Borders at Bottom Wood.

11.55 am.

XV Corps telephoned 17th Division Headquarters and Major-General Pilcher was informed that the 23rd Division, of III Corps, was going to attack Contalmaison in conjunction with his Division's attack on Quadrangle Support Trench. This message was then repeated to the 17th Division in a telegram.

D battery of the 79th Royal Field Artillery was ordered to fire upon Quadrangle Alley until 12.15 pm. The gunners of B battery busied themselves 'sniping' at enemy troops who could be seen by the Forward Observation Officers entering Contalmaison from the east. The artillery paid special attention to the areas where German machine guns had been reported and they shelled the area around the German 'stop' at the junction of Quadrangle Alley and Quadrangle Support Trench.

12.00 Noon.

51st Field Ambulance noted that the stream of wounded had once again increased and the quiet period had ended. The casualties were being cleared by the buses and motor lorries so there was no congestion at the Aid Stations. The Commanding Officer of the 51st Field Ambulance visited Queens Redoubt and found his men dirty and resting.

12.15 pm.

As XV Corps sent a situation report to Fourth Army Headquarters the British Artillery barrage ceased and the 7th Yorks launched the next bombing attack up Quadrangle Alley, aiming once again at the junction with Quadrangle Support Trench. The barrage had lasted for an hour and a half and special attention had been given to the junction of Quadrangle Alley and Quadrangle Support Trench as well as known machine gun positions. A Stokes Mortar section had arrived and moved into the positions that the 7th Yorks had prepared for them. Their job was to give close support to the attacking troops.

Once again machine gun fire held up the attack and once again the attack failed. The 7th Yorks reported that this time the machine gun fire came from different positions. The Stokes Mortars were unable to participate in the action, because the ground was too soft and muddy to set the weapons up properly. Despite the intense shelling of suspected German machine gun positions the guns had not been knocked out because their crews had simply moved them.

The 50th Brigade recorded that this was actually their sixth attack on the junction of Quadrangle Alley and Quadrangle Support Trench. They noted that machine gun fire made movement in the open, by day, impossible. Brigadier-General Glasgow then suggested to the battalions that they might try a surprise night attack with artillery support.

17th Division recorded that the 12.15 pm attack failed because of the state of the trenches and the heavy rifle and machine gun fire from the flanks.

As recorded at 8.20 am this attack should have been a co-operative bombing effort between 50th and 51st Brigades, and apparently in conjunction with a 23rd Division attack on Contalmaison. However no mention is made of 51st Brigade or 23rd Division attacking at 12.15 pm. The 7th Lincolns were in the left hand portion of Quadrangle Trench at this point, having taken over from the 7th Borders earlier in the day. Their war diary makes absolutely no mention of an assault at this time up Pearl Alley or on Quadrangle Support Trench.

The 17th Divisional history *implies* that the attack took place on both flanks but by which formations it does not say. The 51st Brigade war diary does not mention an attack at this time by any of its battalions.

A Forward Observation Officer reported to XV Corps that the Germans had started a heavy bombardment on the XV and III Corps fronts. III Corps sent up an SOS rocket and the British guns replied. Within moments the air throbbed, the ground shook and exploded as a furious artillery duel began.

12.30 pm.

As the artillery duel raged C Section, 50th Brigade Machine Gun Company, in Willow Trench, added extra noise to the cacophony as they began indirect fire against Strip trench. Obeying orders to support an attack upon Strip Trench they opened their fire on the junction of Wood and Strip Trenches, sweeping the latter trench. Then from here they traversed their guns along the edge of Mametz Wood. But who was attacking Strip Trench at this moment? The 38th Division was not and nor were the 6th Dorsets.

Later in the day, it is not recorded when, enemy troops were observed moving about in a gap of Quadrangle Support Trench where it joined the Wood. A Section of the 50th Machine Gun Company based in Bottom Wood was ordered to open fire on them. They reported that fire was successfully directed at these troops.

12.40 pm.

While talking to two of his officers, Lieutenant-Colonel Cardew received telephone orders for his guns. As part of the preparations for the forthcoming attack on the German second line his brigade was to concentrate upon cutting the belts of wire near Bazentin-le-Grand. They were to open fire at 1.15 pm and continue the operation until dusk.

1.00 pm.

C Company of 8th South Staffords were sent up from Bottom Wood to assist the 7th Lincolns in the front line.

Back in Fricourt the 10th Notts & Derbys had stood by, as ordered, for an hour. No orders to move forward had arrived so the 10th Notts & Derbys stood down. No orders had arrived for them to move forward because no forward movement had taken place ahead of them. The plan was probably for the 7th Lincolns to move into Quadrangle Support once they had captured it. The 8th South Staffords were to then to have moved into the front line in place of the 7th Lincolns and so on.

79th Royal Field Artillery reported that the heavy German barrage on the 17th Division front line was still going on and it had certainly extended to the III Corps front on the left flank.

1.15 pm.

The batteries of the 80th Brigade Royal Field Artillery opened fire on the wire in front of the German line near Bazentin-le-Grand.

2.00 pm.

Lieutenant-General Horne contacted both 17th and 38th Divisions saying that intelligence gathered from prisoners, recently captured on the XV Corps front, showed that all that was needed was a strong British attack to ensure complete success. The prisoners had told intelligence officers that their forces were withdrawing and there would be little opposition to a British attack. Lieutenant-General Horne urged both divisional Commanders to show determination in the forthcoming attacks; both today and in the coming days.

Lieutenant-General Horne told his Major-Generals

All prisoners captured in the last 24 hours express astonishment that our infantry does not attack in greater strength instead of bombing up trenches in twos or threes. The enemy is much in confusion there being small groups here and there of every regiment. There are some stretches of country without any enemy in it at all. If our infantry attacked in strength they could sweep the whole of them back... All communications trenches to the rear are smashed. This information confirms that already received from aircraft and other sources. Corps commander impresses on all commanders the necessity of utmost vigour and determination in the attacks to be delivered today and great results which accrue there from. He looks to divisional commanders ensuring his directions on this point are carried out.[43]

It seems plain that Lieutenant-General Horne, trusting the prisoners' information, did not think that his Major-Generals had not been trying hard enough. In Phillips' case that appears to have been true. Major-General Watts, proven in battle, successful and now commanding the 38th Division did not need to be told about determination and vigour. Though the advice was probably not aimed at him. Major-General Pilcher could not mistake the implied

43 In Colin Hughes, *Mametz – Lloyd George's Welsh Army at the Battle of the Somme*, p.98

threat in this communiqué. He was being watched by the XV Corps Commander. In fact General Haig had been concerned about Major-General Pilcher since February 1916. On the very day that the 17th Division was facing its first real test in action at 'The Bluff' he had written in his diary that he felt that Pilcher, among others, was not fit for his appointment.[44]

Wilhelm Wegener, an officer of the 8th Company, 3rd Battalion, the 9th Grenadier Regiment had been captured on 7 July and had described how the British artillery had wreaked havoc on the German lines. He described the situation behind the lines as chaotic. He told the interrogating officers that the German artillery had been put out of action by British fire. The story of chaos was supported by other prisoners and deserters taken in the XV Corps area. Prisoners talking among themselves had been overheard saying that the British would break the German lines with a determined attack.[45] It was just what the British High Command wanted to hear. It seemed to prove their theory that the Germans were in a bad way and would break under relentless pressure.

Captain Mozley and any other soldier in and around Bottom Wood could say with absolute conviction that the German gunners were far from out of action. They had been shelling the British trenches for days. Lieutenant-General Rawlinson himself knew very well that the German defenders and machine gunners were sticking to their task with dogged efficiency.

Yet Lieutenant-General Horne had been briefed on all of these reports so he urged the 17th Division to make another, surprise attack on Quadrangle Support Trench in the evening, using rested soldiers. He told Pilcher

Machine guns should not stop fresh troops if they mean to get in. Impress upon your troops that they are going to be relieved tomorrow night, that it is up to them to make their reputation by taking the trench before they go... [46]

[44] Haig in Sheffield & Bourne, *Douglas Haig War Diaries and Letters 1914-1918.* p. 181

[45] TNA: PRO. WO95/468. XV Corps Intelligence Summaries, July 1916.

[46] In Colin Hughes, *Mametz – Lloyd George's Welsh Army at the Battle of the Somme,* p.98

Chapter Eight : 9 July 1916 2.15 pm to 11.30 pm

At some point during this day General Haig wrote to Lieutenant-General Rawlinson to express his opinion that the withdrawal from Contalmaison on 7 July and the failure of the 38th Division to take Mametz Wood were not creditable performances.[47] The High Command was stepping up the pressure and not only on the enemy.

52nd Field Ambulance officers returned to Sunken Road, after the front line Aid Posts had been completely cleared of wounded. The remainder of the wounded who had been brought back from in front of Quadrangle Trench had also been brought down. Captains Dougal and Bury went up Pearl Alley and brought in seven more cases. Mud was making the work arduous; the trenches were almost impassable so the bearers had to work mostly in the open,

51st Field Ambulance bearers took over from the 52nd but no fresh casualties reported at this time. Despite being relieved some of the 52nd Field Ambulance bearers proceeded to search Shelter Wood and the local vicinity for possible casualties that had not been reported.

The 52nd Field Ambulance reported that over the last three days Private Hartley had been wounded on 7 July. Private Wise had been shell shocked on 8 July. Lance Corporal King had been wounded on 9 July. Private James Carlisle, 41518, was killed by a single rifle bullet on 7 July.

2.15 pm.

The 7th East Yorks, who were under constant German artillery fire in the reserve trenches of Railway Alley and Crucifix Trench, recorded that they had received the message saying that they would be relieved on the night of 10 July.

At around this time XV Corps recorded that the German heavy artillery fire that had begun at 12.15 pm had slackened off.

---

[47] TNA: PRO. WO95/5. War Diary, G.H.Q., General Staff, July 1916.

2.20 pm.

Major Hughes-Onslow of the 6th Dorsets sent a message back from the front line to Lieutenant-Colonel Rowley at battalion headquarters.

He reported that his men were now sixty yards from Mametz Wood. They had set up a 'stop' in the trench. This advance meant that the Dorsets now held practically all of Wood Trench now. There was still no sign of the 38th Division and the Major pointed out that he could not withdraw C Company and replace them with A Company until contact had been made with the 38th Division.

2.30 pm.

A message came into 17th Division's headquarters saying that the 38th Division would not now be attacking at 4.00 pm; the attack was postponed until the following day. Major-General Pilcher issued verbal orders to 50th and 51st Brigades to the effect that they should prepare to carry out a surprise assault on Quadrangle Support Trench at 11.20 pm.

Major-General Pilcher ordered the 51st Brigade to make a preliminary bombing attack up Pearl Alley to capture and hold the junction with Quadrangle Support. A garrison there would protect the left flank of the forthcoming attack. Major-General Pilcher ordered that this bombing attack should be made 'at once.'

The main attack was to be delivered over the open to a point three hundred and fifty yards south east of Pearl Alley/Quadrangle Support junction. He told Brigadier-Generals Trotter and Glasgow that their Brigades would attack Quadrangle Support Trench simultaneously, 50th Brigade would attack over the open against Quadrangle Alley/Quadrangle Support junction, and their attack would extend fifty yards west of the above junction. Once taken both junctions were to be consolidated and turned in to strong points, the section of Quadrangle Support Trench in between the two junctions was then to be evacuated by daybreak.

2.40 pm.

A warning order was sent out to the 17th Division, from XV Corps, advising them of their relief by the 21st Division on the night of the 10/11 July.

3.00 pm.

In Willow Trench, C Section, 50th Brigade Machine Gun Company, ceased firing on Strip, Wood Trenches and the edge of Mametz Wood.

50th Brigade received news from 17th Division headquarters that the proposed attack at 4.00 pm by the 38th Division was once again postponed. The attack would now be made early in the morning of 10 July.

XV Corps received a report from 17th Division about the 12.15 pm attack. Major-General Pilcher said that their attack on Quadrangle Support Trench had been unsuccessful owing to machine gun fire. The machine guns had been shelled but they had moved position and were undamaged. Major-General Pilcher informed Lieutenant-General Horne that, in accordance with his orders, a new attack would be put in with fresh troops after dark.

3.15 pm.

Fifteen minutes later Major-General Pilcher sent another message to XV Corps headquarters. Major-General Pilcher had been expecting support from the 23rd Division on his left but that had been unforthcoming and he communicated this to XV Corps. Lieutenant-General Horne bluntly responded by ordering that Quadrangle Support Trench must be taken that night by the 17th Division; with or without an attack by 23rd Division.

3.30 pm.

D Section, 50th Brigade Machine Gun Company, relieved C Section in Willow Trench. C Section returned through the crowded and mud filled trenches to Wicked Corner where they were to be the Company reserve. Once they had set up D Section commenced firing on Strip Trench.

4.00 pm.

The 6th Dorsets recorded that the planned attack by the 38th Division for this time was again postponed. Major Hughes-Onslow would have to relieve C Company with A Company without getting in touch with the 38th Division.

4.05 pm.

D Section, 50th Brigade Machine Gun Company, ceased firing on Strip Trench from Willow Trench.

4.50 pm.

The 7th Lincolns' bombers supported by two platoons of their B Company were sent out to clear Pearl Alley of any enemy troops that may be there. They had orders to capture and hold the junction of Pearl Alley and Quadrangle Support Trench. As usual the conditions were playing their part. Lieutenant Jones reported back that the mud in Pearl Alley was making it difficult for the men to throw their grenades effectively. Two hours and twenty minutes had passed since Major-General Pilcher had ordered this bombing attack be made at once.

5.30 pm.

In their positions at Fricourt the 10th Notts & Derbys received new orders. They were warned to be prepared to move up to the line of Hedge at short notice after 9.00 that evening. The 10th Notts & Derbys adjutant, Captain 'George Jimmy' Partridge, recorded in the war diary that from this time, in anticipation of the coming assault, the battalion provided carrying parties to the front line. They carried bombs, Verey lights and small arms ammunition up to the troops in the front line. Sixty-four men were specifically detailed to take rations up the line for the 8th South Staffords.

5.35 pm.

General Haig and Lieutenant-General Rawlinson visited Lieutenant-General Horne at XV Corps Headquarters. They impressed upon him the need for the 38th Division to make head way against Mametz Wood. They also made it clear that the performance of both the 17th and 38th Divisions had so far been a disappointing.

Lieutenant-General Horne agreed with them. He told his superiors that he "was very disappointed with the work of the 17th Division and 38th Division."[48] General Haig later noted in his diary that both

---

[48] In Colin Hughes, *Mametz – Lloyd George's Welsh Army at the Battle of the Somme* p. 95

17th and 38th Divisional Generals had been removed from their posts. [49]

Major-General Phillips had indeed been replaced. However, Major-General Pilcher remained in command of the 17th Division. He had not been replaced, not yet, though it would seem that Lieutenant-General Horne had made up his mind about Major-General Pilcher. He would have to go.

5.50 pm.

The 7th East Yorks received orders for the next attack upon Quadrangle Support Trench. Their only part, however, was to take over the strong point at the junction of Quadrangle Alley and Quadrangle Support Trench at dawn. This was assuming that the junction had been captured by the 7th Yorks and the strong point had in fact been built by the Pioneers, the 7th Yorks & Lancs.

The orders from 50th Brigade Headquarters to the 7th Yorks, 7th East Yorks and 6th Dorsets were as follows.

They were informed that the 51st Brigade was at that moment attempting to capture and hold the junction of Pearl Alley and Quadrangle Support Trench. At 11.20 pm the 50th and the 51st Brigades were to deliver a surprise attack over the open on a front of three hundred and fifty yards with the left flank on Pearl Alley. The 7th Yorks were going to attack astride Quadrangle Alley with their left flank extended fifty yards West of Quadrangle Alley. Their attack was timed so as to arrive in Quadrangle Support Trench at 11.20 pm. On their arrival in Quadrangle Support Trench the 7th Yorks were to bomb along the trench towards the 51st Brigade troops. The 51st Brigade would do the same and bomb towards the 7th Yorks.

Once the attack was underway and the junction of Quadrangle Alley and Quadrangle Support Trench was taken a strong point was to be constructed there, at once, by a detachment of Pioneers. The officer in charge of the Pioneers detachment was ordered to report to Lieutenant-Colonel Fife of the 7th Yorks to receive further information and orders. The trenches at the junction were be 'stopped' to the North and East and manned by the 7th Yorks.

---

[49] Haig in Sheffield & Bourne, *Douglas Haig,* p.201

Though any part of the trench occupied North West of the strong point at the junction would have to be evacuated before daylight. The German machine guns at Acid Drop Copse and at the top of Quadrangle Alley would be dealt with by artillery. They were informed that there would be no regular bombardment on the trench before the assault. Lieutenant-Colonel Clive of the 7th East Yorks was ordered to visit Lieutenant-Colonel Fife of the 7th Yorks to arrange the take over of the new Strong Point at the junction of Quadrangle Alley and Quadrangle Support before dawn.

6.00 pm.

The 93rd Field Company, Royal Engineers, received orders that they were to report at Fricourt at 7.00 pm for work.

The softening up process on the German second line carried on. 79th Royal Field Artillery received orders and their zone for nightly firing on the second line. They were to commence firing at 10.00 pm each night using the batteries in shifts of one and a half hours each.

6.40 pm.

Major-General Pilcher issued Operation Order No. 64 concerning the forthcoming attack. The orders reinforced the verbal orders that he had given to the 50th and 51st Brigades at 2.30 pm that afternoon. The attacks were timed to reach the enemy trench at 11.20 pm.

7.00 pm.

The 93rd Field Company, Royal Engineers arrived at Fricourt as ordered and were promptly sent back as they were not required.

7.20 pm.

Lieutenant-General Horne was informed of 17th Division's orders for a surprise attack on Quadrangle Support Trench at 11.20 pm.

The 8th South Staffords received orders to take Quadrangle Support Trench. They were informed that the attack would begin without the usual, preliminary barrage. They were also told that 50th Brigade was to provide a simultaneous assault on the right probably attacking up Quadrangle Alley. The 7th Lincolns were going to bomb up Pearl

Alley on the left. In a similar operation to the right flank a single Company of Pioneers were to follow up this assault and to build strong points at the junction of Pearl Alley and Quadrangle Support Trench, once these trenches were in the hands of the 8th South Staffords.

7.45 pm.

7th Lincolns reported that they remained in Quadrangle Trench and began consolidating the position. They reported that they were occupied with the task of consolidation for the rest of the night coming under regular sniper and artillery fire. Lieutenant A. H. Bird and Second Lieutenant J. A. Levette were both wounded during the night.

No mention is made about their earlier, 4.50 pm, bombing attack and attempt to capture the junction of Pearl Alley and Quadrangle Support Trench. Nor is there any mention of when it was called off. Yet as can be seen from the diary entries later and on the following day, made by both the 8th South Staffords and 7th Lincolns, the battalion bombers and two platoons of B Company, the 7th Lincolns, were still in Pearl Alley.

Therefore Lieutenant Jones's earlier report about the conditions in Pearl Alley must mean that the Lincolns' attack was called off. The 7th Lincolns made no record of being told that they were to bomb up Pearl Alley alongside the 8th South Staffords in the main 11.20 attack.

Captain Mozley and his men arrived in Wood Trench to relieve C Company. Captain Mozley expected to be greeted by the two NCOs that he had sent ahead earlier in the day but there was no sign of them. He enquired after them and soon discovered that they were dead. They had made their way up Bottom Alley but then they had climbed out of the trench and tried to head for the front line over the open ground. In full view of the Germans they were inevitably fired upon and apparently killed. Captain Mozley wrote that he could not understand what had possessed these two level headed NCOs to do such a 'reckless thing'. Even though a few days before he himself had remarked upon the state and congestion of this communication trench.[50]

---

[50] See Appendix 04

He had little time to dwell on their loss as the business of taking over a section of the front line had to be dealt with. C Company left him their four Lewis guns and he noted that his company was supported by a Vickers gun team posted on higher ground than Wood Trench at the eastern end of Quadrangle Trench. Captain Mozley wrote in his diary that his company had varying fields of fire. On the right he could bring Wood Support Trench under fire but on the left he had a fairly short field of fire as the ground rose steeply towards Contalmaison. Only the Vickers gun, because of its elevation, was able to fire up the small valley towards Acid Drop Copse.

8.00 pm.

Lieutenant-Colonel Barker, of the 8th South Staffords, went out into no mans land with his company commanders and reconnoitred the ground that their men had to cross in their attack. Lieutenant-Colonel Barker had planned the operation well. Linesmen had run telephone wires up from the 8th South Staffords battalion headquarters to Quadrangle Trench so that he could stay in constant touch with his men.

He had laid out his plans to the companies. B and D Companies were detailed to attack in three lines. B Company was to advance on the right, with their bombers watching right and D Company on the left, with their bombers watching left. The front rank of both Companies carried wire cutters just in case the German wire was still intact. A Company was to be held in reserve and C Company was detailed to hold the front line, Quadrangle Trench.

To gain maximum surprise the men were ordered to be completely silent. All unnecessary equipment was removed and their bayonets were smeared with mud to prevent them glinting in the moonlight that shone intermittently through the scudding rain clouds. Some of the 8th Battalion's bombers were sent to assist the 7th Lincolns in Pearl Alley because the South Staffords had noticed that the Lincolns were making no headway there.

Having learned from the previous attacks the 8th South Staffords knew that Quadrangle Support Trench was not visible until the attacking troops were virtually on top of it. So Captain Gibson took men from C Company to act as markers for the assault. They had white streamers tied to their backs and they had to be in the open, in front of Quadrangle Trench, and on an alignment parallel to the line of Quadrangle Support Trench by 11.00 pm. These markers were to give a line on which the attackers would form.

At this time 50th Brigade issued Brigade Message 143. The 38th Division would attack on the right with two brigades at 4.15 in the morning. Their objective would be just south of where Wood Support Trench joined Wood Trench. The 7th East Yorks and the 6th Dorsets were ordered to be ready to co-operate at about 6.00 am and push up Quadrangle Alley and the Railways and get a footing in Wood Support Trench. They were to co-operate in every possible way with the 38th Division.

Pioneers of the 7th Yorks & Lancs, along with men of the 78th Field Company, Royal Engineers carried concertinas of barbed wire to Bottom Wood. Shortly after dark three hundred and fifty yards of concertina wire had been deposited in the Wood.

8.35 pm.

The 10th Notts & Derbys received an order from Brigadier-General Trotter at 51st Brigade Headquarters. Two companies were required to take over the front line from the 8th South Staffords when they attacked that night. Lieutenant-Colonel Banbury was ordered to send one officer from each company to report to the 8th South Staffords headquarters at 10.30 pm. Lieutenant-Colonel Barker would give these officers instructions as to where he wanted the incoming companies to go.

8.50 pm.

The 50th Brigade diary recorded that the 6th Dorsets had now completely captured Wood Trench.

10.00 pm.

A and D Companies of the 10th Notts & Derbys were sent forward to the front line as instructed by Brigadier-General Trotter.

52nd Field Ambulance had moved their headquarters to the Advanced Dressing Station at Fricourt. They received a message from the 7th Yorks reporting that there were wounded men in Bottom Wood. Squads of bearers were duly sent out. Captain Levis of the 51st Field Ambulance was also sent to investigate.

Lieutenant-Colonel Cardew sat down to keep his diary. Along with other notes about the day, he wondered about the effectiveness of his batteries during the afternoon and evening. Major O'Malley-Keyes had apparently done good work with his battery but the other two batteries had only done 'fairly'. Lieutenant-Colonel Cardew wrote that he thought the range, of over three thousand yards, was too long for his guns and he was not sure how much wire had been cut. Worryingly he set down on paper that one of his battery commanders, a Captain, (his name is illegible in the diary) did not seem to take an interest in how his guns were operating and they were always firing awry. This officer's battery had guns away from the gun line being repaired as did the third battery commanded by an officer named Preston.

Lieutenant-Colonel Cardew's mind turned to a safe billet again and he noted that he was still in his tent, while the others had made a new dug out in a brick shed. Finally he wrote that he received some rock cakes, a new pair of field glasses but no letters.

17th Signal Company recorded that on the night of the 9th July a good many artillery Brigades moved forward and good deal of cable was issued so that the lines from the Brigade to the batteries could be extended and also from the batteries to the Forward Observation Officers. They now found that lines laid previously from the old front line trenches to Crucifix Trench in anticipation of artillery movement were now used. Some of these lines were also used by the 23rd Division as it side slipped to the east covering a large amount of the original 17/21st Divisional area.

10.32 pm.

The 7th East Yorks and the 6th Dorsets received the following orders from 50th Brigade headquarters. This was Brigade Message 145 cancelling Brigade Message 143.

The objective of 38th Division was now to secure the whole of Mametz Wood from South East. The British artillery would be shelling up to a line half way into the wood. At 6.15 am the barrage would lift and the 38th Division infantry were to move into the wood and occupy that line. At the same hour the 7th East Yorks would endeavour to take the South West corner of the wood and the piece of wood that protruded south and that ran across Wood Support Trench.

The 7th East Yorks would then send a party to capture the West end of Wood Support Trench and then bomb east to join up with 38th Division. The 7th East Yorks and the 6th Dorsets were told that if the attack on Quadrangle Support Trench, due to take place within the next hour, was unsuccessful then the commander of the 7th East Yorks must be made to understand that he had to watch the progress of any troops on the right and seize any opportunity that may present itself to achieve his objectives. The 6th Dorsets objective was to hold Wood Trench and join hands with infantry of the 38th Division which should come level with Wood Trench before 6.15 am.

Pencilled below this message was a note made by the 7th East Yorks Commanding Officer, Lieutenant-Colonel Clive.

> *Brigadier stated on telephone that I was not to attack till 38th Division on right came up level to corner of Wood Support. I asked for this in writing. 11.20 pm.*[51]

Captain Mozley wrote that during the night they were informed that the long expected attack of the 38th Division against Mametz Wood would take place at 5.00 a.m. the following morning.

10.45 pm.

An officer patrol from the 8th South Staffords went out into no-man's-land to find enemy listening posts and reconnoitre the ground to be traversed in the coming attack.

11.00 pm.

The 8th South Staffords were ready for the attack. Two Companies of the 10th Notts & Derbys moved into the Hedge previously occupied by the 8th South Staffords.

One gun from D Section, 50th Brigade Machine Gun Company, moved into Quadrangle Trench.

---

[51] TNA: PRO. WO95/2002. War Diary, 7th East Yorks, July 1916.

11.05 pm.

Under undirected sweeping bursts of machine gun fire from Contalmaison the assault upon Quadrangle Support Trench began again. The 8th South Staffords were well ahead of the 11.20 pm deadline that had been set for them to be in the enemy trench. The war diary of the 7th Lincolns, who were to make a bombing attack up Pearl Alley, makes no mention of this action at all. Their bombers and two platoons of B Company were in Pearl Alley and ready to co operate with the 8th South Staffords.

But the attack began in confusion. At the time that the 8th South Staffords attacked the 7th Yorks were away down the hill on the right flank preparing for their part of the attack, the advance up Quadrangle Alley. Apparently they did not attack at the same time as the 8th South Staffords.

There is a discrepancy in the written orders. The 7th Yorks had been told to attack at 11.20 pm and they had also been told that the 51st Brigade would attack at the same time.

> *At 11.20 pm LACK (50th Brigade) and LAWN (51st Brigade) will deliver a surprise attack on a front of 350 yards with left on Pearl Alley." These same orders also stated that the "Attack to be timed so as to arrive in Quad Support at 11.20 pm.* [52]

11.10 pm.

A, B and C batteries of 79th Royal Field Artillery received orders to barrage the western edge of Mametz Wood.

11.18 pm.

The 8th South Staffords had successfully reached their objective. Proudly they recorded that by this time they had taken Quadrangle Support Trench at bayonet point. Men of the German 11th Company, the 122nd Regiment, had fought back with bombs and machine gun fire but the 8th South Staffords had taken the trench. Their operation had been a success. If the time is correct then they had taken the trench in thirteen minutes. The 8th South Staffords recorded that the 7th Lincolns had made no progress up Pearl Alley

---

[52] TNA: PRO. WO95/2002. 7th East Yorks, July 1916.

at all. In fact the attacks up the communication trenches on both flanks had been failures. The 8th South Staffords had got into the left hand section of the trench but it was still occupied on the right by the 10th and 12th Companies of the 122nd Regiment.

German resistance and awful ground conditions in Pearl Alley made certain that the joint operation stalled. The bombers of both battalions and two platoons of the 7th Lincolns' B Company were stuck and unable to move forward. In order to make headway the 8th South Staffords' bombers climbed out of the trench and attacked the German defenders of Pearl Alley from the open. This brave and determined action gained the British about one hundred yards of Pearl Alley, but the cost in casualties to the 8th South Staffords bombers was high.

11.20 pm.

17th Division waited for the attack to play out and recorded simply that the attacks were delivered as ordered.

On the right flank the 7th Yorks began their attack, at the time that they had been given. The 7th Yorks recorded their version of events.

C Company with Captain A. J. Barmby in command had been ordered to attack the junction of Quadrangle Alley and Quadrangle Support Trench. They had been ordered to attack with the bayonet over the open and then set up stops in Quadrangle Alley and Wood Support Trench to cover the extreme right flank. According to the plan bombing parties from the 7th Yorks were to work down Quadrangle Support Trench and join hands with 51st Brigade who would be coming in the opposite direction. Lieutenant-Colonel Fife wrote in his diary that he had chosen Barmby's C Company because the orders for the attack had stated that only a small force should be employed. C Company was indeed a small force; it was down to 60 men.[53]

The 78th Field Coy, Royal Engineers, recorded that an attack was to be made on Quadrangle Support Trench. Number one Section and a platoon of Pioneers, the 7th Yorks & Lancs, were ordered to consolidate the junction of Quadrangle Alley and Quadrangle

---

[53] Lieutenant-Colonel Fife's personal diary, courtesy of The National Trust and The Green Howards Museum, Yorkshire.

Support, and to build a strongpoint there while C Company, 7th Yorks, held the stops and covered them.

The attack by the 8th South Staffords had alerted the German troops and the 7th Yorks could not get past the rifles and machine guns of the 10th and 12th Companies, the 122nd Regiment, who were manning this section of Quadrangle Support Trench. Captain Barmby and Lieutenant George Duncan MacIntyre led their men over the top and tried their best to get into to their objective. They came under very heavy fire. Their attack was, like so many before, doomed to failure. Captain Barmby was wounded and Lieutenant George MacIntyre went missing. He was later found and brought in to an aid station but died of his wounds on 10 July. The 78th Field Company, Royal Engineers, recorded that the attack was not a success. The only thing that Number one Section and the platoon of Pioneers could do was to carry bombs for the attacking infantry. The 7th Yorks reported to Brigade that the attack had failed. When the 17th Division heard this Major-General Pilcher immediately ordered that another attack be sent in and then later on he countermanded the order; there would be no further attack on the right flank that night.

With this British attack pacified Lieutenant Irion, the commanding officer of Quadrangle Support Trench, was able to turn his attention on the 8th South Staffords and the 7th Lincolns who were pushing down towards him from the direction of Pearl Alley. The German infantry began to counter-attack the British with bombs. B Company, the 8th South Staffords, who were attempting to work their way down the trench in the belief that they would join up with the 7th Yorks met the German bombing attack. Under the direction of Second Lieutenants Whitehead, S. Baker and T. H. Baker, B Company managed to hold off this heavy attack.

The Pioneers got to within five hundred yards of the junction and then apparently got lost. The strong point which they were to build was badly needed to prevent any counter-attack from the left flank. Desperate to protect his men from attack on at least one flank Lieutenant-Colonel Barker sent six runners out into the chaotic night to find them but to no avail. The Pioneers were not where to be found; they seemed to have vanished. Very soon, on the left, the machine guns of Contalmaison got to work and wrought havoc among the 8th South Staffords.

After the operation had started so well things were now going wrong for the 8th South Staffords. His carefully laid plans had succeeded but now Lieutenant-Colonel Barker was furious. He looked for aid and found none. The Pioneers had disappeared and the 7th Yorks were not advancing on the right. The 8th South Staffords recorded this of the 7th Yorks.

OC South Staffs never realised for one moment that Regt. on right, after an initial attempt, would be content to sit down and do nothing for the remainder of the night.[54]

He did not know that the 7th Yorks were not sitting down doing nothing. They had been specifically ordered to attack with a small force and that small force had been decimated. Barker did not know that the 7th Yorks were going to prepare to attack again but that attack was going to be cancelled because it was going to be too late to save the situation.

Meanwhile three platoons of the Pioneers had been ordered to carry up materials and wire. The remaining three sections of the 78th Field Company, Royal Engineers, and two platoons of the Pioneers wired three hundred yards of Railway Alley and made the trench fightable. A portion of the trench dug the night before was filled in and strong points were constructed. One man, Sapper Andrew McLanachan, of the 78th Field Company, was killed by a stray bullet, while the section was withdrawing down Willow Avenue.

11.25 pm.

D Section, 50th Brigade Machine Gun Company, opened indirect fire along a line 100 yards north of Quadrangle Support Trench from Willow Trench in an attempt to provide some support for the 8th South Staffords.

11.30 pm.

The guns of 79th Royal Field Artillery commenced their barrage of the western edge of Mametz Wood. They were ordered to cease fire at 12.30 am.

---

[54] TNA: PRO. WO95/2007. War Diary, 8th South Staffords, July 1916.

In Quadrangle Support Trench, having met the German bombing attack, the 8th South Staffords were steadily pushing the Germans back towards the junction with Quadrangle Alley. The 11th Company had already been almost completely wiped out by the ferocity of the 8th South Staffords attack. Seeing that the situation was serious the German senior officer, Lieutenant Irion, had his men set up a machine gun protected by sand bags a little way away from the junction with Pearl Alley. With this weapon firing down the trench and no longer bothered by attacks from Quadrangle Alley the German troops were able to successfully halt the complete capture of the trench. They forced the British into a stalemate. From the British held portion of the trench the South Staffords tried to maintain the impetus of the attack but were unable to get past the machine gun.

It appears that a group of British soldiers, either from the 8th South Staffords or the 7th Lincolns pushed forward and made their way to Acid Drop Copse. These men may well have set up a machine gun in the remains of the copse. There is no mention of this machine gun in the diaries of the 8th South Staffords or the 7th Lincolns; the only report is from the German 122nd Infantry Regiment and they were adamant that the British had a machine gun in Acid Drop Copse at this time.[55]

Despite the fact that the 11th Company had been wiped out both the 10th and 12th Companies were still capable of holding off attacks by the 8th South Staffords on the left and any British attacks made up Quadrangle Alley. With the machine guns of Contalmaison firing on the left flank of the 8th South Staffords the prospects were not good for the British. The 8th South Staffords blamed the 7th Yorks for not getting forward and the 7th Yorks firmly blamed the 8th South Staffords for the failure of the attack. They said that the 8th South Staffords had attacked far too early and alerted the German troops to the coming attack. Sadly, it seems that the devil was in the detail of the orders but the night was not over.

The night of 9 July.

On the night of the 9th July the German 122nd Wuttemburg Regiment had the 1st Battalion, 1st, 2nd, 3rd, and 4th Companies in

---

[55] See Appendix 03

Contalmaison and the trenches to the west of the village. The 3rd Battalion, 10th and 12th Companies held Quadrangle Support Trench, the 11th Company having been wiped out, and the remainder of the 9th Company held Wood Support Trench down near Mametz Wood. During the course of the day the 9th Company, manning Wood Support Trench, had lost up to fifty percent of its strength to a British artillery barrage so the 5th Company of the 2nd Battalion, who were in reserve in the second line, were sent forward to re-enforce them.

Chapter Nine : 10 July 1916 12.10 am to 6.00 am

XV Corps recorded the weather was fine to begin with.

7th Borders settled into positions in Fricourt Wood.

51st Field Ambulance recorded that the flow of wounded was steady throughout the night and into morning.

12.10 am.

At this time the 17th Division received a message from 51st Brigade saying that the 7th Lincolns had pushed beyond Acid Drop Copse and that the 8th South Staffords had taken their objective and were holding Quadrangle Support Trench. There was no news, however, of the attack on the right by 50th Brigade. Perhaps this message gives a clue to the identity of the machine gun team in Acid Drop Copse. The 7th Lincolns had pushed forwards beyond Acid Drop Copse. The machine gun team may have belonged to them.[56]

12.20 am.

D Section, 50th Brigade Machine Gun Company, ceased fire on targets north of Quadrangle Support Trench. Two guns were then made ready to move to Bottom Wood where they would relieve two guns of A Section.

12.30 am.

B Section, 50th Brigade Machine Gun Company, left Wicked Corner with two guns, bound for Willow Trench.

Instead of ceasing fire, the 79th Royal Field Artillery was ordered to continue firing at the western edge of Mametz Wood using battery at a time. They were ordered to fire salvoes at five minute intervals.

78th Royal Field Artillery bombarded Wood Support Trench and Quadrangle Support Trench.

---

[56] See Appendix 03

12.35 am.

Lieutenant Brooke of the 7th Yorks managed to return to the front line, Quadrangle Trench. Here the 7th East Yorks were waiting in reserve with orders to move forward and hold the German 'stop' in Quadrangle Alley once the 7th Yorks had taken it. Lieutenant Brooke reported that the attack had been a failure and that Captain Barmby of 7th Yorks had been severely wounded in the ill-fated assault. Barmby and his men had attacked over the open ground earlier in the night. The orders for the 7th East Yorks were immediately changed; fifty men under Second Lieutenant Calvert were ordered forward as reinforcements for the 7th Yorks who, according to Lieutenant Brooke, were pinned down by the defenders of the 'stop' in Quadrangle Alley. Far from doing nothing the men of the 50th Brigade were determined to batter their way through the 'stop'. An additional forty men of the 7th East Yorks led by Second Lieutenant Goodwin attempted to carry more bombs up Quadrangle Alley to the embattled 7th Yorks.

In the left hand section of Quadrangle Support Trench the 8th South Staffords, were having a rough time. Lieutenant-Colonel Barker was looking for British support on either flank, but even though men were available, no support seemed to be forth coming either from either the 50th or 51st Brigades. The machine guns of Contalmaison were harrying the left hand end of Quadrangle Support Trench and taking a toll on the Staffordshire men. At the right hand end the German commander, Lieutenant Irion, no longer troubled by British assaults up Quadrangle Alley, was able to launch his own attacks upon the 8th South Staffords. These attacks were spearheaded by his company bombers. The 8th South Staffords held the Germans back but took casualties in the process. Lieutenant-Colonel Barker knew that his men's position was made even worse by the fact the Pioneer unit that should have arrived to consolidate and reinforce the trench were still missing. Much needed men and supplies, vital to the operation were lost somewhere in the muddy darkness. Attacked on both flanks and lacking support, the 8th South Staffords grimly hung on.

1.00 am.

17th Division received a wire message from the 50th Brigade. They had no news of their attack upon Quadrangle Support Trench as the communications had again been cut. Shortly after this message arrived at 17th Division headquarters the 50th Brigade telephoned to report that the attack had been a failure.

The 6th Dorsets recorded the relief of their C Company in Wood Trench by A company. C company returned to Bottom Wood. The German guns were busy and the shelling was recorded as heavy.

Two guns of D Section, 50th Brigade Machine Gun Company, left Willow Trench and moved towards Bottom Wood. They were subjected to severe shelling as they moved and one soldier was wounded. Private Pandy repeatedly carried messages to and fro, under heavy shell fire, to the commander of D Section in Willow Trench.

The two guns from B Section, 50th Brigade Machine Gun Company, in Wicked Corner arrived in Willow Trench.

1.05 am.

Knowing now that the attack by his Brigade had been a failure Brigadier-General Glasgow issued orders that the 7th Yorks should keep attacking. He also ordered that one company of the 6th Dorsets be placed at the disposal of the 7th Yorks. The commanding officer of the company was ordered to report to the 7th Yorks headquarters immediately.

2.00 am.

17th Division noted that the situation on the right with 50th Brigade remained vague. At this time Major-General Pilcher knew that the 7th Yorks had attacked but had been held up by heavy rifle and machine gun fire and had suffered severe losses. He informed 50th Brigade of the successful situation on the left flank and ordered them to "go in again and press home the attack".[57]

In their position in reserve the 10th Notts & Derbys received 'sudden' orders to send up the remainder of the battalion and they were to take as much small arms ammunition as they could carry. The company officers were to go on ahead of their men to meet with Colonel Barker of the 8th South Staffords. As ordered, B and C companies immediately turned out and proceeded to the dump at

57 TNA: PRO. WO95/1981. War Diary, 17th Division, July 1916.

Lonely Copse to draw ammunition and bombs. Up at the front line A and D Companies were in position in Quadrangle Trench as they had taken over from the 8th South Staffords when they attacked Quadrangle Support Trench.

When they arrived at Railway Alley B and C Companies of the 10th Notts & Derbys were ordered forward to Quadrangle Trench, emphasis was placed that their battalion bombers must go forward as well. Lieutenant-Colonel Banbury of the 10th Notts & Derbys set up his own headquarters alongside that of the 8th South Staffords in a dugout in Railway Copse. It now looked as if some concerted help was being organised for the beleaguered 8th South Staffords.

2.30 am.

17th Division noted that Brigadier-General Glasgow had ordered the 7th Yorks to attack the junction of Quadrangle Alley and Quadrangle Support Trench. The 7th East Yorks were to be in support.

The 50th Brigade recorded that at this time the 51st Brigade had failed in their attack. Because of this the 7th Yorks were warned by 50th Brigade to discontinue their action if they were not already committed. This order was reported to Major-General Pilcher at 17th Division headquarters but he refused to approve it. He knew that the left hand of the attack had been successful and he wanted to keep up the pressure. So the 50th Brigade was obliged to order the 7th Yorks into the attack again. It was not recorded in the 17th Division war diary that Major-General Pilcher had countermanded Brigadier-General Glasgow's order to discontinue the attack.

After about two hours it became obvious to Lieutenant-Colonel Barker of the 8th South Staffords that a no assault had materialised on the right flank. However, the Pioneers did finally reach Quadrangle Support Trench. They were too late to be of any use.

2.40 am.

17th Division received a message from 51st Brigade. Brigadier-General Trotter reported that things were going badly in Quadrangle Support Trench. The 8th South Staffords were holding on but nearly all of their officers were killed or wounded and they were being hard pressed. Division assured the 51st Brigade that reinforcements had been sent forward.

2.45 am.

Despite their assurances about reinforcements reports began to filter back to 51st Brigade headquarters that the attack had failed and the 8th South Staffords were withdrawing. The battalion had done magnificently, holding on for three hours with their flanks in the air and with no support.

Lieutenant-Colonel Barker of the 8th South Staffords took only a short time to decide that his men's position in Quadrangle Support was now completely untenable. They were being gradually pushed back as the Germans recaptured more and more of their trench. So he decided that withdrawal was the only course of action left to his remaining men and the wounded. The 8th South Staffords were ordered to withdraw not only from Quadrangle Support Trench but from the front line as well. Having been rushed up to the front the 10th Notts & Derbys took over from the South Staffords in the centre of the line in Quadrangle Trench. They, in turn, were supported by three companies of the 7th Lincolns who were spread out on the left in Pearl Alley and on the right in Quadrangle Trench.

As no progress being made on the right and no doubt fully aware of the situation on the left, 50th Brigade once again ordered its units to disengage and withdraw all of its troops from Quadrangle Alley before dawn.

3.08 am.

When Major-General Pilcher heard the news that 50th Brigade had again ordered a withdrawal he immediately countermanded the order, issuing new orders that the attack must be pressed home. Communications with the front were a shambles so Major-General Pilcher was forced to send out runners. The 50th Brigade withdrawal order had already reached the forward units by the time Major-General Pilcher sent out his runners. The surviving men of the 50th Brigade battalions were coming back from the German lines. Finding the trenches of Pearl and Quadrangle Alleys choked by reinforcements, equipment, wounded men, and mud the withdrawing British soldiers simply went back to their rear positions over the open ground; in doing so they missed or ignored Major-General Pilcher's runners. It would seem that the British were falling back in some chaos.

3.15 am.

51st Brigade contacted 17th Division to let them know that the 8th South Staffords were being forced back by the enemy to the junction of Pearl Alley.

3.30 am.

Even though the runners had gone out with orders to continue the attack, the news that the 8th South Staffords were retiring forced Major-General Pilcher to talk to Brigadier-Generals Glasgow and Trotter about the situation. They persuaded him that as it was nearly daylight and that the 8th South Staffords were being pushed back it was no use trying any more attacks at that point. 50th Brigade, therefore, was ordered by Major-General Pilcher to cease the attack if they were not already committed. These orders, 17th Division noted, were received in time to stop a further attack.

Lieutenant-Colonel Fife had been preparing to personally lead his men into another attack up Quadrangle Alley when the orders came in and cancelled his orders to attack. It certainly looked like he had either not received the withdrawal order sent out by 50th Brigade or he was obeying the Divisional orders to renew the attack. He evidently believed that he and his men should try to get forward and support the embattled 8th South Staffords. The 7th Yorks were not content to "sit down and do nothing for the remainder of the night" as the 8th South Staffords suggested. They had tried to go forward and at great cost. They simply could not get through the mud or past the machine guns and rifles of the 122nd Regiment.

Lieutenant-Colonel Fife said in his diary that at 1.00 am he was ordered to make another attack and was given a depleted force of the 6th Dorsets and 7th East Yorks to augment his dwindling numbers. They arrived at 2.00 am. When Fife arrived in the front line he found his men in a very demoralised state. Lieutenant MacIntyre was believed to be dead and Captain Barmby was seriously wounded. Fife seriously doubted if his men could be encouraged to attack again so soon. The new attack was hastily prepared as dawn was breaking and Fife realised that his men would provide easy targets for the machine gunners in the morning light. He decided that the only chance he had of getting the attack underway was to lead it himself. He knew that his officers trusted him and would follow him. He hoped that his men would come willingly if he went as well. As they prepared to go, the attack was cancelled.[58]

Something had to be gained from this failed attack so Major-General Pilcher issued orders to 51st Brigade that they must hold the junction of Pearl Alley and Quadrangle Support Trench at all costs and to consolidate their position there. In accordance with his orders the 7th Lincolns set up and held a bombing post in Pearl Alley.

By dawn the remainder of the 8th South Staffords were back in Quadrangle Trench and from there they went back behind the lines taking all of their wounded with them.

No orders to withdraw reached the men in Acid Drop Copse, if indeed any were sent to them at all. Sitting behind Quadrangle Support Trench they proved that they were in an excellent position. Advancing over the open ground from the German second line came the German 6th Company, 122nd Regiment led by Lieutenant Kostlin. They had orders to reinforce their comrades in Quadrangle Support Trench.

Lieutenant Kostlin later wrote that as they advanced his company came under machine gun fire from Acid Drop Copse. In the half light he had misjudged the distance to Quadrangle Support Trench, so he and his men were forced to run a distance of three hundred yards while under fire from the machine gun.

In the predawn light the machine gun proved to be deadly. Lieutenant Kostlin reported that only thirty men of the relief company made it to the trench unscathed, those who were not killed or seriously wounded took cover in shell holes; a lucky few managed to get back to their own second line.

Lieutenant Kostlin arrived in Quadrangle Support Trench without injury. As he was senior to Lieutenant Irion he took command of the trench and took stock of the situation. Their numbers had dwindled during the fighting with the 8th South Staffords. The 11th Company had been wiped out, the 10th and 12th Companies were severely depleted; and his own 6th Company was not in much better shape. All told they numbered six officers and one hundred and sixty other ranks. Fortunately for the Germans, the British were not aware of this. The British machine gun team in Acid Drop Copse

---

58 Lieutenant-Colonel Fife's personal diary.

continued to hound the men in Quadrangle Support Trench until, according to the German account; they were put out of action by a direct hit from a British shell.

The 79th Royal Field Artillery ceased the single battery barrage on the western edge of Mametz Wood and began a new bombardment on the south western edge of the Wood employing A and B Batteries. C and D batteries began a bombardment on Quadrangle Alley, north of the junction with Quadrangle Support Trench. The batteries fired one round per minute at their targets.

On the right the 4.5-inch howitzers of the 81st, Brigade, R. F. A., commenced a heavy bombardment of Mametz Wood, preparatory to the attack by the 38th Division at 4.15 am. The 81st recorded that the Wood was penetrated and after further heavy bombardment the attackers made more progress.

3.40 am.

XV Corps received a telegram from 17th Division to say that the attack that had begun at 11.30 pm on 9 July had been a failure. Prisoners had been taken in the fighting; men from the 2nd and 3rd Battalions the Lehr Regiment, 2nd and 3rd Battalions the 122nd Regiment and the 3rd Battalion, Bavarian Regiment were being sent back to the Divisional cage[59] of interrogation.

4.00 am.

The 7th East Yorks under Lieutenant Calvert arrived back at their HQ as ordered by Lieutenant-Colonel Fife of the 7th Yorks.

Captains Dougal and Baker of the 52nd Field Ambulance arrived at the front line with ten squads of bearers. Captain Dougal and three squads proceeded to the 7th Yorks headquarters. There were no casualties in Bottom Wood but they were told that there were three men needing evacuation in Quadrangle Trench. A heavy barrage had prevented them being cleared sooner. Captain Dougal and his men discovered that their route to Quadrangle Trench, Bottom Alley, was impassable because of the mud. Like Captain Mozley's two unfortunate NCOs Captain Dougal and his three squads went over

---

[59] Wire enclosure erected by all of the divisions engaged in the fighting to hold prisoners.

the open to get to Quadrangle Trench and they were forced to clear the three casualties over the open. As they worked they came under machine gun fire and two men, Privates U. Keegan and J. Morgan were hit and wounded. Later that day a recommendation for an award was sent back for Private E. A. Davis after he went out into the open twice to bring both men to safety.

The remaining seven squads under Captain Baker went on to Railway Copse and cleared the Aid Posts there. Captain Levis who had been working at Railway Copse was relieved. Sub-divisions of bearers were left at the Aid Posts to clear wounded men as required and they were visited regularly by their officers. The 52nd Field Ambulance reported that as they worked the Village of Contalmaison came under heavy shellfire which preceded an attack.

4.15 am.

The 7th Yorks recorded that the 38th Division attack on Mametz Wood had begun. The 38th Division had been ordered to secure all of Mametz Wood. In their part of the front line the 6th Dorsets and the 7th East Yorks peered through the early morning mist for any sign of the Welsh as they had been ordered to co-operate with the 38th Division in anyway they could.

As the attack began 38th Division contacted XV Corps and informed them that their attack on Mametz Wood was underway. Behind an extremely accurate and very heavy British barrage, they attacked the Southern edge of the Wood that was held by the 2nd Battalion, Lehr Regiment. Making use of the barrage the left and right hand units of the attacking Brigades, the 113th and 114th, were able to take trenches before the German defenders could emerge from their dug outs. In the centre the attack was held up, largely because of the open ground that the Welshmen were forced to cover. Gradually, because of the capture of trenches on both flanks the 2nd Battalion Lehr Regiment was either forced to attempt to retire. Many were surrounded by the Welshmen. The 2nd Battalion Lehr Regiment must have been exhausted; they had been in the front line for a long time without re-enforcement or relief.

79th Royal Field Artillery barrage lifted slowly and searched into Mametz Wood with a slow rate of fire.

4.55 am.

Two guns of B Section, 50th Brigade Machine Gun Company, commenced indirect fire against one of the rides inside Mametz Wood.

Captain Mozley wrote in his diary that his battalion were ordered to provide a strong bombing squad to work alongside and connect up with the Welshmen attacking on their right. He was also ordered to prepare mortar artillery support for the Welsh attack.

5.00 am.

C company of the 7th East Yorks and the bombers of D company were sent forward to Quadrangle Trench to watch the situation on the right and patrol forward if possible.

Two guns of D Section, 50th Brigade Machine Gun Company, in Willow Trench, opened fire on the North West positions of Mametz Wood.

5.15 am.

The two guns of B Section, 50th Brigade Machine Gun Company, ceased firing against Mametz Wood. Each gun expended 500 rounds of ammunition.

5.30 am.

Two messages containing welcome news came into Major-General Pilcher's Divisional Headquarters at Meaulte. The 38th Division had taken the southern part of Mametz Wood and the 23rd Division, on the left, had taken Bailiff Wood.

6.00 am.

17th Division produced a summary of the current situation. The 23rd Division on the left held Bailiff Wood but were unable to advance against Contalmaison. The 17th Division had a post in Peake Wood, and Pearl Alley was held up to and now including the junction with Quadrangle Support Trench. Quadrangle Alley was held up to a point two hundred yards south of the junction with Quadrangle Support Trench. Wood Trench was held by the Division and the troops in that trench were in touch with the 38th Division on the right. A dump of bombs and small arms ammunition had been made in Wood Trench and the 38th Division had managed to get into Strip Trench

Captain Mozley and A Company watched the Welshmen go into the Wood. Their leisurely pace and mixture of formations certainly made an impression upon the commanding officer of A Company. He noted that most of them had their rifles slung on their backs; and he wrote that it was fortunate for the Welshmen that they did not encounter a barrage. When they arrived at the edge of the wood most simply plunged into it, only a few went up the outside. Following orders, the 6th Dorsets bombing squad set off down the eastern end of Wood Trench and joined up with the Welsh troops.

Lieutenant Davidson M.C., the 2 i/c of A Company, who was posted in the eastern end of Wood Trench directing the consolidation work in the far end of Wood Trench, was shot by a sniper. The bullet struck his arm and then went into the side of his body. Though he was evacuated immediately and taken to the 36th Casualty Clearing Station at Heilly Station, the thirty year old officer died of his wounds the next day.

It was a blow to Captain Mozley as he and Lieutenant Davidson were great friends. However, when writing about these events some time later Mozley simply noted, with the understatement of a veteran trench fighter, that the eastern end of the trench was in a 'smashed state' and that it was hard to move around there without being exposed to hostile fire.

When Lieutenant Davidson was hit Captain Mozley was in the middle of the trench. Minutes after his friend was shot Captain Mozley said that there was a sudden burst of gunfire. The Lewis Guns posted in the western end of the trench opened fire as did the Vickers Gun that was set up on the high ground looking over the eastern end of the trench. Captain Mozley rushed to the end of Wood Trench and found that the Welsh advance had dislodged a large group of German soldiers from the edge of Mametz Wood.

Surprised, the Germans dashed right across the front of Wood trench as they desperately tried to reach the safety of Wood Support Trench. The Lewis and Vickers Guns did an efficient job, very few of the German soldiers made it to safety. Captain Mozley recorded that he only saw one man get into the Western end of Wood Support Trench.

Out of the mist, just as the echoes of the gunfire died down, a lone German soldier came running towards A Company in Wood Trench. He was unarmed, wore no equipment and was obviously panic stricken. No one fired as he dashed towards the British. Suddenly he stopped in his tracks, as he realised in horror that he was heading for a British trench. Captain Mozley wrote that about twelve rifles were pointed at the terrified soldier and his men shouted for him to give the order to fire. Captain Mozley said that he was tongue tied and unable to issue the order to fire. The German soldier turned on his heels and fled; he made good his escape.

This episode says a good deal about the discipline in the ranks of A Company. Though why the Lewis Gunners and Vickers gun did not fire at the solitary soldier is not explained.

According to German sources the troops dislodged by the Welshmen and fired upon by Captain Mozley's A Company were the 5th and 9th Companies of the 122nd Wuttemburg (Reserve) Regiment who evacuated their positions because they suddenly found themselves outflanked.

In Carnoy Valley Lieutenant-Colonel Cardew had managed to get a peaceful night as the Germans seemed to have altered their range. Their shells were now going some four hundred yards over his position. He rode around the batteries in the morning and then he had a walk to Major O'Malley-Keyes' observation post. Cardew remained here for two hours helping Major O'Malley-Keyes to direct fire upon groups of Germans that they could see trying to cross open ground.

He did not say where this open ground was but he does mention Mametz Wood. It may have been the same piece of ground where the 5th and 9th Companies of the 122nd Regiment tried to cross.

Major O'Malley-Keyes and Lieutenant-Colonel Cardew spotted single men and groups of men and each time called the guns to fire upon them. According to Lieutenant-Colonel Cardew the trick was to catch them with a shell before they reached the opposite wood. Then groups of four and five tried to get back to Mametz Wood and they "bagged lots".[60] One man was seen to stop and pick up a wounded comrade; they did not call upon the guns to shoot at them. Lieutenant-Colonel Cardew and Major O'Malley-Keyes then noticed a large number of Germans, in what Cardew called a new trench, so they "hammered them for a bit."

Lieutenant-Colonel Cardew noted that no shells landed near the observation post while he was there and they were only troubled by one or two rifle bullets. However, after he left the men in the post had a very narrow shave but Cardew did not say what that narrow shave was. His visit to the post "was most exciting" wrote Cardew when he updated his diary later that night.[61]

On the left flank, things had gone quiet since the failure of the attack upon Quadrangle Support Trench. Captain Partridge, the adjutant of the 10th Notts & Derbys, recorded that an advance on Mametz Wood was observed on the right. The 10th Notts & Derbys pushed patrols (though this was later amended to 'patrol') forward to see if the advance on the right would cause the defenders of Quadrangle Support to retire. As Pearl Alley was now held by the British they must have probed beyond the junction of Pearl Alley and Quadrangle Support Trench and were subsequently fired on. Deducing that Quadrangle Support Trench was still 'well occupied' the patrol withdrew.

Arrangements were being made for an attack on the south east corner of Mametz Wood, Railway Strip and the West end of Wood Support by the 7th East Yorks.

Meanwhile the 7th Yorks had been ordered to assist the 38th Division in their assault on Mametz Wood by pushing up Quadrangle Alley and getting a footing in Wood Support Trench.

The 7th Yorks had suffered badly during the night and their ranks were sadly depleted. Despite the best efforts of the 8th South Staffords, Quadrangle Support Trench was still occupied by men of the 122nd Regiment. As had been proved many times before, to try and get past the junction would be difficult, if not impossible. To make matters worse German troops occupied the northern portion of Quadrangle Alley.

---

[60] Lieutenant-Colonel G. A. Cardew, C.M.G., D.S.O., C. O., 80th Brigade, Royal Field Artillery. (IWM 86/92/1)

[61] Ibid.

It was recorded by Lieutenant-Colonel Ronald Fife that the 7th Yorks did not move forward during the day. Instead they 'materially assisted' the 38th Division with their Lewis Guns and the Vickers machine guns attached to them. Fire was directed at the point where Wood Support Trench joined Mametz Wood. He wrote that the Lewis Guns and machine guns did great damage to the enemy.[62]

---

[62] Lieutenant-Colonel Fife's personal diary.

Chapter Ten : 10 July 1916 6.45 pm to 11.00 pm

6.45 am.

XV Corps informed 17th Division that their task for the day was to prepare to be relieved.

In the rear the 9th Northumberland Fusiliers paraded at Ville-Sous-Corbie and then marched 3 miles to Mericourt railway station.

7.00 am.

XV Corps received a telegram from the 38th Division to say that three battalions had entered Mametz Wood and had gained their objective. News arrived from the17th Division reporting that the 50th Brigade was now in touch with the 38th Division in Strip Trench.

Major-General Pilcher received further orders from Lieutenant-General Horne saying that his Division was to co-operate with 38th Division.

7.15 am.

News of the success in Mametz Wood soon filtered down to the Brigades. 50th Brigade sent Message 164 to the 6th Dorsets headquarters. Lieutenant-Colonel Rowley was informed that the Royal Welsh Fusiliers had advanced to the northern edge of Mametz Wood and were holding a line there. The 6th Dorsets were ordered to send forward patrols to clear up the situation on their front.

7.25 am.

Major Hughes-Onslow commanding the 6th Dorsets in the front line sent a situation report to Lieutenant-Colonel Rowley at his battalion headquarters. Major Hughes-Onslow informed his Commanding Officer that the 38th Division were still pushing the enemy through Wood. The enemy had been observed, however, retiring over the hill near Acid Drop Copse on the left. He informed Lieutenant-Colonel Rowley that he and his men were consolidating Wood Trench and that he should be glad of more picks as the trench was in a very bad state at the eastern, Mametz Wood end.

Major Hughes-Onslow's message appears to indicate that he thought that his men would be better employed in their work of consolidation than patrolling forward into unknown danger. Perhaps no one was ready to believe Brigade or the claims of the neighbouring Division just yet.

8.00 am.

Major King arrived in the 7th East Yorks portion on of the front line, the centre of the 17th Division front. He had orders to take command of the men there and prepare for and implement an attack.

Major King wrote that he joined C Company in Quadrangle Trench. His orders were to take Quadrangle Alley on the right of Quadrangle Support Trench, get into and hold a portion of Quadrangle Support Trench on the left and push on to the northern end of Quadrangle Alley. There he was to set up a line that could join up with the 38th Division. This line should be at the north end of the Alley where a siding of the railway ended, the spur of wood began. Crucially, it would be north of Wood Support Trench.

Bombers of C Company would lead the attack and D Company, already on their way to the front line, would be in support.

Safe in the knowledge that his right flank was at last secure Captain Mozley and his men continued repairing and consolidating the smashed eastern end of Wood Trench. All the while the men worked they were harried by snipers. Captain Mozley wrote that the Germans held a strong point in the corner of the wood opposite his trench. It was receiving the personal attention of a British field gun which was firing an accurate succession of shrapnel shells. The shells, though regular and on target, did not suppress the snipers.

It was hot now and the sun had burned away the morning mist. With Lieutenant Davidson gone Captain Mozley took over the job of directing the work of consolidation. He found that it was best to supervise his men by dashing from shell hole to shell hole. Captain Mozley and his men had had no more than one hour's sleep in the past four nights. He wrote in his diary that while he was in one of the shell holes, over come by the heat and fatigue, his head nodded forward and he fell asleep.

His rest was short and the work continued. Despite the efforts of the snipers his company did not suffer any more casualties and the work was completed. They set up a 'stop' a few yards short of the wood because A Company did not have enough men to spread along the whole length of Wood Trench.

8.15 am.

The 79th, Brigade R. F. A., barrage lifted from Mametz Wood and now fell on the German second line. At this point the 79th recorded that it had been reported that Mametz Wood was in the hands of the British infantry.

8.25 am.

50th Brigade Message 193 arrived at the 6th Dorsets battalion headquarters.

Lieutenant-Colonel Rowley was informed that Wood Support Trench was now unoccupied by the enemy. Therefore the 6th Dorsets should send patrols forward to occupy it, leaving a garrison in Wood Trench. The enemy was retiring on his front, he was told and the battalion should endeavour to support the 7th East Yorks by getting into, and bombing down, Quadrangle Support Trench. The 7th East Yorks had suffered heavily and were in need of support.

Yet, as Captain Mozley had already observed, A Company did not have enough men to hold all of Wood Trench. A Company did not send any patrols forward to Wood Support Trench. They were fairly certain that it was still occupied by the enemy.

8.30 am.

17th Division issued Operation Order No. 65 ordering 50th Brigade to co-operate with 38th Division and to consolidate their present line.

9.00 am.

Major King of the 7th East Yorks had, by now, familiarized himself with the front line situation and the troops had prepared for the next attack. Major King therefore sent a bombing patrol, from C Company, up Quadrangle Alley. Their aim was to take the 'stop' set up by Lieutenant Kostlin's men at the junction of Quadrangle Alley and Quadrangle Support Trench.

Their orders were to bomb left along Quadrangle Support Trench and set up a stop there in the trench. Then they were to bomb in an easterly direction so that D Company, who he ordered to advance up Quadrangle Alley and consolidate the objective, would have both left and right flanks protected. Lieutenant Gale was in command of C Company and Captain Heathcock commanded D Company.

9.25 am.

Pearl Alley, up the hill on the left flank, shallow and over looked by Contalmaison and not an easy place to defend, had been abandoned by the British. But the 7th Lincolns sent their battalion bombers and two platoons from their B Company back into the trench with orders to hold the bombing post at all costs. The remainder of the battalion stayed in Quadrangle Trench. Lt G. H. Redinnick was wounded in the action.

9.30 am.

Forward observation posts reported back to the 79th Royal Field Artillery that they could see a good deal of enemy infantry movement around Contalmaison Villa and in the north eastern corner of Contalmaison Village itself. The guns opened fire and this movement was checked. The 79th Royal Field Artillery then barraged from Lower Wood to Pearl Wood; an area between the German second line and Mametz Wood.

D Company of the 7th East Yorks arrived in the front line and was placed under the command of Major King. Later, Major King sent a report about the day's events back to the 7th East Yorks Headquarters.

He said that C Company bombers could not push through the German defenders of the stop at the junction of Quadrangle Alley and Quadrangle Support Trench. (Lieutenants Kostlin and Irion had seen to it that the 'stop' was well manned). Major King wrote in his report that he ordered D Company's bombers forward to support C Company bombers but despite their efforts no headway could be made. Three men did try to get over the German 'stop'[63] but they were shot down. Then his bombers came under rifle grenade bombardment. Major King was unsure if the 'stop' was defended by a sniper or a machine gun but the intensity of the German defence led him to conclude that the position was held "in force by the enemy." It seems that he suspended operations at some point during the morning.

Lieutenant Kostlin also wrote about the attack by the 7th East Yorks. His sentries in Quadrangle Alley, Lieutenant Kostlin called it 'the sap', saw steel helmets above the parapet of the trench and kept a careful watch. The Tommies got to within twenty yards of the German position. Then the British began to climb out at the sap head and ran towards the German defenders in order to bomb them from above. Each time the British tried this Lieutenant Kostlin's men met them with point blank fire. Lieutenant Kostlin noted that there were other British troops crowded into the sap head, they repeated the effort; they too failed.

9.55 am.

XV Corps received reports from observation posts at the front that parties of enemy infantry were seen entering Mametz Wood from the north. These reports continued to come in for the next forty minutes.

10.00 am.

The 6th Dorsets Battalion Headquarters sent a message to Major Hughes-Onslow, commanding the 6th Dorsets in Wood Trench. His message, sent at 7.25 am, had been received and noted.

He was now informed that the 38th Division was reported to be holding and consolidating a line in the middle of Mametz Wood and not the northern edge as had been previously reported by 50th Brigade headquarters. He was told that if Wood Support Trench was not occupied by the 38th Division then he was to push forward two or three platoons forward to occupy it if possible. In response to his request for more digging tools he was told that the battalion

---

[63] It does appear that the German defenders had a small trench dug out from Quadrangle Support that gave them a superior view of the enemy operations.

would try to send more. Lieutenant-Colonel Rowley told Major Hughes-Onslow that he had sent his letter on by orderly. 10,000 rounds of small arms ammunition, in bandoliers, arrived along with the message.

Shortly after this message, orders arrived from 50th Brigade via battalion headquarters for Captain Mozley, the commander of A Company.

His company was to make a reconnaissance of their left flank. Captain Mozley was puzzled by the orders from Battalion headquarters so he discussed them with Major Hughes-Onslow. In the light of previous messages both of the officers were wary. They decided to send out a patrol of six men under the command of twenty-two year old Second Lieutenant Walter Clarke. The young officer and his men were told to work up the edge of the strip of trees that jutted out of Mametz Wood at a right angle towards the western end of Wood Trench.

It was towards the start point of this strip of trees that Major King's 7th East Yorks had been ordered to go. They were still trying to get past the German block at the junction of Quadrangle Alley and Quadrangle Support Trench. Perhaps Captain Mozley's orders had something to do with this action.

As instructed Second Lieutenant Clarke led his patrol up the belt of trees running from the west end of Wood Trench to Mametz Wood.

Meanwhile orders arrived for the 93rd Field Company, Royal Engineers, to go up to the front line to work. Work had to be done in Bottom Wood and the 93rd were needed to build strong points there.

The 79th Royal Field Artillery was ordered to barrage the line of Lower Wood and Pearl Wood to behind the German second line.

10.35 am.

Reports came into XV Corps informing Lieutenant-General Horne that the enemy troop movements into Mametz Wood from the north had ceased.

Sometime before 11.00am

Four men from Second Lieutenant Clarke's patrol returned to Wood Trench.[64] Second Lieutenant Clarke and one other man were missing. Second Lieutenant Clarke was known to have been wounded and, quite without orders, a stretcher bearer dashed out of the trench to try and find the young officer. He too was shot and wounded but his comrades managed to get him back into their trench. He later died of his wounds.

After listening to their report Captain Mozley concluded that Second Lieutenant Clarke and his men had got quite a way forward. They had been seen by the Germans in Quadrangle Support Trench and had come under heavy fire. Quadrangle Support Trench over looked the strip of wood from the left.

Captain Mozley wrote that the Germans were holding the trenches opposite his in strong numbers, and for most of the day, on their left flank, he and his men could see British troops of the 7th East Yorks making what he called futile attacks upon the strongly held enemy positions. Second Lieutenant Clarke's loss compounded his misery at losing his friend Lieutenant Davidson.

Lieutenant Kostlin wrote that he had been astonished to see the 5th and 9th Companies of his regiment suddenly bolt from their positions towards Wood Support Trench. Therefore Lieutenant Kostlin was keeping a sharp look out upon events to his left and he kept a particular eye on Mametz Wood. As he watched the battlefield through his binoculars one of his sentries called to him and pointed out a man dressed in khaki some four hundred yards to their rear on the left flank.

Lieutenant Kostlin watched the patrol advance under cover of the strip of trees in the bottom of the valley and surmised that they must have had something to do with the sudden withdrawal of the 5th and 9th Companies. He ordered his men to open fire and as they did so the patrol vanished into the cover of the strip of trees. Lieutenant Kostlin did not know at this point that the 38th Division were now inside Mametz Wood in considerable numbers. Yet he deduced that in all probability the patrol meant that the British now held Mametz

---

[64] No time has been given for the return of the patrol, but it must have before Major Hughes-Onslow was killed at 11.00 am.

Wood. If this was the case, he reasoned, his line of retreat to Bazentin was under serious threat.

Captain Mozley said later that he had sent out Second Lieutenant Clarke's patrol against his judgement. Originating from 50th Brigade, and passed on to him via battalion headquarters, the orders were badly worded and unclear. Had Captain Mozley or Major Hughes-Onslow requested clarification of the orders it would have taken time so the patrol had to go out. It had got further forward than Captain Mozley had realised. He made it very clear in his writing that from this time on he became "distrustful of all Brigade messages".[65]

11.00 am.

Not long after the patrol had returned a further disaster occurred. Major Hughes-Onslow was shot in the back of the head and killed. He and Captain Mozley had been sitting together in Wood Trench, Onslow was writing a situation report and Mozley was bending forwards, reading a map. Though the war diary of the 6th Dorsets originally stated that he had been shot by a sniper Captain Mozley maintained that Hughes-Onslow had been killed by a stray bullet. The war diary was amended accordingly.

Major Hughes-Onslow had been mentioned in despatches earlier in the war and was very popular with the men. His death cast a shadow over the whole battalion. Apparently he had been wounded in the hand earlier on in the day but had concealed the wound with his glove. Captain Mozley was terribly shocked by the episode; now three of his friends were gone. When the battalion came out of the line they took the Major's body with them and buried him in the military cemetery at Meaulte.

Reports filtered back to the Brigade headquarters from the battalions in the line saying that the Germans were still defending their positions in strength. XV Corps received patrol reports from 17th Division saying that the Germans were still holding on to Wood Support Trench. Also, machine gun fire from Contalmaison was making the post at the junction of Pearl Alley and Quadrangle

---

[65] Captain B.C. Mozley, D.S.O., C.O., A Company, 6th Battalion, Dorsetshire Regiment. (IWM 01/45/1)

Support untenable. The post had therefore moved and been re-established fifty yards short of the original position.

XV Corps sent out orders for a smoke demonstration for later in the afternoon. This was to come from Pearl Alley to assist III Corps with an attack on Contalmaison.

Major King, of the 7th East Yorks, wrote a report about the events of the day. He had continued to direct bombing attacks upon the junction of Quadrangle Alley and Quadrangle Support all morning. Each attack had been met by bloody failure. In the report that he wrote later, he said that his attack was to be in concert with one by the 38th Division but although they were watched for this attack there were no signs of it.

In Major King's report he stated that he received orders from Brigade, sent via his Commanding Officer, at 12.00 o'clock noon. He wrote that he was informed that the neighbouring battalion, the 6th Dorsets, was preparing to support the 38th Division with Stokes Mortars and that an infantry 'rush' was going to take place on Wood Support Trench from Mametz Wood after the mortar bombardment. He and his men were ordered to do all they could to push up to the Mametz Wood end of Strip Wood and "take Wood Support in the flank and rear."

At this point he prepared his two companies, in Quadrangle Alley, to attack once again. C Coy was to attack through to north of Quadrangle Alley and D Coy was to attack over the open to the railway in the valley to the south west of Mametz Wood and work up to point N.K. The battalion bombers would attack the left flank of Wood Support Trench.

Major King wrote that he waited to launch his attack until he considered that conditions were favourable. He said that "this moment arrived" when he saw that British troops were visible on the right and in the Wood itself. These men could either have been Second Lieutenant Clarke's patrol or the Welsh. Major King went on to say that at the same time that he saw these British soldiers, 'large numbers' of German troops were seen coming out of the west of the wood.[66] They ran across the open and his Lewis gunners

---

[66] This group of German soldiers might have been the same one reported by Captain Mozley earlier in the morning. Then again it may not. The men were exhausted, the situation was extremely confused and communication was erratic at best.

opened fire on them. The appearance of the British troops and the withdrawing Germans convinced Major King that the time had come to launch his second attack of the day.

Major King's attack must have begun shortly after noon (for reasons that will be shown later). It went ahead as he had organised; the only change being that he ordered two platoons of C Company, under the command of Lieutenant Cracroft, to climb out of Quadrangle Alley and go over the open to get back into the alley again, north of the troublesome German 'stop' if and when he came under fire. C Company's Bombers were detailed to take on and capture the 'stop'.

As with the attack in the morning no headway was made against the 'stop' in Quadrangle Alley. Inevitably Lieutenant Cracroft and his men came under fire, Major King thought from Acid Drop Copse. Lieutenant Cracroft was killed trying to get his men over the open ground.

Meanwhile Captain Heathcock and his men had climbed out of their trench and were advancing over the open, in extended order and in two lines. Major King says that they too came under heavy fire; from two machine guns. One sited at the point where the strip of trees joined Mametz Wood and from the other was dug in at the right of Wood Support Trench. Like Lieutenant Cracroft, Captain Heathcock was killed leading his men against the objective.

Major King wrote that though it was certain that large numbers of the enemy had retired, machine gunners and bombers had remained at their posts and while they held their strong points they dominated the whole area. He confirmed that when he launched his attack he sent orderlies to bring A and B Companies forward in support. However, he did not feel justified in committing them to the same attack. He stated that the attack had been determined and if it could have succeeded then it would have done.

Once it was evident that the attack had failed Major King reorganised his men, sent a report to his Commanding Officer, and awaited further instructions. Major King was furious with the British troops that he had seen in the right flank position. Why had they not assisted his attack? Wood Support would have easily fallen to them while his men were taking the enemy's attention.

The 16th Royal Welsh Fusiliers, operating on the right of the 6th Dorsets and at this time they were battling to take control of the southern portion of Mametz Wood.

Lieutenant Kostlin wrote about Major King's second attack. Alerted by the earlier withdrawal of the 5th and 9th Companies and the appearance of Second Lieutenant Clarke's patrol he was still keenly watching the valley. He was concerned that his line of withdrawal to the safety of the main German line was about to be cut.

As he watched the large open clearing in Mametz Wood, bisected by Wood Support Trench, or the Weirgraben as the German forces had named it, through his binoculars Lieutenant Kostlin saw what he described as 'lines of skirmishers' advancing directly upon the trench. As the British advanced no fire or sound came from Wood Support Trench. It seemed to Lieutenant Kostlin that the men there had vanished. The lines of enemy troops gave his men, over looking them in Quadrangle Support Trench, a superb target that could be enfiladed at a range of six hundred yards. Lieutenant Kostlin recorded that he hardly needed to give the order to open fire; his men had seen the target and needed no bidding.

Captain Heathcock's D company, it could only have been them, advancing in lines, in the open, stood little chance. Every German soldier who could shoot was doing so; even Lieutenant Kostlin's officers picked up rifles and joined the fusillade. The garrison kept firing until their rifle barrels were red hot. After a short while a large number of British dead and wounded lay out in the open and Lieutenant Kostlin declared that not a single Englishman seemed to reach Wood Support Trench.

Just after this Lieutenant Kostlin and his men noticed the advance of another line of men, this time appearing from a fold in the ground near the strip of trees in the valley. These men were probably the first of Lieutenant Cracroft's platoons advancing upon the left of Lieutenant Kostlin's trench in an attempt to destroy the 'stop' at the junction. They were shot down in their line within a few yards of Quadrangle Support Trench. Moments later the second platoon advanced in the same fashion and was dealt with by Lieutenant Kostlin's men in the same, deadly, fashion.

Lieutenant Kostlin said that the men in the sap head, or Quadrangle Alley, remained silent which was fortunate for him and his men. An attack from there at this time would probably have proved fatal.

12.10 pm.

After a four hour wait in showery rain the Northumberlands finally entrained for Ailly-sur-Somme. The train moved off at 12.35 pm demonstrating the fact that it did not take long at all for the battalion to board.

12.35 pm.

Lieutenant-General Horne wanted information about the situation in and around Wood Support Trench. He needed to know if it was safe for the heavy artillery to fire on its eastern end where it met Mametz Wood. Orders had been given by XV Corps to the Brigade General of Royal Artillery, for the Field Artillery to bombard the whole northern portion of Mametz Wood.

12.45 pm.

A change of wind direction forced XV Corps to change the orders concerning the distraction smoke barrage from Pearl Alley for 23rd Division. Instead the 7th Lincolns in Pearl Alley were instructed to cause a distraction by flashing and fixing bayonets.

1.00 pm.

Colonel Collins of the 17th Division Staff visited the 7th East Yorks headquarters. The local situation was explained to him and he was informed that the left flank was held by the 7th Lincolns and 10th Notts & Derbys from the 51st Division. Colonel Collins requested that Lieutenant-Colonel Clive's men once again attack the junction of Quadrangle Alley and Quadrangle Support Trench and then move towards the south-west end of Mametz Wood.

Lieutenant-Colonel Clive and his officers were told that this new assault was to be in conjunction with the 38th Division. Colonel Collins told them that they were to be informed of the start time, that afternoon, and that it would be earlier than 5.00 pm. The new attack would be preceded by a forty-five minute bombardment.

B Section, 50th Brigade Machine Gun Company, opened fire with two guns on the Western side of Mametz Wood. They reported that they fired at irregular intervals.

51st Field Ambulance recorded that the motor vehicles that they had been loaned to ferry the wounded from the front had to be returned to their own respective headquarters. Evacuations to Vequemont and Maricourt continued using their own ambulances and any motor vehicle that they could commandeer.

1.50 pm.

17th Division headquarters warned the 50th and 51st Brigades that the 23rd Division was going to attack Contalmaison from the direction of Bailiff Wood at 4.30 pm. Because of the wind change the smoke screen could not be employed. Instead the 51st Brigade men stationed in Pearl Alley, the 7th Lincolns, were ordered to prepare to make their demonstration of fixing bayonets in an attempt to distract the German defenders of Contalmaison.

2.00 pm.

In preparation for their next attack Lieutenant-Colonel Clive and the battalion Adjutant of the 7th East Yorks started out for the front line with their A and B companies. Major King had sent back a request to Battalion headquarters for A and B Companies to be sent forward.

Then, just after they had left, something odd happened. Corporal Frost arrived at the 7th East Yorks headquarters with a verbal message from Major King in the front line. His message stated that the junction of Quadrangle Support Trench and Quadrangle Alley had been captured. Corporal Frost was then sent back to Colonel Collins of 17th Division Staff bearing Major King's message.

Perhaps this message was the report that Major King said that he sent back to his Commanding Officer. After seeing that his men stood no chance, he had suspended operations, and decided to await further orders. There is no explanation made as to why Corporal Frost was told to tell his Commanding Officer that the junction had been captured when it had not been.

The 16th Royal Welsh Fusiliers recorded that a large portion of the southern end of Mametz Wood was in their hands.

2.24 pm.

The 9th Northumberlands reached Ailly-sur-Somme and detrained. From here they marched 10 miles via Picquigny-Cavillon-Oissy to Riencourt.

The 12th Manchesters had also entrained for the rear at Mericourt and had travelled via Ailly-sur-Somme to their rest billets in Picquigny-Cavillon-Oissy.

2.40 pm.

17th Division received a message from the 50th Brigade saying that the Germans appeared to be withdrawing on the right and that British patrols were being pushed into Wood Strip, the strip of wood jutting out at right angles towards Wood Trench. Significantly, British troops were reported to be at the junction of Quadrangle Support and Quadrangle Alley. These were probably men from the 7th East Yorks.

When Colonel Collins received Corporal Frost's message from Major King he immediately had the bombardment stopped and asked that patrols be sent out.

Lieutenant-Colonel Clive of the 7th East Yorks and his two companies joined Major King in the front line and discovered that the junction had not been taken and the situation there was unchanged.

Arrangements were made for a fresh assault so that the 7th East Yorks would be ready when zero hour was announced. Following Colonel Collins' orders a patrol was sent up Quadrangle Alley towards the junction with Quadrangle Support Trench. It was halted by what was termed as 'distant machine gun fire', rather than the usual heavy point blank fire that the 7th East Yorks had experienced that morning. The junction was most definitely not in British hands.

3.00 pm.

17th Division and 50th Brigade recorded that men of the 38th Division were seen to the north east of Wood Support Trench. 50th Brigade attacked with the 7th East Yorks to give them support. The 38th Division troops moved further east into the wood and no co-operation occurred between the two units. The 7th East Yorks,

Major King's second attack, were initially successful and reached their objective but they failed to hold on there and were forced to withdraw with considerable casualties.

3.30 pm.

Two guns of B Section, 50th Brigade Machine Gun Company, ceased fire against the Western side of Mametz Wood.

4.00 pm.

The Commanding Officer of the 51st Field Ambulance visited the A.D.M.S at Ville and received notice that his unit was to withdraw from all stations when relieved by the 21st Division. In preparation for the hand over the Commanding Officer of the 65th Field Ambulance, 21st Division, visited the File Factory at Meaulte and was shown around.

38th Division attacked northwards from their line inside Mametz Wood.

4.10 pm.

A message came into 50th Brigade headquarters from the Ordinance officer of the 17th Division informing them that the travelling kitchen and other stores were waiting for them at the Ordinance dump. He wanted the kitchen and stores collecting that day.

4.20 pm.

B Section, 50th Brigade Machine Gun Company, was ordered to move to Railway Alley. An A Section gun team in Quadrangle Trench reported that they had fired successfully at several targets. They had been moving their gun from Quadrangle Trench to Wood Trench and back again, firing at any targets that offered themselves. They reported that in the process they had killed several of the enemy.

4.24 pm.

The 7th Yorks recorded that the 7th East Yorks had not been successful in their attack on Wood Support Trench.

4.30 pm.

III Corps began their attack upon Contalmaison from Bailiff Wood.

4.40 pm.

Both the 17th and 38th Divisions sent messages to XV Corps Headquarters reporting that British troops could be seen in the open at Wood Support Trench.

Major-General Pilcher and his staff at Divisional Headquarters had become increasingly irritated that Quadrangle Support Trench had not been captured and held before the relief took place. Lieutenant-Colonel Banbury at the 10th Notts & Derbys headquarters received orders to the effect that his battalion was to be relieved by the 110th Brigade. He would be notified later as to which positions in the rear the battalion would take up.

4.45 pm.

A report was sent back to Brigade by the 7th Lincolns saying that the Germans appeared to be evacuating Quadrangle Support Trench.

D Section, 50th Brigade Machine Gun Company, was ordered to lift its fire from the north edge of Mametz Wood and concentrate on the road running to the north east of Contalmaison. It was hoped that this fire would catch any German troops that were falling back towards their second line.

4.50 pm.

To draw the enemy's attention away from the west of Contalmaison, where III Corps were about to attack, the 7th Lincolns in Pearl Alley were ordered to put on their demonstration of rapid fire and 'flashing' bayonets.

5.00 pm.

Fifteen minutes after receiving their orders D Section, 50th Brigade Machine Gun Company, commenced firing at the road north east of Contalmaison.

The roving gun of A Section, 50th Brigade Machine Gun Company, operating in the front line, Quadrangle and Wood Trenches gave covering fire to the 7th East Yorks as they continued to attack Mametz Wood. This proved to be extremely efficient and the crew was complemented. The Sergeant in command of the gun and Lance Corporal Lyderman were recorded as being responsible for the efficiency of the gun at this time.

5.10 pm.

B Section, 50th Brigade Machine Gun Company, was in position in Railway Alley and opened fire with two guns on the 'Cutting'.

After tea, Lieutenant-Colonel Cardew took a turn around the gun batteries and then visited three observation posts. While he was visiting one of these he watched British soldiers being shot down by machine gun fire; he thought that it was during an attack upon Contalmaison. He wrote that he believed that Contalmaison and Mametz Wood had been captured during the day.

5.45 pm.

79th Brigade, Royal Field Artillery, was ordered to assist III Corps in their assault by shelling a section of Pearl Alley beyond the Cutting and up to the vicinity of Pearl Wood, near the German second line.

In Quadrangle Trench, near the junction with Wood Trench, the 7th East Yorks watched and waited for the preliminary barrage that would herald their attack. Despite being told by Colonel Collins that their zero hour for attack would be before 5.00 pm no such barrage had occurred. British troops were spotted moving at the back of Wood Support Trench and Lieutenant-Colonel Clive realised that there would not now be a preliminary barrage. He ordered his men to attack the junction of Quadrangle Alley and Quadrangle Support Trench as requested by Colonel Collins earlier in the day.

This was their third attack of the day.

5.50 pm.

50th Brigade issued Order 184. 50th Brigade was to be relieved that night by two battalions. Headquarters of the battalion in line was to go to the 7th Lincolns headquarters and the reserve battalion was to go to Railway Copse. Each unit was to send one officer guide and others to 50th Brigade headquarters at Fricourt Chateau by 9.00 pm that night. These guides would help to bring the relieving battalions into position.

The 6th Dorsets were to provide 4 guides for Wood Trench, two guides for Sunshine Trench, two guides for Willow Trench and two guides for Post number five.

The 7th East Yorks were to provide four guides for Quadrangle Trench and four guides for Railway Copse.

The 7th Yorks would send eight guides for Bottom Wood, two with specific knowledge of the 7th Lincolns headquarters.

5.55 pm.

B Section, 50th Brigade Machine Gun Company, ceased fire on the 'Cutting' beyond Contalmaison.

6.15 pm.

A situation report from the 6th Dorsets was sent to 50th Brigade headquarters at Fricourt Chateau.

They reported that at 6.15 pm they had received a message from Major Hughes-Onslow in command of Wood Trench. He had reported that the Royal Welsh Fusiliers were digging a front line trench on the south side of the ride through Mametz Wood. Their support line was now practically a continuation of Wood Trench and the intention was to work through Mametz Wood to the next track. The 7th East Yorks were attacking on the left.

This message was late. Major Hughes-Onslow was dead. The news that the Welsh were consolidating a line on the road through Mametz Wood had been received earlier on in the morning.

Above message sent off to Brigade headquarters at 6.50 pm.

Two machine guns cut the 7th East Yorks assault to pieces. As usual they tried to push on but one gun situated on the left in Acid Drop Copse and another, placed by the Germans at the end of the strip of wood jutting out of Mametz Wood, halted the attack. (Major King had already reported the existence of this machine gun earlier in the day).

Later, on 12th July 1916, Lieutenant L. Holroyd of the 7th East Yorks wrote the following report to Lieutenant-Colonel Clive about his part in this attack. It demonstrates the difficulty faced by the infantry, not only in this particular attack but in all of the attacks since 6 July.

Lieutenant Holroyd's report told how two platoons of B Company were to attack the stop at the junction of Quadrangle Support and Quadrangle Alley. Like earlier attacks, they had to go over the open, jump into the enemy trench and start to throw bombs. They had to cover fifty yards of open ground that was, according to Lieutenant Holroyd, "swept by machine guns". When he got to within fifteen yards of the enemy trench he noticed that he only had four men left. He and these men promptly got back into their own trench (presumably they were running parallel with Quadrangle Alley) and were joined by another six men.

He organised his small command and discovered that he had three bombers among his men. They were given all the bombs that the other men had and were made into a small bombing squad. Lieutenant Holroyd knew that he did not have the men or resources to bomb along both the Alley and Support so he opted to find out how strongly Quadrangle Alley was held.

As they advanced two men were shot by rifle fire from the front. They continued until they reached the 'stop' and two of his men, Corporal Farr and Private Bagley, climbed over it. Here they were met by a barrage of bombs from the German side of the stop and Lieutenant Holroyd and his men were forced to fall back. He now sent a man back as a messenger, leaving him with a force of six men. The Germans continued to hurl bombs at him and his small party and he realised that they could throw their bombs further than his men could. The Germans were in the advantageous position of being up hill. Rifle grenades may have made a difference but the small group had none. Lieutenant Holroyd decided to sit tight and wait for reinforcements. Shortly afterwards the orders came to fall back.

Two of Captain Mozley's men in Wood Trench were buried by shelling in the afternoon, but neither was seriously hurt.

6.30 pm.

Captain Michell, temporary Commanding Officer of the 93rd Field Company, Royal Engineers, handed over to Captain W. J. N.

Glasgow R.E. Captain Michell had been in command since the Major had dislocated his ankle on 5 July.

III Corps reported to XV Corps that the attack on Contalmaison had been a success and the village had been captured.

This report was confirmed by the 7th Lincolns. Obviously this was a relief to them because the sniping from the village at British troops in Pear Alley had finally ceased. It had been a "nuisance" they said.

Now that they were threatened on three sides, the position of Lieutenants Kostlin and Irion and their men in Quadrangle Support Trench was truly precarious. The remainder of the 6th, 10th, the shattered 11th and the 12th Companies waited in the trench knowing that, very soon, another assault would come and this time they would be hard pressed to defend against it. Lieutenant Kostlin had no illusions as to the outcome of another assault, he saw that the only chance that they had was to hold on and try to escape when it fell dark. He assumed that should they survive, he and his men would be captured. Nor did Lieutnenat Kostlin have any illusions about the state of his men. He wrote that at this time his men were completely exhausted and very thirsty. They were forced to quench their thirst by drinking from the polluted, yellow water in the trench sump.

6.35 pm.

50th Brigade reported to 17th Division that a Forward Observing Officer had seen groups of German troops retiring from Quadrangle Support Trench. News came in to 17th Division headquarters, at the same time, that 23rd Division had, in fact, captured Contalmaison. Division at once issued instructions to the 51st Brigade to advance up Pearl Alley and swing left to the Cutting north east of Contalmaison and join up with the 23rd Division. 50th Brigade was also instructed to make Quadrangle Support Trench good and join up, in the trench, with units of the 51st Brigade.

6.45 pm.

As a consequence of the capture of Contalmaison by III Corps, XV Corps gave the 17th Division verbal instructions to push up Pearl Alley to the east of the 'Cutting', establish a post there and get in touch with III Corps. As has been seen, ten minutes before, 17th Division had already acted.

In Quadrangle Support Trench, despite the desperate situation, Lieutenant Kostlin thought that help was almost at hand. Despite the obvious advances being made by the British on both flanks, an attack upon Quadrangle Support Trench did not materialise. Lieutenant Kostlin knew that he and his men could not last long and he was almost resigned to falling into enemy hands. For a moment there was a strand of hope when they heard machinegun and rifle fire opening up from their second line. For a while the men of the 122nd Reserve Regiment hoped that it was a counter-attack that would drive the British back and save the position that they had so doggedly defended. Their hope was short lived however because the British artillery opened up and the ground between the second line and Mametz Wood erupted in great black and green explosions. The infantry fire suddenly died and with it went their last chance of escape; or so they thought.

6.50 pm.

XV Corps confirmed their verbal orders to 17th Division.

A message received by the 10th Notts & Derbys said that the enemy were apparently retiring from Quadrangle Support Trench under intense British artillery fire. Immediately patrols were ordered forward to get into, or close to, the trench. Shortly afterwards they received news that Contalmaison had fallen. A joint attack on Quadrangle Support by the 10th Notts & Derbys and 7th Lincolns was ordered. Accordingly Lieutenant-Colonel Banbury of the 10th Notts & Derbys conferred with the Lieutenant-Colonel Forrest of the 7th Lincolns and between them they decided that the attack should go forward at 9.45 pm. A strong patrol led by Lewis Gunners, was to go out at 9.30 pm and establish itself on the ridge in front of Quadrangle Support Trench to give supporting fire for the attackers.

7.00 pm.

79th Brigade, Royal Field Artillery, recorded that III Corps had captured Contalmaison. All batteries therefore lifted their barrage to north of the Cutting to prevent German reinforcements arriving and to catch any German troops retiring.

7.30 pm.

B Section, 50th Brigade Machine Gun Company, received orders to move again, this time back to Wicked Corner.

The Commanding Officer of the 51st Field Ambulance visited Queens Redoubt and found that the bearers had been ordered to rest for the night. Knowing that they were to be relieved, he decided to send them back to billets in Meaulte. On returning to the File Factory he sent the section wagons to Queens Redoubt to pick up the weary bearers. At this time the bearers of 21st Divisional Field Ambulance had arrived at the dressing stations at Fricourt and the Subway.

7.50 pm.

Lieutenant-Colonel Rowley of the 6th Dorsets sent orders to his Quartermaster. As the battalion was to be relived that night it was believed that, on relief, they would head for and billet for the remainder of the night in Meaulte. Lieutenant-Colonel Rowley requested that the Quarter Master have guides ready to lead the out going companies to their billets in Meaulte. Wherever the battalion was to billet they would stop in Meaulte for hot tea and rum; the Quarter Master was asked to have these available. All of the officers' horses were to be sent to the ration dump at 9.30 pm and the leading company should be expected at 10.20 pm.

Captain Mozley also received orders for the relief. A Company was to be relieved at 10.00 pm and unless heard differently the men would be billeted in Meaulte. A limber was to be waiting for them on the far side of Number Five Post with their crocks. Captain Mozley had three of his platoons in Wood Trench and one platoon in the new section that had been dug to connect up to Quadrangle Trench. Lieutenant Moss and four men from Headquarters had been detailed to act as guides for the platoons as they came out of the front line. Captain Mozley was instructed to take D Company's platoons out with him, they were supporting A Company, and to send two of C Company's machine gun teams out of the trench as soon as it was dark enough. They did not have to wait to be relieved. Lieutenant-Colonel Rowley was specific in his orders that Second Lieutenant Clarke and other wounded men must be recovered.

7.55 pm.

Lieutenant-Colonel Rowley sent orders to the commander of C Company stationed in Bottom Wood. His orders were largely the same as Mozley's. C Company was to leave Bottom Wood as soon as it was dark and they were not to wait until they were relieved by the incoming battalion. Their first stop was to be Number five post where their crocks would be waiting. A party was to be left behind to help the two machine gun teams sent out of the line by Captain Mozley.

8.00 pm.

9th Northumberlands finally reached Riencourt where they went into billets.

D Section, 50th Brigade Machine Gun Company, ceased firing at the road north, north east of Contalmaison. The two guns were withdrawn to Wicked Corner, as were the two D Section guns who had been posted in Bottom Wood.

52nd Field Ambulance recorded that bearer officers of the 64th Field Ambulance arrived with five squads to take over. Five squads were not sufficient, so some of the exhausted 52nd Field Ambulance bearers had to carry on working.

In Quadrangle Support Trench Lieutenant Kostlin watched tensely for any movement by the British against his position. He knew that the end was going to come very soon. Therefore he decided to exercise his authority to order a withdrawal. Now that Mametz Wood was in British hands Lieutenant Kostlin and his men expected to be attacked at any moment. By dusk no attack had materialised either from the British front line or Mametz Wood but it was only a matter of time before it came. Lieutenant Kostlin held a conference with his officers. They decided that they should evacuate their positions and make for the safety of their second line as soon as darkness fell.

To cover their withdrawal a group of men were selected to, at the allotted moment, run down towards the British front line throwing hand grenades as if an attack was about to begin. During this diversion Lieutenant Kostlin's remaining men were to dash from their trench with orders to keep Mametz Wood on their right. This way no one should get lost, and hopefully, they reach their own lines.

8.05 pm.

50th Brigade sent a message to 17th Division reporting that the 7th East Yorks were meeting stiff resistance at the junction of Quadrangle Alley and Quadrangle Support and that heavy fighting was in progress. Despite the impeding relief men of the 6th Dorsets were sent to reinforce them.

A later report to Division from 50th Brigade said that the 7th East Yorks had seen the enemy retiring and had gone forward to capture the junction of Wood Support and Quadrangle Support Trenches with Quadrangle Alley to try and cut off the enemy's line of retreat.

8.10 pm.

Plans and preparations continued for the relief that night. Lieutenant-Colonel Rowley sent his orders now to D Company, two platoons of which were stationed in Railway Alley.

Like A and C Companies they were to proceed to Number five post to collect their crocks from the limber and then move on to Meaulte where they would be billeted for the night. D Company commander was informed that his departure time was to be 9.00 pm and that his two platoons in Wood Trench would be marching out with A Company and he need not wait for them. He should not wait to be relieved by the incoming battalion.

8.25 pm.

XV Corps ordered the Motor Machine Gun Battery, attached to both 17th and 38th Divisions, to withdraw that night. One section of the battery was detailed as an escort for No. 3 and No. 4 Kite Balloon sections.

8.30 pm.

50th Brigade recorded further progress in Mametz Wood and Contalmaison was reported to be completely in the hands of the 23rd Division.

9.00 pm.

B Section, 50th Brigade Machine Gun Company, arrived back at Wicked Corner and remained in reserve. C Section was also stationed here and the men were used to carry the gun gear of A and D Sections when they too were relieved.

In Wood Trench Captain Mozley and his men were thinking about the relief and getting away from the front line for a while. However, at 9.00 pm a message arrived ordering him to advance upon Wood Support Trench, that was now deemed empty, and occupy said trench with two platoons. Two platoons of C Company would come forward from Bottom Wood to replace the two platoons who would go into Wood Support Trench. Captain Mozley was unimpressed with this order; despite the facts that he and his thinly stretched men were exhausted and he, at his own admission, was viewing messages from Brigade with suspicion. He was totally convinced that Wood Support was strongly held by the enemy. A good deal of sniper fire had been directed at him and his men from that trench and he had seen the 7th East Yorks attacking it since 5.00 pm, without any measure of success.

On that point he did say that the 7th East Yorks had attacked without warning him. Had they done so he could have supported them with the Vickers gun that was stationed on his left flank.

He freely admitted that at this point on 10 July he was "not feeling at all offensive". Perhaps if he and his men had not been so fatigued then things may have been different. As it was, he prepared a squad to try and get in touch with the Welsh on the right and make a reconnaissance of Wood Support Trench. However, by the time the bombs had been sent up to the squad, the Germans had put a heavy barrage down around Wood Trench, the left flank and the edge of Mametz Wood. The patrol did not go out straight away.

9.20 pm.

79th Brigade, Royal Field Artillery, barraged along Pearl Alley to the North West as ordered. Each battery fired one round per minute until further orders arrived

The British had put a barrage down all around Quadrangle Support Trench but the fire all but ceased and Lieutenant Kostlin saw that he and his men had a chance to escape. His plan worked perfectly and though a number of men were wounded by bullets and shells five officers and one hundred and twenty men managed to regain the safety of their second line.

Moving cautiously they arrived at their wire at about 1.30 am (12.30 am British time) and were immediately fired upon by an alert machine gun team. Hurling themselves to the ground they shouted at the machine gunners to cease fire, which they did, and fortunately Lieutenant Kostlin's command suffered no more losses.

9.45 pm.

The attack on Quadrangle Support Trench by the weary and muddy 10th Notts & Derbys began. Despite heavy shelling of the British front line, the adjutant of the 10th Notts & Derbys, Captain George 'Jimmy' Partridge, recorded that two companies of the 8th South Staffords came forward and took charge of Quadrangle Trench as the 10th Notts & Derbys left it. As his men advanced Lieutenant-Colonel Banbury moved his battle headquarters into Quadrangle Trench and almost immediately lost telephone communication with the rear as the heavy German barrage, once again, cut the telephone wires.

The 7th Lincolns recorded that they supported the 10th Notts & Derbys when they assaulted Quadrangle Support Trench. They also recorded that the German artillery barrage was heavy, falling on all trenches, and all supporting points. The barrage also severed all communications for four hours. Second Lieutenant Basil Liddon Kimber was killed during this German barrage.

10.00 pm.

Fifteen minutes after the attack had begun a wounded runner arrived at Lieutenant-Colonel Banbury's Headquarters in Quadrangle Trench. He reported that the 10th Notts & Derbys had successfully captured Quadrangle Support Trench. They had met little resistance as the Germans had abandoned their position. The runner also reported that the 7th Lincolns had not attacked. As has been mentioned earlier the attack had been planned by both battalion commanders. Other than the entry about supporting the attack no mention was made about the operation in the 7th Lincolns diary.

Private Harlow wrote in his diary that the divisions on the left and right flanks took both Contalmaison and Mametz Wood. The 10th Notts & Derbys went over the top again and took Quadrangle Support Trench from the Germans, who had found it as impossible to hold as the British had when they were enfiladed.

The 8th South Staffords recorded that the 10th Notts & Derbys now occupied Quadrangle Support Trench, which had not been held. The 8th South Staffords must have been irritated considering how hard they had fought to try and hold on to the trench.

50th Brigade diary recorded that the 7th Yorks' patrols had found the stop at the junction of Quadrangle Alley and Quadrangle Support Trench deserted. The 7th Yorks occupied it. The west end of Mametz Wood was also found to be empty of enemy units. By now the relief of the 17th Division by the 21st Division had begun.

Five more bearer squads of the 64th Field Ambulance arrived at 52nd Field Ambulance HQ allowing most of the 52nd Bearers to stop work. The 53rd Field Ambulance, which was waiting in reserve at Advanced Dressing Stations, were sent back to their headquarters at the Subway. A sub-division of 52nd Field Ambulance was also sent to the rear. B & C sub-divisions remained at the front.

10.30 pm.

A heavy German barrage fell upon Quadrangle Trench and the immediate rear area. German troops had been reported to be moving in Pearl Alley. So the 79th Brigade, Royal Field Artillery, received orders to speed up their rate of fire on Pearl Alley to one round every thirty seconds. .

As he wrote his diary for the day, Lieutenant-Colonel Cardew noted that was a furious counter-attack going on in Contalmaison. The German guns were shooting accurately from the northern end of Mametz Wood and his batteries had been shooting back for a while.

10.55 pm.

News came into 17th Division Headquarters from both the 50th and 51st Brigades and this time it was the news that Major-General Pilcher had been hoping for. The 51st Brigade reported the successful capture of Quadrangle Support Trench and 50th Brigade reported that they had occupied and were holding Quadrangle Alley up to and including the junction with Quadrangle Support Trench. They added that they had also taken the west end of Wood Support Trench.

11.00 pm.

Lieutenant-Colonel Banbury received the information that the 7th Lincolns had not attacked because they had received no orders to do so.

The 6th Dorsets recorded that the relief by the 21st Division, 110th Brigade, began at 11.00 pm. Captain Mozley noted that the German shelling abated and at 11.00 pm and the patrol, ordered at 9.00 pm was able to set off. By 11.30 pm they had returned with the news that Wood Support was still held by German machine guns. This information was duly sent back to 50th Brigade headquarters. Captain Mozley noted that the German guns now turned their attention on the light railway, the route along which the relief had to travel.

The 10th Notts & Derbys reported that the night passed quietly for them in Quadrangle Support Trench and that the Germans did not counter-attack. The 110th Brigade relieved them, as planned and this difficult relief was completed by 4.00 am.

17th Division made out a situation report. The 23rd Division on the left now held Contalmaison; the 17th Division held Pearl Alley up to the junction with Quadrangle Support Trench and was advancing north east towards the Cutting. Quadrangle Support Trench, Quadrangle Alley and part of Wood Support was held, and men of the Division were advancing along this trench to join hands with the 38th Division. That Division was advancing on the northern edge of Mametz Wood and had their left flank on the central ride of the wood. 17th Division troops were also in Wood Trench and in touch with men of the 38th Division at the eastern end of said trench. Operation order No. 66, with details of the relief, had been issued at 10.20 pm and the relief of the 17th Division by the 21st Division was now under way.

During the day General Haig had written to his wife saying:

216

The battle is being fought out on lines which suit us. That is to say the Enemy puts his reserves straight into battle on arrival, to attack us, thereby suffering big losses.[67]

---

[67] Haig in Sheffield and Bourne, *Douglas Haig*, p.202

Postscript : 11 July 1916

It was noted at XV Corps headquarters that the weather on this day was fine, but dull and much cooler than of late. It was also recorded that the situation on the 17th Division front was still confused.

With Contalmaison, Quadrangle Support Trench and Mametz Wood in British hands the units of the 50th and 51st Brigades, 17th Division, began their journeys to the rear. The Division was now spread out in a line that stretched from the front line to the 'Cavillon Area' north west of Amiens. Some of the journeys went smoothly, others went badly. Some units were forced to wait until the next day for transport to the rear. Others were ordered off their trains by Transport Officers well before they reached their destinations. Despite the protestations of their officers, the men were forced to march to the rear. Even the wounded were put off the trains and those that could, went on by foot.

According to the Divisional history a spectator, who witnessed the 50th and 51st Brigades leaving the front line to entrain at a rail head near Meaulte, told how the battalions were so reduced in numbers that the marching columns "seemed to be chiefly transport."[68]

Before he and A Company left the line, Captain Mozley attempted to find Second Lieutenant Clarke. In the dark, he scouted up the narrow strip of trees where the young officer and his patrol had gone. It was a hopeless task; Captain Mozley failed to find the youngster. On relief by a battalion of the Leicesters, he and his men left the front line and took the body of Major Hughes-Onslow with them.

The artillery remained in the line and continued to engage German targets. The 79th Brigade, Royal Field Artillery, continued to shell Pearl Alley.

For part of the morning the 78th Brigade, Royal Field Artillery, fired on the Northern edge of Mametz Wood and Lower Wood. Then, when it became clear that the infantry had captured the whole of Mametz Wood, the 78th Brigade barrage lifted and concentrated their fire upon targets just in front of the German second line.

---

[68] A. Hilliard Atteridge, *17th Division*, p.139

Lieutenant-Colonel Cardew's 80th Brigade, Royal Field Artillery, was ordered to cut the German wire. He wrote in his diary that Lieutenant Dobb got the orders confused and A and B Batteries shelled the wrong targets. Lieutenant Dobb sent no orders at all for C Battery so they did not fire. Lieutenant-Colonel Cardew had to sort the problem out himself and get the batteries firing on the correct targets. He thought that he had sorted the problem out and that the wire had been cut.

The R.A.M.C were still busy in the line. Captain Dougal and several bearer squads of the 52nd Field Ambulance worked until the last minute, tirelessly searching trenches, dugouts, shell holes and Mametz Wood for casualties. They found plenty from both sides.

At day break the men of the 6th Dorsets and 10th Notts & Derbys arrived at Meaulte. Hot food and drinks were doled out and the men settled down to a brief rest.

Lieutenant Hoyte remembered that as the men arrived at Meaulte they were sleepy, unshaven and "Muddy in that special and peculiar way that the Somme can make a man muddy."[69] He later noted that there was no lack of cheerfulness among the men.

Private Harlow remembered how tired everyone was as the 10th Notts & Derbys marched through the mud from the trenches. The mud was thick and clung heavily to their clothing; the men were forced to cut the lower portions of their great coats away just to help them move. Each man who did this got into a great deal of trouble when the damage to Army property was discovered.

The 7th Yorks arrived at their bivouacs in a railway siding. They were reduced to 394 effective men. Lieutenant-Colonel Fife had gone five days and nights without sleep. On the way to the sidings he had fallen asleep on his pony and then when he was standing once they arrived. He simply lay down on the earth and slept.[70]

At 7.45 am Lieutenant-General Horne sent orders to 17th Division for Major-General Pilcher to report to XV Corps headquarters as soon as the Division relief had been completed. While preparing to

---

[69] W.N. Hoyte, in M. T. F. J. McNeela ed, *10th (S) Battalion The Sherwood Foresters The History of the battalion during the Great war.* (Naval and Military Press, 2003), p.16

[70] Lieutenant-Colonel Fife's personal diary.

dismiss their commanding officer Lieutenant-General Horne sent a congratulatory message to the men of the 17th Division.

After a brief rest Captain Mozley and others from the battalion attended the funeral of Major Hughes-Onslow at the small military cemetery that had sprung up on the outskirts of Meaulte. Afterwards he returned to his temporary billet and picked up an out of date copy of the *Daily Mail*. Captain Mozley read two communiqués that had been issued by G.H.Q shortly after the opening of the Battle of the Somme. The concluding sentence of the first communiqué remained with him ever since that morning. "So far the day goes well for England and France."

Later in the day Major-General Pilcher arrived at the Cavillon Area where the Division had set up Headquarters. He only stayed for one night. On the next day, 12 July, he toured units of the Division that were billeted in the immediate area and bade them an emotional farewell. He was temporarily replaced by Brigadier-General Clarke who in turn was replaced, on the afternoon of 13 July, by Major-General Philip R. Robertson.

The 6th Dorsets did not discover that Major-General Pilcher had been replaced until 15 July. Captain Mozley later wrote about Major-General Pilcher's dismissal. The officers and men often felt bitter towards the Major-General but they were surprised and displeased at his dismissal. Captain Mozley himself was no admirer of the higher ranks and he noted that the staff officers at Army Corps level were far too optimistic in their views during the first days of the Somme battle. He thought that they had been far too reckless in the way they had expended human life. The battalion heard that Major-General Pilcher had been sent home because he had stood up to Corps and refused to allow his already depleted Division to be thrown into another "useless frontal attack."[71] Captain Mozley felt that if this was the true reason for Pilcher being sent home then the affair did the Major-General credit.

Lieutenant-Colonel Cardew chose to put down in writing that in his opinion the Generals and staff should come up to the front line more often. So that they could see things for themselves rather than trying to run the battle by map and telephone.

---

[71] Captain B.C Mozley, D.S.O., C.O., A Company, 6th Battalion, Dorsetshire Regiment. (IWM 01/45/1)

By this day the German units had regrouped in their second line and were preparing to face the British once again. The German reaction was to give a great deal of credit to their troops and they praised the courage and tenacity of their men. The 183rd Regiment was, at the time of the British attacks on Quadrangle Support Trench, recorded as being at the peak of its performance. Though it could be argued that by dawn on 11 July it was a spent force.

The German writers praised the determination and courage of the British soldiers but were scathing about the apparent lack of intelligence behind their attacks. The British senior officers did not, in the German point of view, appear to possess any tactical skill at all. The British artillery was the main problem faced by the German units over these few days, a problem to which they had no real answer.

The historian of the 122nd Wuttemburg (Reserve) Regiment maintained that it forced the British to waste a great number of lives and ammunition to capture an intermediary position. This is undeniably true, but it was an indisputable fact that the Germans had been forced to abandon their positions and withdraw to their second line. Nor did they mount the counter-attack that the British expected. The historians of both regiments recorded their losses up to 11 July. In the defence of Contalmaison the 183rd Regiment had lost nearly one thousand men of all ranks, killed, wounded or missing. The 122nd Regiment had lost thirty officers and one thousand one hundred and eighty one other ranks, killed, wounded or missing, in the defence of intermediary positions.

By the end of the day the 17th Division, less the divisional artillery, was out of the line. Like the 23rd and 38th Divisions the 17th Division had persevered and had taken its objectives. It had done what had been asked of it but had paid a high price. One hundred and ninety seven officers and four thousand five hundred and seventy four other ranks had become casualties since 1 July. Of them ninety one officers and one thousand six hundred and thirty four other ranks were killed or missing. The gaps in the ranks would be filled by 'green' soldiers straight from Britain and men from other formations. The advance of the British right flank continued and on 1 August the 17th Division was to return to the front line, at place called Delville Wood.

Appendix 01 : Casualties mentioned in the text or found during research[72]

Allen, John Stanley, Captain, 9th Northumberland Fusiliers. He was taken back down the line to a dressing station and then onto the File Factory, from there he went to the field hospital at Mericourt L'Abbe and ultimately he arrived in Britain. Allen recovered from his wounds and was sent back to the Battalion. Later Allen was awarded the Military Cross and promoted to Major but on 11 April 1918 he was killed in action near Ploegsteert aged 26. He is commemorated on panel 2 of the Ploegsteert Memorial.

Ashington, Henry Sherard Osborn, Lieutenant, 7th East Yorks. Recovered from his wounds and was later promoted to Captain. He was wounded once again in January 1917. He died of his wounds on 31 January 1917 and is buried in grave III. B. 23. in Combles Communal Cemetery Extension.

Attwell, W, Private, 78040, 51st Field Ambulance. Aged 29 and husband of Cissies Attwell, of Wharf Cottage, Andy Magyar, Newport. He was killed by a shell on 7 July and is buried in grave III. F. 8. in Gordon Dump Cemetery.

Bacon, Second Lieutenant, 10th West Yorks. Wounded while in a carrying party on 9 July. He recovered from his wounds.

Borrett, George Frederick, Private, 3765, of B Section, 52nd Brigade Machine Gun Company aged 23, was killed in action on 7 July 1916 and buried in grave III B 8 at Gordon Dump Cemetery.

Bottom, Thomas, Private, 12683, 7th East Yorks. Killed in action 7 July 1916. commemorated on Thiepval Memorial, pier and face 2 C.

Brumpton, William, Private, 15046, 7th East Yorks. Killed in action 7 July 1916. Commemorated on Thiepval Memorial, pier and face 2 C.

Carlisle, James, Private, 41518, of the 52nd Field Ambulance was killed by a single rifle bullet on 7 July and is commemorated on Thiepval Memorial Pier and Face 4c.

---

[72] Using *Soldiers Died in the Great War* (Naval and Military Press), *Ancestry.com* and The Commonwealth War Graves Commission website.

Chapman, Albert Edward, Lance Corporal, 3665, of the 51st Brigade Machine Gun Company was killed in action on 8 July and is commemorated on Thiepval Memorial, pier and face 5c and 12c.

Clarke, Samuel Stephen, Private, 13180, of the 6th Dorsets. Aged 41, son of Samuel Clarke and husband to Sophia who lived at 13, Shorncliffe Road, Old Kent Road, London. He was killed in action on 12 July 1916 and is buried in Dantzig Alley Cemetery in grave VIII. H.3.

Clarke, Walter Stanley Arnold, Second Lieutenant, A Company, 6th Dorsets. Killed while leading a patrol on 10 July. He was the son of Walter and Jessie Clarke of 4, Chalcroft Road, Lee, London and was aged 22. He is commemorated on Thiepval Memorial.

Cowie, A. W. S., Second Lieutenant of the 7th Lincolns was killed in the process of relieving the 7th Borders at 7.20 pm on 8 July 1916. He is buried in grave VII H7 over looking part of the battlefield, at Dantzig Alley British Cemetery, Mametz.

Crawhall, Neil Grant, Lieutenant. Went missing in action 7 July during the Manchester's disastrous attack; it later emerged that he had been killed. He had been attached to the 12th Manchesters from the 2nd East Lancs. He is commemorated on the Thiepval Memorial, pier and face 13a and 14c.

Davidson, Gerald Louis, M.C., Lieutenant of A Company 6th Dorsets. Posted in the eastern end of Wood Trench directing the consolidation work in the far end of Wood Trench. He was shot by a sniper; the bullet struck his arm and then went into the side of his body. Though he was evacuated immediately and taken to the 36th Casualty Clearing Station at Heilly Station, he died of his wounds on 11 July. Age 30, the son of F. Gerald and Mary Davidson. He is buried in grave I. E. 12. at Heilly Station Cemetery, Mericourt L'Abbe.

Fisher, John Wilfred 'Fishcakes' Captain, D.S.O., of D Company, 10th Notts & Derbys. Buried in grave I. A. 15 at Heilly Station Cemetery, Mericourt L'Abbe. Captain Fisher was the son of Horace and Kate Fisher who lived in Arno Vale Nottingham and had been at Trinity College Cambridge. The twenty-three year old Captain had been a popular officer with his men; wounded twice before and mentioned in despatches he had been with the Battalion since it had been formed in 1914. Fisher was wounded and some of his men brought him back from the battlefield. Though he was rushed through the casualty clearing system and arrived at the at Heilly casualty clearing station he died the next day.

Fletcher, D. H., Lieutenant. 9th Duke of Wellingtons. Wounded on 7 July 1916. He underwent the first 'plastic' operation on his right eye socket just behind the lines. He was recorded by the M.O. as doing well. He underwent a further plastic operation in England. After attending a medical board at Millbank on 22 August 1916 that comprised of a Lieutenant-Colonel and a Captain of the R.A.M.C he was recommended six months leave. He returned to duty, and was promoted to Staff Lieutenant (1st Class) on 2 July 1917. He became an Embarkation Officer and was promoted to Captain (temporary) on 20 September 1918.

Gardner, Ernest, Private, 11842, of C Coy 7th Yorks and Lancs (Pioneers), age 36. Son of Selina Gardner and husband of Edith Caroline Gardner, 163 Solly Street Sheffield. Killed by shell fire on 7 July 1916 and buried in grave L. A. 90. in Norfolk Cemetery Becordel- Becourt.

Gibbs Ernest William, Private, 3795, 52nd Machine Gun Company. Of 24, Harrow St, Lisson Grove, Marylebone, was killed in action on 06/07/16 and is commemorated on Thiepval Memorial, pier and face 5c and 12c.

Gresham, Lawrence, 11609, 7th East Yorks. Killed in action 7 July 1916. Buried in grave F. 2. in Fricourt New Military Cemetery.

Hall-Brown, John, Major of 10th Notts & Derbys, aged 45, is buried in Dantzig Alley British Cemetery. His grave is lost therefore the Major is commemorated on Special Memorial II.

Hughes-Onslow, Denzil, Major, of the 6th Dorsets, aged 52 and from Ayrshire was killed in action on 10 July and is buried in grave D 12 in Meaulte Military Cemetery.

Kimber, Basil Liddon, Second Lieutenant of the 7th Lincolns was killed during a German barrage on 10 July. He was the son of Frederick and Fanny Kimber of 48, St Thomas Road, Brentwood, Essex. He was 22 and had served in France since November 1914 in the London Regiment, London Rifle Brigade.

Kirby, Harold, 12566, 7th East Yorks. Killed in action 7 July 1916.buried in grave VIII. B. 5. in Gordon Dump Cemetery.

Longdon, Charles, Private, 30835, of 10th Notts & Derbys. Killed in action 7 July 1916 and buried in grave IV L9 Dantzig Alley British Cemetery Mametz.

MacIntyre, George Duncan, Lieutenant of the 7th Yorks, was wounded on 9 July and he died of his wounds the next day. He was aged 34 and had been a Chartered Accountant in civilian life. His parents lived at 57, Clifton Hill, St. John's Wood London. He is buried in Gordon Dump Cemetery, La Boiselle in grave V. F. 6. Gordon Dump was opened on 10 July and closed for use in September 1916, by then it contained 95 graves. George MacIntyre must have been one of the first men buried there.

McLanachan, Andrew, Sapper, 49323, of the 78th Field Company RE of Paisley, Renfrewshire was killed by a stray bullet at 11.20 pm on 9 July 1916. He is buried in plot I. A. 92. at Norfolk Cemetery at Becordel-Becourt. The unit were withdrawing down Willow Trench at the time.

Molineux, John, Private, 12282, 7th East Yorks. Killed in action 7 July 1916. Commemorated on Thiepval Memorial, pier and face 2 C.

Morris, Henry Augustus, D.C.M., Sergeant, 14275, of 10th Notts & Derbys. Killed in action 7 July 1916 and buried in grave II M 2 Dantzig Alley British Cemetery Mametz.

Nelson, William Horace Vere, Lieutenant of 10th Notts & Derbys, aged 20, was wounded 7 July and taken to Mericourt L'Abbe Casualty Clearing Station. Where, on 8 July, he died and is buried in grave I A 16 at Heilly Station Cemetery Mericourt L'Abbe.

Nowell, G. A. H., Sergeant, 19087, of 10th Notts & Derbys. Killed in action 7 July 1916 and buried in grave IV L6 Dantzig Alley British Cemetery Mametz.

Osborne, John R. Private, 11323, of Lincolnshire and formerly of the 2nd Battalion Notts & Derbys was killed in action on 7 July, probably during the 8.00 pm attack. John Osborne was born in 1890 to Andrew and Elizabeth Osborne in Boothby-Pagnell in Lincolnshire. He enlisted on 8 January 1910 in the market town of Derby and given the service number 3257. He was recorded as being 5 feet six ¼ inches tall, he weighed 127 pounds, had a fresh complexion, had hazel eyes, brown hair and had a scar on the outer of his left knee. He gave his profession as farmer. He served in the 3rd Special Reserve Battalion until 9 April 1910 when, weight 17 more pounds, he joined the 2nd Battalion and was renumbered to 11323. On 27 September 1910 he was sent to Plymouth. His pre-war military service was spent at home with the 2nd Battalion. On 7 September 1914 that home service ended. The 2nd Battalion crossed to France on 9/10 September 1914. On 9 May 1915 he sustained an injury to his foot (*not* a wound) in the field and he spent a few days in Hospital at Rouen and Boulogne. After being discharged to the base depot in Rouen on 27 May 1915 he was transferred to the H.T. (Horse Transport) depot at Abbeville as a driver in June 1915. What happened from then up to his death on 7 July is unknown because his service documents have been very badly damaged. All that is known is that he was transferred to the 10th Battalion at some time before July 1916.

It is not certain which Company John belonged to. It could have been in C Company as it had been heavily reinforced in February/March of 1916 after the mine explosion virtually wiped the company out near Ypres; 350 casualties. He had been a regular soldier and though his Medal Index Card records his entrance into France in 1914 John, curiously, does not appear to be entitled to a 1914 or 1914/15 Star. Entitlement to these medals ceased in December 1915 and he was certainly in France before then, the paper work proves it. There must have been some kind of mistake or mix up. His elderly father Andrew collected his medals, as the receipt for the British War and Victory medals shows. Andrew had to collect John's brother's medals as well. Osborne is commemorated on Thiepval Memorial, pier and face 10c, 10d, 11a.

Peel, Robert, Driver, 36794, of C Battery 80th Brigade RFA. Age 19 and son of Mr and Mrs Peel of 73, Great Portwood Street, Stockport. He was killed in action on 11 July and is buried in grave L. 25. in Carnoy Military Cemetery.

Pratt, Neville Herbert, Captain, 10th Notts & Derbys, aged 23, from 23 Meadow Lane Nottingham, and of B Company. Wounded 7 July died of his wounds on 8 July. He is buried in grave II B 22 in Mericourt L'Abbe Communal Cemetery Extension.

Reynolds, Charles Edward, Private, 3514, 50th Machine Gun Company, age 19 was killed in action on 7 July 1916. He lived at Long Cottages, Great Melton, Norwich. He is commemorated on Thiepval Memorial, pier and face 5c and 12c.

Robinson, F. W. Private, 21286, of 10th Notts & Derbys. Killed in action 7 July 1916 and buried in grave IV L 10 Dantzig Alley British Cemetery Mametz.

Shorter, V. B., Lieutenant. Returned to the Queens Regiment after his service with the 7th Lincolns and was promoted to Captain. The unmarried Shorter of Old Road West in Gravesend was killed in action 28 September 1917 and is buried in grave I. J. 13 in Godewaersvelde British Cemetery.

Stanbury, Lionel Duncan, Lieutenant, O.C., of B Section, 52nd Brigade Machine Gun Company aged 20, was killed on the morning 7 July and is now commemorated on Thiepval Memorial, pier and face 5c and 12c.

Taylor, Edward, Sergeant, 3750, of the 52nd Brigade Machine Gun Company was killed in action on 6 July and is commemorated on Thiepval Memorial, pier and face 5c and 12c.

Taylor, J. W., Private, 17269, of 7th Yorks and Lancs (Pioneers) Killed by shell fire on 7 July 1916 and buried in grave L. A. 91. in Norfolk Cemetery Becordcl-Becourt.

Winter, Thomas, Private, 15045, 7th East Yorks. Killed in action 7 July 1916. Commemorated on Thiepval Memorial, pier and face 2 C.

Wood, James, Private, 12117, 7th East Yorks. Killed in action 7 July 1916. Commemorated on Thiepval Memorial, pier and face 2 C.

Wooley, James, Private, 3/5506, 7th East Yorks. Killed in action 7 July 1916. Commemorated on Thiepval Memorial, pier and face 2 C.

Appendix 02 : The dismissal of Brigadier-General Fell

On 11 July Lieutenant-Colonel Cardew wrote sadly in his diary

Preston told me that poor Gen Fell had been sent home – he was quite out best Brig and his Bde did very well but he apparently let the show be hung up in Fricourt for 4 hours.[73]

An examination of the war diaries of the units that made up 51st Brigade gives a picture of what happened. On the evening of 1st July the 51st Brigade moved to the front line facing Fricourt village to take over from the 50th Brigade. At 11.00 pm XV Corps sent orders to the 17th Division saying that they should push forward to Fricourt Wood, towards Bottom Wood. The Divisions on either side would advance at the same time and the 17th would be the link between them. The 51st Brigade was to attack for the 17th Division; the Brigade had three objectives, the last of which was the capture of Fricourt Farm.

Orders for the attack were issued the morning of 2 July and the operation got underway at 12.15 pm. The attack began well, the 8th South Staffords attacking on the left moved through Fricourt village which had been evacuated by the enemy. The 8th South Staffords gained each of their three objectives but were forced to halt as the attack on the right by the 7th Lincolns was delayed and then held up.

The delay lasted nearly four hours during which time no one could get a clear picture of what was happening on the 51st Brigade front. The 10th Notts & Derbys, in reserve for the assault, could not obtain any information about the delay, even from the front line troops themselves. Significantly the 10th Notts & Derbys recorded that they could not contact 51st Brigade headquarters and that headquarters was suffering communication problems.

17th Division and XV Corps headquarters only had a very confused picture of what was happening. At 4.50 pm Lieutenant-General Horne saw an artillery report stating that the 17th Division was held up by one machine gun near Fricourt Farm. The attack did move

---

[73] Lieutenant-Colonel G. A. Cardew, C.M.G., D.S.O., C. O., 80th Brigade, Royal Field Artillery. (IWM 86/92/1)

forward again but even by 6.55 pm no definite information could be obtained and the situation remained confused for sometime.

When the situation finally cleared up it emerged that the 7th Lincolns had been held by extremely difficult terrain, multiple enemy machine guns and some caution on the part of the battalion. The damage had been done; the attack had been held up. At 11.00 pm the 7th and 21st Divisions received congratulatory telegrams from General Sir Henry Rawlinson. The 17th Division received nothing; this rebuke would not have gone noticed at either 17th Division or XV Corps headquarters. Someone would have to pay the price for the delay and that someone was the Brigadier-General whose headquarters had suffered communication problems during those crucial hours.

It is also worth mentioning that shortly before the opening of the Somme Battle Brigadier-General Fell had lost his trusted, right hand man, Captain Franklyn the Brigade Major. He had been promoted to the 23rd Division staff literally days before 1 July. Franklyn had been with the General since the early days at Ypres in 1915. Franklyn always kept Fell informed of situations and he knew the battalions in the brigade and indeed the other brigades in the division well. At the time of the Fricourt incident Fell was having to work with a new Brigade Major who had come from a completely different unit, knew no one and who was effectively learning his new job.[74]

---

[74] Osborne, *A History of the 10th Battalion, The Notts & Derbys, Volume Two.*

Appendix 03 : The Missing Machine Gun Team

The identity of and the unit of the men in Acid Drop Copse and reported by Lieutenant Kostlin as manning a machine gun remains a mystery. Both the 7th Lincolns and the 8th South Staffords had been in action in and around Pearl Alley and Quadrangle Support Trench on the night of the 9/10 July. Two platoons of B Company and the battalion bombers of the 7th Lincolns attacked up Pearl Alley in co operation with the 8th South Staffords attack upon Quadrangle Support Trench. Therefore the men in the copse had to belong to one of these battalions.

There was a report, at 12.10 am on 10 July, stating that the 7th Lincolns had pushed *beyond* Acid Drop Copse, at the time that the 8th South Staffords were occupied with the task of holding on to Quadrangle Trench. The men in the copse could well have been from the 7th Lincolns. It has been suggested, in the documents held with Captain Mozley's diary that the gun team belonged to the 8th South Staffords. If the 8th South Staffords had set up the gun in the copse they would have recorded it in their diary. This battalion kept a thorough diary that was never shy to proclaim their feats. By contrast the 7th Lincolns kept a sparse diary that often failed to mention events of importance. Also when the orders came to retire from Quadrangle Support Trench Lieutenant-Colonel Barker tried to make sure that everyone got back, including the wounded, so it does not seem probable that he would leave anyone behind if it was humanly possible. It is really impossible to say why these men remained behind enemy lines when their comrades withdrew. Perhaps they simply did not receive the orders to retire. They evidently did an extremely good job because the Germans did record their presence. Lieutenant Kostlin's attempt to substantially reinforce the German defenders of Quadrangle Support Trench was severely hampered by the men in Acid Drop Copse.

The men in the copse may well have not been manning a machine gun. Time and again both sides confused rapid rifle fire with machine guns. It was most certainly not a Vickers gun as the Machine Gun Companies generally kept good records and had they lost a gun and team they would have recorded it. It is possible that the men in the copse had a Lewis gun with them.

A search of the *Soldiers Died* data base shows that fourteen men of the 7th Lincolnshires are recorded as being killed in action on 9 and

10 July 1916. Eleven were killed on 10 July, ten of which are commemorated on Thiepval Memorial. Men who were missing and whose bodies were not recovered or identified are remembered here. Men were often blown to pieces by shells, or their bodies left unrecovered for so long that they were constantly pulverised by more shelling or became so decomposed that when they were found identification was impossible. Lieutenant Kostlin stated that the machine gun was knocked out by British artillery. It is possible that all or some of these men were part of the small garrison who died at Acid Drop Copse.

Ashley, George Harold, Private, 19188.

Harrison, William Harold, Private, 12175, age 26.

Houghton, Jasper, Lance Corporal, 19268.

Jervis, Ernest, Private, 11999, age 24.

May, Fred, Private, 11544.

Plant, Benjamin, Private, 16722.

Rayson, Harry, Private, 15079.

Sayer, Francis, Private, 12519.

Wild, Tom, Lance Sergeant, 14917, age 22.

Williamson, Alfred Henry, Private, 13470, age 19.

Appendix 04 : The incident of the two "level headed NCOs" of A Company, 6th Dorsets

A check on the 'Soldiers Died' disc shows that no NCOs of the 6th Dorsets were killed in action from 9 to 14 July. However, three died of their wounds and two of them must be the men sent out by Captain Mozley.

Salt, James, Lance Corporal, 12156, died of his wounds on 9 July and was buried in grave D. 15 at Meaulte military cemetery.

Milner, Frederick William, Corporal, 11846, died of his wounds on 10 July and was buried in grave II. A. 23 at Heilly Station Cemetery Mericourt L'Abbe.

Cole, Henry Alfred, Lance Corporal, 11560, died of his wounds on 12 July and was buried in grave II. A. 50 at Heilly Station Cemetery Mericourt L'Abbe.

Evidently the two men were wounded and not killed outright, either by bullets or artillery fire. They were spotted and got back into either Bottom Trench or Quadrangle Trench. Still alive they were sent down, through the aid post in Fricourt, to a medical facility in the rear. Heilly station was a rear hospital and clearing station.

Who brought them in?

On 7 July the 51st Field Ambulance were moving casualties with two motor buses, horse drawn carts and ambulances. They took stretcher cases to the 64th Field Ambulance at Mericourt L'Abbe. They carried sitting cases to the 36th Casualty Clearing Station at Heilly.

Were the two casualties 'sitting' cases?

So Mozley sent out two reliable NCOs to the front line in advance of A Company's move to the front. They travelled along Bottom Trench but, as had been reported by many others, it was crammed full of troops and difficult to move along because of the mud. Perhaps the men had tried to push through and failed, perhaps they were waiting to get through. Very probably they wanted to obey their orders and get into the front line trench to carry out Mozley's orders. It was certain that they had got some way along the trench.

Sources and Bibliography

Unit War Dairies, The National Archive

GHQ, General Staff, (TNA: PRO WO95/5)

XV Corps, (TNA: PRO WO95/921)

XV Corps Intelligence Summaries, (TNA: PRO WO157/468)

17th Division, (TNA: PRO WO95/1981)

50th Brigade, (TNA: PRO WO95/1998)

51st Brigade, (TNA: PRO WO95/2005)

52nd Brigade, (TNA: PRO WO95/2009)

113th Brigade, (TNA: PRO WO95/2552)

6th Dorsets, (TNA: PRO WO 95/2000)

7th East Yorks, (TNA: PRO WO95/2002)

7th Yorks (Green Howards), (TNA: PRO WO95/2004)

10th West Yorks (Prince of Wales' Own), (TNA: PRO WO95/2004)

7th Lincolns, (TNA: PRO WO95/2007)

10th Notts & Derbys (Sherwood Foresters), (TNA: PRO WO95/2008)

8th South Staffords, (TNA: PRO WO95/2007)

7th Borders, (T N A PRO WO95/2008)

9th Duke of Wellingtons, (TNA PRO WO95/2014)

10th Lancashire Fusiliers, (TNA PRO WO95/2012)

12th Manchesters, (TNA PRO WO95/2012)

9th Northumberland Fusiliers, (TNA: PRO WO95/2013)

13th Royal Welsh Fusiliers, (TNA: PRO WO95/2555)

14th Royal Welsh Fusiliers, (TNA: PRO WO95/2555)

15th Royal Welsh Fusiliers, (TNA: PRO WO95/2556)

16th Royal Welsh Fusiliers, (TNA: PRO WO95/2556)

50th Brigade Machine Gun Company, (TNA: PRO WO95/2004)

51st Brigade Machine Gun Company, (TNA: PRO WO95/2008)

52nd Brigade Machine Gun Company, (TNA: PRO WO95/2014)

7th Yorks and Lancs. Pioneers, (TNA: PRO WO95/1995)

51st Field Ambulance, (TNA: PRO WO95/1996)

52nd Field Ambulance, (TNA: PRO WO95/1996)

78th Field Coy, RE, (TNA: PRO WO95/1993)

93rd Field Coy, RE, (TNA: PROWO95/1993)

78th Brigade Royal Field Artillery, (TNA: PRO WO95/1991)

79th Brigade Royal Field Artillery, (TNA: PRO WO95/1991)

80th Brigade Royal Field Artillery, (TNA: PRO WO95/1991)

81st Brigade Royal Field Artillery, (TNA: PRO WO95/1991)

17th Signal Company Royal Engineers, (TNA: PRO WO95/1991)

The War diaries of the 4th Army HQ and the 77th Field Company R.E., for this week were not available.

Publications

Hilliard Atteridge, A. *The History of the 17th (Northern) Division* (Naval and Military Press, 2003)

Brown, M. *The Imperial War Museum Book of The Somme* (Pan,1996)

Chapman, G. *Vain Glory* (Cassell, 1937)

Dunn, J.C. *The War The Infantry Knew 1914 – 1919* (Abacus, 1999)

Farrar-Hockley, A.H. *The Somme* (Pan, 1983)

Graves, R. *Goodbye To All That.* (Penguin, 1980)

Griffith, W. *Up to Mametz* (Gliddon Books, 1988)

Hoyte, W.N. McNeela, M.T.F.J. (Ed) *10th (S) Battalion Sherwood Foresters. The History of The Battalion During The Great War.* (Naval and Military Press, 2003)

Hughes, C. *Mametz – Lloyd George's 'Welsh Army' at the Battle of the Somme* (Orion Press, 1990)

Lewis, C. *Sagittarius Rising* (Greenhill Books, 1993)

McCarthy, C. *The Somme The Day By Day Account* (Arms and Armour Press, 1993)

Munby, J.E. *A History of the 38th (Welsh) Division.* (Naval and Military Press, 2003)

Renshaw, M. *Mametz Wood.* (Leo Cooper Pen and Sword Ltd, 1999)

Sandilands, H.R. *The 23rd Division* (Naval and Military Press, 2003)

Sheffield, G, & Bourne, J. (Eds) *Douglas Haig War Diaries and Letters 1914-1918* (BCA, 2005)

Westlake, R. *British Battalions on the Somme* (Leo Cooper, 1998)

Winter, D. *Death's Men* (Penguin, 1979)

Osborne, W. *A History of the 10th Battalion, The Notts & Derbys, Volume One* (Salient Books, 2009)

Atkinson, C.T. *The Seventh Division 1914-1918,* (Naval and Military Press)

Unpublished Papers, Imperial War Museum

Lieutenant-Colonel G. A. Cardew, C.M.G., D.S.O., C. O., 80th Brigade, Royal Field Artillery. (IWM 86/92/1)

Captain O.P. Eckhard, 12th Battalion, Manchester Regiment. (IWM 78/42/1)

Private E.H. Harlow, M.M., 10th Battalion, Notts & Derbys Regiment. (IWM 03/15/1)

Captain B.C. Mozley, D.S.O., C.O., A Company, 6th Battalion, Dorsetshire Regiment. (IWM 01/45/1)

Lieutenant Kostlin, C.O., 6th Company, 122nd Wuttemburg, (Reserve) Infantry Regiment, German Army. The report appeared in the Army Quarterly 1925, kept with Captain Mozley's papers at the Imperial War Museum.

Colonel F. P. Cook. A Sapper in the 78th Field Company R. E., during July 1916. (IWM 81/44/1)

Other Sources

Soldiers Died In The Great War, 1914-19, (Naval and Military Press)

Commonwealth War Graves Commission website (www.cgwc.org)

Lieutenant (later temporary Captain) D. H. Fletcher's papers. (Author's collection)

The diary of Lieutenant-Colonel Fife, from a copy held by The Green Howards Museum, Richmond, Yorkshire.

Ancestry.com

Index

6th Dorsets, 24, 32, 39, 43, 47, 49, 60, 64, 74, 77-80, 88, 93-5, 104-11, 113-5, 120-1, 129-7, 143, 145-7, 154, 158-9, 161, 165-7, 177, 180, 183, 185, 189, 191, 193, 196-8, 206, 210, 212, 216, 220, 221, 224-5, 233

7th Borders, 58, 61, 64, 78, 107, 113, 121-2, 124, 127, 135, 136, 146, 149, 152-3, 175, 224

7th East Yorkshires, 19, 20-1, 24, 33, 39, 47, 60, 63-4, 66-7, 72-4, 77, 79-80, 86, 88-9, 95-6, 99-100, 103-4, 106-7, 109-11, 115, 120-1, 125, 127, 130, 157, 161-2, 165-8, 176, 178, 180, 182-4, 187, 190-5, 197, 200-3, 205-6, 212-3, 223, 225-6, 228

7th Lincolns, 35, 74, 80, 108, 113, 123, 136, 146, 153-4, 160, 162-4, 168-70, 172, 175, 179, 181, 192, 200-1, 204-6, 208-9, 214, 216, 224-5, 228-31

7th Yorkshires, 24, 37, 39, 80, 87, 91-3, 95, 115, 120-4, 127, 129-30, 134-6, 139-40, 144-5, 148, 152-3, 161, 165, 168-72, 176-8, 180, 182-3, 187-8, 203, 206, 215, 225-6, 228

7th Yorks and Lancs, 37, 87, 91, 225, 228

8th South Staffords, 35, 74, 87, 98, 109, 121, 149, 152, 154, 160, 162-5, 167-72, 175-81, 187, 214-15, 229, 231

9th Duke of Wellingtons Regiment, 43, 53, 56, 58, 66, 70, 71, 72, 73, 77, 82, 83, 97, 99, 106, 133, 144, 225, 235

9th Northumberland Fusiliers, 23, 25, 29, 33, 39, 43-4, 47, 49, 50, 52-6, 58-9, 63, 70, 77, 86, 99-100, 133, 143-4, 189, 202, 211, 223

9th Royal Welsh Fusiliers, 83

10th Lancashire Fusiliers, 25-6, 36, 39, 43, 44-5, 47, 49, 52, 53-4, 57-8, 60, 77, 82-3, 103, 133, 144, 235

10th Notts & Derbys, 5, 11, 35, 38, 44, 58, 63, 75, 77, 80, 82, 85-6, 95-6, 103, 107, 109, 110-14, 121, 122, 150, 154, 160, 165, 167, 177, 178-9, 187, 200, 204, 209, 214-16, 220-30

10th West Yorkshires, 24, 77, 133, 145, 223

12th Manchesters, 11, 43, 55, 63, 65-7, 69, 70-4, 77-9, 85-6, 99, 108-9, 119, 144, 202, 224

14th Royal Welsh Fusiliers, 43, 49

15th Royal Welsh Fusiliers, 97, 106

16th Royal Welsh Fusiliers, 123, 198, 201

Royal Army Medical Corps
34th Casualty Clearing Station, 87
36th Casualty Clearing Station, 87, 185, 224, 233
21st Field Ambulance, 37, 210
50th Field Ambulance, 126
51st Field Ambulance, 32, 34, 39, 45, 54, 57, 87, 90, 98, 115, 122, 126, 146, 152, 157, 165, 175, 201, 203, 210, 223, 233
53rd Field Ambulance, 39, 41, 90, 108, 133, 215
54th Field Ambulance, 94
64th Field Ambulance, 87, 96, 108, 125, 211, 215, 233
65th Field Ambulance, 203

Royal Artillery
78th Brigade, Royal Field Artillery, 33, 34, 219
79th Brigade, Royal Field Artillery, 33, 34, 38, 116, 205, 209, 213, 215, 219

GERMAN FORMATIONS

GENERAL INDEX

Other Publications from Salient Books

A History of the 10th Battalion, The Notts & Derbys, Volume One.
By Wayne Osborne.

The 10th Battalion, the Notts & Derbys, The Sherwood Foresters, spent the whole of the Great War on the Western Front. Consequently , this Kitchener Battalion saw action in most of the major engagements of the war. Written using unpublished personal diaries from the Imperial War Museum and unit war diaries held at The National Archive, this book, Volume One, spans the time from the formation of the Battalion in Dorset in 1914 through its baptism of fire and service in the trenches of the Ypres Salient in 1915.

A Boer War Sharpshooter.
Edited by Keith Case and Wayne Osborne.

The Diary of Colonel Alexander Weston Jarvis, commanding officer of the 21st Battalion, Imperial Yeomanry in the Boer War 1901-1902.

Equally at home in the saddle and in high society Alexander Weston Jarvis kept a diary that captured the mood and atmosphere of the time. He takes the reader bivouacking under the African stars, riding long miles on patrol, skirmishing with a wily and elusive enemy. Then in stark contrast he tells of the luxury of dinner parties, nights in the mess and visits to the theatre with the famous, great and notorious. The diary is a valuable and evocative record of the British Empire at its height of power and a forgotten war.

For a full, up-to-date list of titles by Salient Books go to www.salientbooks.co.uk

Lightning Source UK Ltd.
Milton Keynes UK
UKHW011530231119
354105UK00001B/11/P